D0166041

Fostering Children's Number Sense in Grades K-2

Turning Math Inside Out

Greg Nelson

Bridgewater State University

PEARSON

Boston   Columbus   Indianapolis   New York   San Francisco
Upper Saddle River   Amsterdam   Cape Town   Dubai   London   Madrid
Milan   Munich   Paris   Montreal   Toronto   Delhi   Mexico City   Sao Paulo
Sydney   Hong Kong   Seoul   Singapore   Taipei   Tokyo

Vice President and Editorial Director: Jeffery Johnston
Vice President, Editor-in-Chief: Aurora Martínez Ramos
Executive Editor: Linda Ashe Bishop
Editorial Assistant: Laura Marenghi
Senior Marketing Manager: Christine Gatchell
Production Editor: Mary Beth Finch
Manufacturing Buyer: Megan Cochran
Cover Designer: Laura Gardner
Editorial Production Service: Element LLC
Electronic Composition: Element LLC

Credits and acknowledgments borrowed from other sources and reproduced, with permission, in this textbook appear on the appropriate page within text.

Copyright © 2014 by Pearson Education, Inc. All rights reserved. Manufactured in the United States of America. This publication is protected by Copyright, and permission should be obtained from the publisher prior to any prohibited reproduction, storage in a retrieval system, or transmission in any form or by any means, electronic, mechanical, photocopying, recording, or likewise. To obtain permission(s) to use material from this work, please submit a written request to Pearson Education, Inc., Permissions Department, One Lake Street, Upper Saddle River, NJ, 07458, or you may fax your request to 201-236-3290.

Many of the designations by manufacturers and sellers to distinguish their products are claimed as trademarks. Where those designations appear in this book, and the publisher was aware of a trademark claim, the designations have been printed in initial caps or all caps.

Library of Congress Cataloging-in-Publication data not available at press time.

10 9 8 7 6 5 4 3 2 1

ISBN 10:   0-13-298151-3
ISBN 13: 978-0-13-298151-4

Contents

PART ②

EMERGENCE OF SECURE PLACE-VALUE AWARENESS

Chapter 3   Place-Value Awareness Launch Points   30

PART 3   SECURE PART-WHOLE AWARENESS AND THE EMERGENCE OF ADDITION/SUBTRACTION FLUENCY

Chapter 5   Addition/Subtraction Fluency Launch Points   65

**PART EXTENDING PLACE-VALUE AWARENESS AND ADDITION/
SUBTRACTION BEYOND THE HUNDREDS**

**Chapter 8   Place-Value Fluency and Multidigit Addition/
Subtraction Checkpoints   126**

Appendices

Preface

I consider it a tragedy of national proportions that so many K–2 classrooms do not tap the intelligence and enthusiasm children could bring to the enterprise of mastering mathematics. The problem is not with the children. Children come to us with an innate fascination with mathematical puzzles. They can be fearless problem solvers, investigating mathematical challenges with eagerness and delight. Given well-crafted resources, subtle guidance, and consistent encouragement to compare their interpretations of mathematical events with each other, children can and do largely figure out the core features of mathematics for themselves. We know this to be true because countries that are teaching math in a more child-centered way are getting much better results than we are in tests of mathematical proficiency (International Association for the Evaluation of Educational Achievement, 1997, 2006; Lee, Grigg, & Dion, 2007; NAEP, 2011).

In this book, I outline my vision of how to foster the development of numeracy in the early grades. Although this is certainly not the only aspect of mathematics children need to master in grades K–2, it is the most critical one according to the National Council of Teachers of Mathematics' *Curriculum Focal Points for Prekindergarten Through Grade 8 Mathematics: A Quest for Coherence* (NCTM, 2006), the National Research Council's *Mathematics Learning in Early Childhood: Paths Toward Excellence and Equity* (NRC, 2009), and the Council of Chief State School Officers and National Governors Association Center for Best Practices' *Common Core State Standards for Mathematics* (2010). Many of the children who later falter mathematically do so because they left the early childhood years without a sufficient grounding in foundational numeracy concepts. Children are expected to leave second grade able to confidently and nimbly manipulate—add and subtract—numbers into the thousands. Almost every child is capable of achieving this goal in a way that prepares him or her for the next stages of mathematics—but not without proper tools to work with or without a supportive teaching and social environment within which to operate.

Turning early childhood math education around requires radical changes in how we teach and what we teach with. I have concluded, based on my 30+ years in the field, that the key is to significantly increase the number of rich mathematical opportunities we provide children, and then give them more opportunities to self-educate. Unfortunately, many of the tasks we typically give young children to do during "math time" do not stimulate deep mathematical thinking, and most teachers do not have the background or training to take full advantage of the mathematical opportunities that spontaneously occur when children are set free to become mathematicians.

What I provide in this book is a detailed set of suggestions and tools for teachers to retool their rooms and their methodologies. I begin with a chapter that provides the conceptual and research basis for what I propose. This is followed by a chapter that provides a detailed, pragmatic implementation template, starting with (a) a blueprint for how to transform the math environment, followed by (b) the key teaching decisions and dispositions necessary to effectively partner with and coach children as they engage in mathematical activity.

The remainder of the book, starting with Chapter 3, deals concretely with the seeding of the mathematical environment. As noted in the research-based policy initiatives cited earlier (Council of Chief State School Officers and National Governors Association Center, 2010; NCTM, 2006; NRC, 2009), there are two major milestones in children's development of number sense during the early grades that lead to addition-subtraction fluency:

- **Part-Whole Fluency.** Children need to understand that numbers can be taken apart, rearranged, and put back together in different configurations without changing the quantity. The early grades are when children need to develop the mental agility, strategies, flexibility, and fluencies that will maximize their potential to take mathematical advantage of this property of numbers.
- **Place-Value Fluency.** Children need to understand that our counting system is not just sequential but has a hierarchical structure of place values, based on the number 10. This is the time when children need to develop the mental agility, strategies, flexibility, and fluencies for comparing relative quantities and navigating comfortably between the different place-value levels.

These two competencies develop in parallel, not separately, and mastery of each informs the other. Therefore, I have chosen to split place value into its emergent and fluency stages. This organization aligns with the learning path that children themselves follow as their ability in mathematics grows and matures. Then, after a brief review of the development of stable counting and early part-whole awareness,[1] I describe how children gradually learn to reconceptualize the counting numbers in base-10 terms, followed by a detailed look at how a deep sense of both numbers and base-10 leads to a flexible ability to take numbers apart and put them back together strategically (which in turn leads to automaticity on the addition and subtraction facts). I conclude with a look at how a mature sense of place value sets the stage for understanding multidigit addition and subtraction algorithms.

Each content section is divided into two kinds of chapters: Launch Points and Checkpoints.

Launch Points

In the first two Launch Point chapters, where age-appropriate, part-whole, and place-value concepts are first discussed, I include a "What Comes Before—And How to Get There" section, where I detail the foundational skills that must come before. In all the Launch Points chapters (Chapters 3, 5, and 7), I include a "Concepts and Skills Being Reinforced in This Chapter" section, where I outline the concepts to be mastered at that stage of numeracy (cross-referencing these to the Common Core standards). The Common Core standards are coded by:

- The *grade level* of the standard: kindergarten (K), first grade (1), or second grade (2).

---

[1] Presented in much greater detail in my earlier work, *Math at Their Own Pace: Child-Directed Activities for Developing Early Number Sense* (Nelson, 2007).

- The *domain* of mathematics: Counting and Cardinality (CC); Operations and Algebraic Thinking (OA); or Numbers and Operations in Base Ten (NBT).
- The *number of the standard* within that domain.

For example, K.CC.4 refers to the fourth standard in the kindergarten Counting and Cardinality domain of the Common Core.

These contextualizing parts of the chapter are followed by examples of high-powered materials and activities for fostering those mathematical concepts in a child-centered, hands-on way. I call these activities *launch points* because they can give children the boost they need to reach the next level of numeracy. Templates are provided in the PDToolkit for many of the materials needed for activities described in this book.

Checkpoints

In these chapters, I provide sample assessment tools for monitoring children's progress. You can't teach well if you don't know what children currently know and how they know it. These materials and activities are learning experiences in their own right (with many including online templates for their construction), but I call them *checkpoints* because (a) they help you judge the progress children are making along the learning continuum and (b) they are useful guides in informing subsequent teaching decisions. I include guiding questions to help you evaluate what the children's actions, choices, and words signify developmentally. In the Appendices, I include some simple templates for recording your observations of an individual child or for the whole class. Also included in some of the assessment chapters are supplemental *Teaching Tips* to help guide ongoing pedagogical decisions.

Those of you teaching a particular grade may be inclined to ask which materials are intended for use in your classroom? The match is made not by age or by grade, but by what children currently know and are interested in. As stated in the preamble to the *Common Core State Standards for Mathematics*:

> What students can learn at any particular grade level depends upon what they have learned before. Ideally then, each standard in this document might have been phrased in the form, "Students who already know A should next come to learn B." (Council of Chief State School Officers and National Governors Association Center, 2010, p. 6)

Children develop different skills at very different rates, and the range of mathematical sophistication within any group of same-age children is enormous. Children who are becoming more competent with numbers will naturally gravitate toward activities in the later chapters,[2] and your own powers of observation and assessment will help you direct individual children to the activities most likely to benefit them.

This book is as much about educating ourselves as it is about educating the children. As I write this, school districts and publishers are scrambling to retool

---

[2] A fact often overlooked in education is that children are drawn more to activities that are *challenging* than to activities that are *easy*. After all, how much pride can they take in completing an activity they can do without effort? We waste so much time in classrooms *forcing* children to do their work. Left to their own devices—and given activities they find meaningful and challenging—they will work their tails off without any prodding whatsoever. I swear it's true!

their classroom practices to align with the new Common Core standards. Many of you reading this book already have a math curriculum that has been adopted by your school or your district, so you already have a suggested (or mandated) scope-and-sequence to follow. That's okay, because what I am offering here is intended to supplement your curriculum, not replace it. More than that, it is intended to get you to rethink all you do in the mathematical classroom. It would be a mistake to skip the teaching recommendations in this book and go straight to the cool manipulatives. The children's learning is more dependent on how you teach than on the specific activities you select. As powerful as the teaching tools provided in this book are, you'll waste their potential if you don't foster their use in a child-centered way.

Although primarily aimed at practitioners already working in classrooms with children, this book can also be a valuable resource for curriculum supervisors and teacher preparation programs. I conclude each checkpoints chapter with a set of *Study Group Discussion Starters* to guide your review of the material in that section and your attempts to put the materials to work in your own classroom. Find some like-minded colleagues who are willing to try something different, and learn together. Once on the right path, I believe it is the *children* who will show you how to perfect your craft as you join them on a wonderful voyage of mathematical discovery. Enjoy.

Acknowledgments

One's journey to understanding is long and convoluted, with no well-defined starting or ending points. I became an educator because I believed in and was fascinated by children's innate intelligence. My quest to understand the unfolding of children's minds started with an eclectic mix of educational theorists such as A. S. Neill, John Dewey, and Maria Montessori. Later, the list expanded to include such diverse influences as Jerome Bruner, Robert Siegler, Mary Baretta-Lorton, Lillian Katz, Constance Kamii, Rheta DeVries, Catherine Fosnot, Kathy Richardson, Marilyn Burns, John Van de Walle, and those folks from a little village in Italy called Reggio Emilia. Of the people I have worked with directly who have influenced the contents of this book, my heart-felt thanks go out to Margaret Loeffler, Bee Pape, Margaret Biggs, Juanita Copley, and Rebecca Corwin. And of course I must thank the many children I have worked with over the years. Every time a child responds to one of my prompts or probes, I learn something new.

Few ideas spring from nothingness, and I understand that some of the unattributed content of this book bears a striking resemblance to ideas found in others' work. If I know an idea originated from a particular source, I have given credit. To the many who have contributed to this field over the years and whose work I have benefited from, I can only say a general "Thank you" and apologize that, over time, it becomes increasingly difficult to reconstruct the origins of my current pedagogy.

I can't conclude without thanking the editors at Pearson for shepherding this book to its current form. I would especially like to thank Kelly Villela Canton for her early recommendations and suggestions on the project. Pearson made this a much stronger and useful offering than it was in its original form.

My gratitude too to the following reviewers for their perspective and suggestions: Meghan Hearn, Veterans Elementary School; Tracie Holland, Somerset County Board of Education; Theresa Koenig, Rocky Run Elementary School; Kathleen M. Morris, Prince William County Schools; Fran Machuga, William Holmes McGuffey Elementary School; Heather Romich, Elkridge Elementary School; Shelley S. Rosen, Neshaminy School District; and Michael D. Sernulka, Williamson Elementary School. And finally, I must thank my wife Ann for understanding that the long hours spent at the computer, the ceaseless assembly and alteration of odd-looking constructions, and the boxes of stuff crammed into too many corners of our living space are what passes for professional activity in my crazy universe.

RETHINKING NUMBER SENSE

What Math Is Not

A big part of our problem in math education is that we spend too much time and energy focusing on two skills we assume are mathematics, even though they are not.

Arithmetic. Arithmetic is a fixed set of predefined procedures (known as *algorithms*) for doing mathematical computations. For example, we teach "When doing subtraction, always subtract the smaller number from the larger number" or "When adding 27 and 36, add the 7 and 6, which is 13; write down the 3, and carry the 1; then add the 1, 2, and 3, and write down the 6 to the left of the 3."

Arithmetic does have to be taught because it involves a fixed way of coming up with an answer. Arithmetic is very useful. It allows people to crank out answers to problems quickly and efficiently without wasting energy pondering why the procedures work. Arithmetic is mindless—and hence is not mathematical (which also explains why it is not very exciting).

More significant to the point being made here, premature teaching of arithmetic sabotages the development of mathematical thinking and can seriously stunt subsequent mathematical proficiency. To teach math well, we need to make arithmetic the epilogue of the mathematical story, not the prologue. You will see in the coming pages that I don't devote much space to teaching arithmetic. In early childhood, it is mathematics that counts.

Math Facts. Math facts are the answers to high-frequency mathematical relationships, such as $3 + 3 = 6$. We can safely memorize these answers because they are indeed facts. They do not change from day to day or under different circumstances. Thus, $5 + 7$ will always equal 12, and $14 - 8$ will always equal 6.

The mathematician's patterns, like the painter's or the poet's, must be beautiful; the ideas, like the colours or the words, must fit together in a harmonious way.

Beauty is the first test: there is no permanent place in the world for ugly mathematics.

—G. H. Hardy,
A Mathematician's Apology

The fastest way to come up with these facts is to know them. But again, memorized math facts are simply known. They are not thought about, and hence, they are not mathematical. Many children can tell you $6 + 7 = 13$ or $6 \times 7 = 42$, but ask them to prove it to you, and they will stare at you blankly. Their eyes will tell you: "It's right because when I put down those answers, I don't get them marked wrong."

When we rush to have children memorize math facts, bypassing their mathematical sense-making, we cripple their deep understanding of mathematical relationships. Mathematical power comes from using flexible mental strategies to see how facts can be arrived at using a variety of strategies. Yes, children must ultimately have the math facts at their fingertips to pave the way to higher levels on their mathematical journey, but if all they do is memorize facts, they will not progress very far. The memorization shortcut is a shortcut to nowhere.

Children's Readiness to Be Mathematicians

We need to be careful not to overestimate children's innate ability to invent mathematics. Children are intelligent, but their intelligence is of a special kind. Let me walk through the problem using the language of Piaget in parentheses. Young children's ability to think logically in the abstract *(formal operational thinking)* is extremely limited. Further complicating the equation is children's tendency to misinterpret what they are seeing *(preoperational thinking)*. Magicians depend on misdirecting us and feeding us false impressions to get us to believe we've experienced the impossible. The process by which children engage in mathematical investigations is similar in nature. Their preexisting interpretations of how the world works *(schema)* are powerful and can cause them to ignore the inconsistencies between their assumptions and the mathematical evidence in front of them *(assimilation)*. However, as children continue to explore and experience, they become increasingly aware of and perplexed by these inconsistencies *(disequilibrium)*. This in turn drives them to experiment, observe, hypothesize, and consult with their peers to arrive at a more satisfying explanation of what's happening *(accommodation)*. In laymen's terms, they are learning math by being mathematicians.

So if we know children are confused and flat-out wrong in many of their preliminary mathematical intuitions, why not bypass all the uncertainty and just tell them the right answers? All this exploration and discovery sounds so darned inefficient! I wish it were possible to just hand children the keys to the kingdom, but every time we take the process of sense-making out of their hands, we short-circuit their mathematical minds. The efficiencies we think we have achieved prove illusory and short-lived.

How We Should Teach Math

The fact that children cannot make much progress mathematically when left to their own devices does not mean we just give up and wait for them to get older. We are educators, after all! By definition, an educator's job is to set up environments and tasks where, with appropriate guidance, children can learn things they cannot or probably will not learn on their own. But if we simply tell children what the mathematical relationships are, they won't understand them in ways that are meaningful and lasting. We seem to be at an impasse. What are we to do?

Think of the children as mathematical scientists. To be scientists, they must be provided with

- A well-equipped mathematical laboratory in which to work;
- Freedom to explore questions of personal meaning and interest to them within that laboratory; and,
- Perhaps most important of all, freedom to arrive at their own conclusions.

As I argued in my earlier book (Nelson, 2007), which focused on children's earlier voyages of mathematical discovery, the best way to make high-quality math happen on a regular basis in the classroom is to implement a *shelf-based curriculum*. By this, I mean

1. Fill the room with mathematical offerings that have been carefully designed so they have embedded within them rich potential for mathematical discovery;
2. Display the materials in an attractive, logical fashion so the children can independently find them, use them, and put them back;
3. Give the children free access to the materials during regularly scheduled choice times;
4. Have in mind a variety of useful ways for children to engage with the materials so you can help individual children use the materials in satisfying and productive ways; and
5. Let the children choose.

Differentiated instruction is a phrase that is used widely in education today. Roughly speaking, this term describes teachers' efforts to make available multiple ways of approaching a core task so children of different interests and ability levels can all be successful. What I am advocating is an efficient and effective means of having all the children learning at their own level, in their own style, and at their own pace.

In this age of high standards and strict accountability, it can be a hard sell to tell teachers and administrators that children should choose the math they will do. Why is it essential that we let children have a say in what they will work on and for how long? Here's why:

- Making children work at skills they are not ready for (or have already mastered) does not work.
- Making children work at tasks they have no interest in does not work.
- Relying on explanation and modeling and having children mimic your example does not work.
- Endlessly pointing out children's errors to them and reteaching the procedures until their performances are error-free does not work.

Why don't these approaches work? That's a book in its own right, but let's start with this. There are three key ingredients in a functional skill:

1. *Durability.* Our goal is results that *last*, not fade. Information memorized in isolation fades rapidly. We see the results of ignoring the durability principle in the common U.S. phenomenon of reteaching the same core knowledge, year after year, with limited cumulative progress. If the foundation keeps crumbling, higher mathematics has nothing to stand on.

2. *Applicability*. We want children to have skills they will use at appropriate times. When information is learned without meaning or context, children do not realize that procedures they know apply to problems that look slightly different. We see the results of ignoring the applicability principle in the long-term trends revealed by the National Assessment of Educational Progress (NAEP, 2009), showing that we succeed in teaching basic computational skills in our elementary schools but fail to move very many students to the problem-solving level.

3. *Flexibility*. We want children to have skills they can use adaptively in solving problems. Information that is simply memorized is learned in a fixed way. It leaves children no way to recover if they fail to recall the appropriate fact or algorithm, and it leaves children unable to adjust the skills they have to match the particular problem at hand. In cognitive science, the ability to nimbly use what you know in novel situations is called *transferability*, and it is considered the hallmark of intelligent action. We see the results of ignoring the flexibility principle in children's tendency, as the pile of memorized algorithms grows higher, to create what I call "algorithm salad," with bits and pieces of various algorithms mixed together and applied in random fashion to mathematical problems.

The National Research Council (NRC) report *Adding It Up* (2001) calls for us to help children gain *mathematical proficiency*. It defines proficiency much as I did a functional skill above, saying it has five interlocking components:

1. Conceptual understanding,
2. Procedural fluency,
3. Strategic competence,
4. Adaptive reasoning, and
5. Productive disposition.

Interestingly, the report also states that this list should apply not just to the students, but also to the teachers that teach them. If we want children to become mathematicians, we must be comfortable in that world ourselves.

This leads us to another advantage of teaching in the manner proposed here. In a functioning mathematical laboratory, we can actually see how the children approach mathematical tasks, which gives us a much better sense of what they understand and what continues to confuse them. Armed with such knowledge, we can better gauge how to subtly intervene or what activities to suggest they try next. My mantra is this: If you don't know where the children are, you don't know where to take them next. Ironically, once teachers start spending the bulk of their time observing rather than teaching, they become better teachers.

What the Experts and the Research Tell Us

So is this approach just my wild pipe dream? Is there any reason to believe this approach will actually work?

We have known since the early days of the international comparison study TIMSS (International Association for the Evaluation of Educational Achievement, 1995, 2006) that our traditional methods of teaching mathematics have been falling short. Referencing this information, the NRC (2001) stated that "the U.S. elementary and middle school mathematics curriculum has been characterized as shallow, undemanding, and diffuse in content coverage" (p. 4).

The National Council for Teachers of Mathematics (NCTM), our national professional body for standards in math education, has led the way in emphasizing understanding rather than memorization (NCTM, 2000), but detailed studies of the TIMSS data show that NCTM's principles are being more faithfully implemented in countries other than our own—and those countries are outperforming us in mathematics. NCTM later issued a joint position statement with the National Association for the Education of Young Children (NAEYC) affirming that early, rich immersion in mathematical content is not incompatible with developmentally based, child-centered practices (NAEYC & NCTM, 2002). Similar summaries of appropriate mathematical instruction in early childhood have been published by the Society for Research in Child Development (Ginsburg, Lee, & Boyd, 2008), the National Mathematics Advisory Panel (2008), and the National Institute for Early Education Research (Brenneman, Stevenson-Boyd, & Frede, 2008). All of them say this:

- Young children are capable of surprisingly sophisticated mathematical thinking.
- We don't have children do nearly enough math in the early years.
- Teachers need a great deal more professional development than they currently receive to maximally impact children's mathematical abilities.

Most recently, NCTM has sought to counter the U.S. tendency to tackle too many math concepts in too small a time frame. In place of a curriculum that is "a mile wide and an inch deep," NCTM (2006) suggests more targeted, developmentally based emphases or *focus points* for math instruction in particular grades:

> When instruction focuses on a small number of key areas of emphasis, students gain extended experience with core concepts and skills. Such experience can facilitate deep understanding, mathematical fluency, and an ability to generalize. . . . A curriculum built on focal points also has the potential to offer opportunities for the diagnosis of difficulties and immediate intervention, thus helping students who are struggling with important mathematics content. (p. 5)

In other words, if we do the mathematics right in the early years, while children are forming their core conceptual schema, we will reap the benefits in the later grades.

NCTM says that in early childhood there should be two areas of emphasis: (1) number sense and operations and (2) geometry. NCTM's (2006) grade-level focus points for K–2 numeracy are as follows:

Kindergarten—Representing, comparing, and ordering whole numbers and joining and separating sets . . .

First Grade—(a) Developing understandings of addition and subtraction and strategies for basic addition facts and related subtraction facts; (b) developing an understanding of whole number relationships, including grouping in tens and ones. . .

Second Grade—(a) Developing an understanding of the base-ten numeration system and place-value concepts; (b) developing quick recall of addition facts and related subtraction facts and fluency with multidigit addition and subtraction. (pp. 12–14)

These are precisely the areas addressed in this book.

Although the NCTM standards are based on what we currently know about the trajectory of children's development, there are those who argue that the standards reflect a belief system rather than science. The NRC has systematically examined the evidence regarding best practices in math education and made recommendations, first in *Adding It Up: Helping Children Learn Mathematics* (NRC, 2001) and more recently in *Mathematics Learning in Early Childhood: Paths Toward Excellence and Equity* (NRC, 2009). The NRC agrees with NCTM that in the early grades the emphasis should be first and foremost on number sense and operations. And, like the TIMSS study, the NRC (2009) sounds the alarm on the gap between what we know about good teaching and actual classroom practices:

> Examination of current standards, curricula, and instruction in early childhood education revealed that many early childhood settings do not provide adequate learning experiences in mathematics. The relative lack of high-quality mathematics instruction, especially in comparison to literacy, reflects a lack of attention to mathematics throughout the [early] childhood education system, including standards, curriculum, instruction, and the preparation and training of the teaching workforce. . . .The committee found that although the research to date about how young children develop and learn key concepts in mathematics has clear implications for practice, the findings are neither widely known nor implemented by early childhood educators or those who teach them. (pp. 2–3)

The NRC argues for a developmental, research-based approach, following what it calls *teaching-learning paths*: "sequences of learning experiences in which one idea lays the foundation for the next" (NRC, 2009, p. 121). Because these paths align with children's normal development, the report states, they are a natural fit for children:

1. They are foundational mathematically and developmentally.
2. They are achievable for children of those ages. . . .
3. They are consistent with children's ways of thinking, developing, and learning when they have experience with mathematics ideas. . . .
4. They are interesting to children. (NRC, 2009, p. 121)

A corollary is that, because these paths follow a natural developmental progression, children will work at them eagerly and without coercion—if, that is, they find themselves in a supportive learning environment that allows them to pursue their mathematical ideas in ways that make sense to them:

> Once started along these numerical learning paths, children become interested in consolidating and extending their knowledge, practicing by themselves and seeking out additional information by asking questions and giving themselves new tasks. Home, child care, and preschool and school environments need to support children in this process of becoming a self-initiating and self-guided learner and facilitate the carrying out of such learning. (p. 127)

The NRC's (2009) research summary identified three *core areas* in children's early number sense development—number, relations, and addition/subtraction operations. A close look at the teaching-learning paths within these three core areas in the early grades (see Appendix A) shows children engaging in increasingly sophisticated problem solving, pattern recognition, and connections across concepts, with little rote memorization. In short, the NRC is lobbying for math instruction similar to what is outlined in this book.

The NRC perspective was the driving force behind the recommendations from the Governors Conference that resulted in the *Common Core State Standards for Mathematics* (National Governors Association Center & Council of Chief State School Officers, 2010)—the closest our nation has ever come to having a national curriculum. The themes in the Common Core standards should seem familiar by now: (1) Fewer math concepts should be emphasized in the early childhood years in order to spend more time concentrating on number sense and geometry, and (2) computational strategies and place-value awareness should be emphasized much more and much earlier than has been common practice. Figure 1.1 summarizes the Common Core critical focus areas related to number sense for grades K–2.

The Common Core standards are not just about the content to be mastered. Like NCTM, they state that desired outcomes are not likely to be achieved without careful attention to *how* the content is taught. Figure 1.2 summarizes the eight Common Core standards for mathematical practice, which also should look familiar by now.

So the approach advocated in this book is not part of some radical fringe of math education. It is public policy. These standards and principles have, at press time, been adopted by 45 of the states. They are the metric against which we should measure our mathematical efforts. More importantly, they signal the current best thinking on how we should be teaching if we want our children to succeed.

Unfortunately, our current workforce is woefully unprepared to turn these recommendations into classroom practice. The need for sophisticated professional development is greater than ever. There are many high-quality resources available that are consistent with the mathematical approach I'm advocating. I highly recommend any or all of them. Mary Baretta-Lorton's classic work *Mathematics Their Way* (1976) and Constance Kamii's *Young Children Reinvent Arithmetic* (1985) helped launch the movement. Excellent case studies of this approach in action in early childhood settings are provided by Dacey and Eston (1999) and Andrews and Trafton (2002). Videos of exemplary programming and assessment also exist (Annenberg Foundation, 1997; Richardson, 2002). Other suggestions for high-quality mathematical activities can be found in the works of many well-known practitioners, teacher trainers, and researchers in the field (Confer, 2005; Copley, 1999, 2000, 2004; Copley, Jones, & Dighe, 2007; Fosnot & Cameron, 2007; Fosnot & Uittenbogaard, 2007; Mokros, Russell, & Economopoulos, 1995; Richardson, 1998; Van de Walle & Lovin, 2006). In short, I am not inventing what I present here out of thin air. It is consistent with what is known in the field and advocated by learned societies and policy makers. But many of those working with young learners still are trying to figure out how to set up powerful math environments and maneuver comfortably within them. This is my own attempt to tip the scales towards better practice.

Figure 1.1 Common Core Critical Focus Areas, K–2

ADDITION/SUBTRACTION AND PLACE VALUE

Kindergarten

1. Students use numbers, including written numerals, to represent quantities and to solve quantitative problems, such as counting objects in a set; counting out a given number of objects; comparing sets or numerals; and modeling simple joining and separating situations with sets of objects, or eventually with equations such as 5 + 2 = 7 and 7 − 2 = 5. (Kindergarten students should see addition and subtraction equations, and student writing of equations in kindergarten is encouraged, but it is not required.) Students choose, combine, and apply effective strategies for answering quantitative questions, including quickly recognizing the cardinalities of small sets of objects, counting and producing sets of given sizes, counting the number of objects in combined sets, or counting the number of objects that remain in a set after some are taken away.

First Grade

1. Students develop strategies for adding and subtracting whole numbers based on their prior work with small numbers. They use a variety of models, including discrete objects and length-based models (e.g., cubes connected to form lengths), to model add-to, take-from, put-together, take-apart, and compare situations to develop meaning for the operations of addition and subtraction, and to develop strategies to solve arithmetic problems with these operations. Students understand connections between counting and addition and subtraction (e.g., adding two is the same as counting on two). They use properties of addition to add whole numbers and to create and use increasingly sophisticated strategies based on these properties (e.g., "making tens") to solve addition and subtraction problems within 20. By comparing a variety of solution strategies, children build their understanding of the relationship between addition and subtraction.

2. Students develop, discuss, and use efficient, accurate, and generalizable methods to add within 100 and subtract multiples of 10. They compare whole numbers (at least to 100) to develop understanding of and solve problems involving their relative sizes. They think of whole numbers between 10 and 100 in terms of tens and ones (especially recognizing the numbers 11 to 19 as composed of a ten and some ones). Through activities that build number sense, they understand the order of the counting numbers and their relative magnitudes.

Second Grade

1. Students extend their understanding of the base-ten system. This includes ideas of counting in fives, tens, and multiples of hundreds, tens, and ones, as well as number relationships involving these units, including comparing. Students understand multi-digit numbers (up to 1000) written in base-ten notation, recognizing that the digits in each place represent amounts of thousands, hundreds, tens, or ones (e.g., 853 is 8 hundreds + 5 tens + 3 ones).

2. Students use their understanding of addition to develop fluency with addition and subtraction within 100. They solve problems within 1000 by applying their understanding of models for addition and subtraction, and they develop, discuss, and use efficient, accurate, and generalizable methods to compute sums and differences of whole numbers in base-ten notation, using their understanding of place value and the properties of operations. They select and accurately apply methods that are appropriate for the context and the numbers involved to mentally calculate sums and differences for numbers with only tens or only hundreds.

Source: Common Core State Standards for Mathematics. © Copyright 2010. National Governors Association Center for Best Practices and Council of Chief State School Officers. All rights reserved.

Figure 1.2 Common Core State Standards for Mathematics

STANDARDS FOR MATHEMATICAL PRACTICE

The Standards for Mathematical Practice describe varieties of expertise that mathematics educators at all levels should seek to develop in their students. These practices rest on important "processes and proficiencies" with longstanding importance in mathematics education. . .

1. Make sense of problems and persevere in solving them.	They analyze givens, constraints, relationships, and goals. They make conjectures about the form and meaning of the solution and plan a solution pathway rather than simply jumping into a solution attempt. . . .They continually ask themselves, "Does this make sense?" They can understand the approaches of others to solving complex problems and identify correspondences between different approaches.
2. Reason abstractly and quantitatively.	Quantitative reasoning entails habits of creating a coherent representation of the problem at hand; considering the units involved; attending to the meaning of quantities, not just how to compute them; and knowing and flexibly using different properties of operations and objects.
3. Construct viable arguments and critique the reasoning of others.	They justify their conclusions, communicate them to others, and respond to the arguments of others.
4. Model with mathematics.	Mathematically proficient students can apply the mathematics they know to solve problems arising in everyday life, society, and the workplace. . . .They routinely interpret their mathematical results in the context of the situation and reflect on whether the results make sense, possibly improving the model if it has not served its purpose.
5. Use appropriate tools strategically.	These tools might include pencil and paper, concrete models, a ruler, a protractor, a calculator. . . . Proficient students are sufficiently familiar with tools appropriate for their grade or course to make sound decisions about when each of these tools might be helpful, recognizing both the insight to be gained and their limitations.
6. Attend to precision.	Mathematically proficient students try to communicate precisely to others. They try to use clear definitions in discussion with others and in their own reasoning. They state the meaning of the symbols they choose, including using the equal sign consistently and appropriately.
7. Look for and make use of structure.	Mathematically proficient students look closely to discern a pattern or structure. Young students, for example, might notice that three and seven more is the same amount as seven and three more, or they may sort a collection of shapes according to how many sides the shapes have.
8. Look for and express regularity in repeated reasoning.	As they work to solve a problem, mathematically proficient students maintain oversight of the process, while attending to the details. They continually evaluate the reasonableness of their intermediate results.

Source: Common Core State Standards for Mathematics. © Copyright 2010. National Governors Association Center for Best Practices and Council of Chief State School Officers. All rights reserved.

MATH INSIDE OUT

I love layers of meaning, and I chose the subtitle *Turning Math Inside Out* accordingly.

The First Level of Meaning. To see how something is put together, you might have to ignore the tidy front view and look at it from the side that hasn't been cleaned up for public display. I want this book to help you do that with the "simple" math we teach to young children. By turning math inside out, the complexities of simple mathematics become apparent. If we as teachers don't take the time to develop a deep understanding of the journey children are on, there is no way we can serve them well as pilots or guides.

It's easy, once you understand something, to forget how hard it was to get to that level of awareness. Teachers of young children can't afford that luxury. We must remember the uncertainty, confusion, cluelessness, embarrassment, and occasional terror of what it is like to not know. Think of yourself as a global positioning system, or GPS. You are observing children on a mathematical map. By knowing where they are and where they have yet to go, you can provide them with helpful tools and advice on planning their next moves. But to best fulfill your duties, you must know intimately the terrain, routes, road conditions, possible detours and delays, alternative routes, dead ends, sites worth seeing along the way, good rest stops, and so on. In other words, you need to know math inside out.

The Second Level of Meaning. Socrates and Freud had it right: Most of the time, we have within ourselves the answers to our most important questions. Sometimes we just need the gift of time, in a risk-free environment, to slowly uncover those truths, although having a friendly ear available to encourage us as we work things out is helpful, too.

Children need to stop looking to their teachers for mathematical sense. The road to mathematical competence is not in the knowing of math but in the *doing* of math. By constantly engaging in meaningful mathematical activity and by challenging themselves and challenging each other to make sense of what they are doing, children develop the confidence, passion, skills, and strategies of successful mathematicians.

Our responsibility as teachers is to convince children that their own mathematical instincts are to be trusted. To do that, we must transform our thinking about how children learn math. The direction of flow is not from the outside in—but from the inside out.

HOW TO TEACH MATH THIS WAY

LOGISTICS

Space

Teaching math in a child-centered, hands-on way requires a significant amount of shelf space allotted to the storage and ongoing display of math materials. One way to free up space is to rethink seating arrangements. In early childhood, children have more need for materials to work with than desks to work on; in fact, having the option of working on the floor offers a welcome change of pace for young bodies.

The materials you are encouraging the children to use need to be highly visible, attractive, and accessible. They should be logically arranged and clearly labeled to show what they are and where they belong so children can

1. Easily find the materials they want to use and
2. Put materials back in their appropriate place when they are finished.

Think beyond shelving that lines the walls: Shelving that extends into the room increases the shelf space available and also helps define a space within the room where mathematical activity is encouraged. But avoid tall storage units with materials only you can reach. Use those spaces only for materials you are holding in reserve.

Should you put *everything* suggested in this book on the shelves at once? Certainly not! The number of choices offered in this book would overwhelm any child (as well as any teacher). There is no need for them all to be available all the time. In fact, periodically changing what's on the shelves helps rekindle children's interest in the math area.

But in deciding which activities to put on the shelf, it is important that you choose activities representing the *range* of skill levels present in your room. You will find children naturally gravitate toward ones that are the right "fit" for them— differentiated instruction as it is meant to be practiced. In order to accommodate the range, you will probably need to put out some activities paralleling each chapter of this book. In addition, you should put out activities children ask for specifically or ones you think would be a perfect next step for certain children. This book (and your adopted curriculum) gives you a pool of options. It is your job to make the day-to-day and moment-to-moment decisions that will keep your math curriculum alive, relevant, and interesting.

Preparing the Learning Materials

In this instructional paradigm, the materials do most of the teaching, not you. That means much of your effort occurs *before* the children enter the classroom. You will have to spend more time than you may be used to acquiring and creating the materials that make up a hands-on curriculum. For many teachers, this is an intimidating concept: "If it's not an easy adjustment of something I already have or can purchase, copy, or download, I'm not interested." But some of the best teaching and assessment materials simply don't exist commercially at this point. Maybe in time they will, but should you make your children wait or skip valuable teaching opportunities because they are inconvenient?

Keep in mind, though, that this is a long-term investment on your part. You are not just developing activities for today or for this week. You are developing materials that different children will use day after day, week after week, and year after year. It pays to take the time to make them well, out of durable materials that last.[1] Try to make them as attractive as possible—your pride in the assembly and display of the materials makes them more appealing, and it communicates to the children that these materials have value. And once you have them, you have them as a permanent addition to your teaching arsenal. I actually think it is much more time-consuming to be coming up with the teaching-props-of-the-day than it is to assemble a durable, high-quality set of teaching and assessment tools.

Although labor-intensive up front, teaching this way need not be expensive. I'm a notorious scrounger, and I would much rather put together a functional activity from scrap and recycled materials than buy a fancy model at the store. Homemade says to the children that math can be found in the materials we use in our day-to-day lives. Most of the materials can be constructed with tools no more sophisticated than a pair of scissors or a good box cutter, a set of permanent markers, and some tag board (the cardboard material that picture frames are made of—you can often solicit donations of tag-board scraps from framing shops). Some materials I generate on the computer, using either the text or the draw function of a good word-processing program. I then print them out, often on glossy photo paper, and mount them on sturdier cardboard or tag board to make them easy for small fingers to manipulate.[2]

Templates for many of the materials I describe are provided in the online resources accompanying this book.

[1] A caveat: Sometimes it pays to make a quick test version of a materials set the first time you put it out. As that trial set is used, you will probably see minor ways you could *improve* on the design. If you put too much time and effort into making the flawed set, you are less likely to replace it with a new, improved version that is attractive and durable enough to serve the long-term classroom.

[2] Design note: When using your computer to make materials, use fonts that are similar to the style you want children to use when they practice their own writing of letters and numerals.

There are some standard commercial materials I refer to frequently as useful math manipulatives, such as *Unifix cubes* (small colored plastic cubes that link together) and *Cuisenaire rods* (small wooden or plastic rods in color-coded lengths). These can be found in many educational supply stores or ordered from catalog suppliers. You might start with Lakeshore (*www.lakeshorelearning.com*), Didax (*www.didaxinc.com*), EAI Education (*EAIeducation.com*), or Discount School Supplies (*www.discountschoolsupplies*) to see what the materials look like and what they typically cost. It will also help you decide if there is a reasonable alternative you already have or can easily make. A handful of the activities use materials that are variations on materials commonly found in Montessori schools. Genuine Montessori materials are very well made but also very expensive, so I usually construct my own. If you're interested in purchasing Montessori materials, a good place to start is the list of suppliers on the Edvisors web page (*http://directory.edvisors .com/Products_and_Services/Montessori/*).

Some of the described materials do require more labor to construct, especially those made out of wood. If you're uncomfortable working with wood, try soliciting volunteers, such as a parent in your program or a neighbor, to make the materials. If you give detailed specifications to someone who knows how to use a table saw, it doesn't take long to cut the pieces needed from scrap wood. However, if you're at a loss for woodworkers, I describe alternative materials that accomplish the same task and are easier to make. I would much rather you use whatever you can manage than have you skip an activity altogether because constructing the materials seemed too labor-intensive.

"Math Time"

It would be nice if we could decide what to teach next, teach it, and then move on. Publisher's teacher guides and district scope-and-sequence charts, built on the assembly-line model handed down from the industrial revolution, are written as if such is possible, and they look really good on paper. The model works well for teachers in that it guarantees that everything is covered in a timely and efficient manner. Unfortunately, as the saying goes, "Teaching is not taught." Children's learning is not linear, not sequential, and not black and white. Your goal should not be to cover everything but rather to *un*-cover everything. Classrooms that successfully transform children's mathematical minds have a fundamentally different definition of "math time."

Having all the children working on the same activity at the same time is like pushing a boulder uphill—much effort is expended, and little is accomplished. There may be times in the school day when all the children need to be choosing math activities,[3] but seldom is it necessary for all the children to be working on the same task at the same time. Differentiated instruction is far easier if a multitude of options is available and children self-select what they want to do based on what they are currently interested in and ready for (and there is a strong correlation between interest and readiness). Remember: The key to real mathematical progress is that (1) the children are mentally invested in the task and (2) they are working at a level they understand.

---

[3] In fact, the NRC (2009) emphasizes that setting aside time explicitly for math within the schedule of the day is important rather than just relying upon the math embedded within classroom routines such as "Calendar Time" or within integrated instruction, which are common strategies in early childhood classrooms.

To control and monitor children's choices, you might set up a *contract system*. Individual children's contacts, negotiated with them on a weekly basis, could specify that they do certain types of mathematical activities during their choice times. Progress on contracts can be reviewed—and new contracts negotiated—on a weekly basis. For older children, journaling can be a useful tool to help you monitor their skills, insights, questions, and progress. Techniques like these are routinely practiced in High/Scope and Montessori programs, but they can work in any classroom.

Workstations are another common way to make different math activities available simultaneously. Task cards describing activities of different levels of complexity can be placed at each station as a way to meet the range of abilities in the class. One advantage of workstations is that they eliminate the problem of having enough materials for every child in the class to use simultaneously. Workstations also free the teacher to move around the classroom and interact with small groups of working children. If you do use workstations, I urge you to resist the temptation to have children rotate through the stations on an assigned schedule. By doing so, you have a situation similar to whole-group instruction; inevitably, some children are

1. Working at tasks they are not interested in,
2. Forced to stop working at tasks they are still interested in, and
3. Not going to be allowed to repeat tasks they find interesting.

Better to have a time when children are to be doing mathematics and allow them to spontaneously create and dissolve their *own* groups at the available workstations.

There are still times when whole-class instruction is called for. At those times, we should borrow a page from the Japanese lesson study model (Fernandez & Chokshi, 2002). Teacher-led, whole-class lessons are common in Japanese early childhood classrooms. Typically, a problem is posed to the whole class, and the class discusses possible ways of tackling the problem. For the bulk of the time, small groups work on the problem while the teacher or teachers circulate amongst the groups: observing, asking children to explain their work, and encouraging collaboration and deeper or more divergent ways of approaching the task. The lesson typically ends with a whole-class sharing time, where the groups compare and discuss their strategies and results and the teachers highlight some approaches or techniques that appear to have been particularly effective or different. As you can see, in this model children are empowered to be active partners in the mathematical process. They are exposed to a much wider variety of problem-solving approaches, and they learn to communicate their own reasoning and listen carefully to the reasoning of others. In short, they practice doing and understanding mathematics. That is "math time" worth having.

Work, Not Play

I am sure that, in the current climate where classroom teachers are increasingly pressured to maximize time-on-task and get results, there are those of you reading this who are uneasy with having math instruction be so activity-based, so individualized, and so lacking in teacher oversight. It is important to communicate to the children a clear and consistent message that, although this form of learning has many of the elements of "play time," this is serious business. Choice is encouraged, but purposeless frittering is not. Fun is encouraged, but silliness is not.

I would be the last to say that play and learning are incompatible, but we have to be very careful about what kind of play we are talking about. Early childhood educators have allowed the concept of play to become a dirty word in policy circles because the term has come to represent lack of rigor, direction, and purpose. DeVries and her colleagues (2002) have done an excellent job of articulating how the most highly functioning learning environments are implementing a very sophisticated form of scaffolded play. Clements and Sarama (2009) provide the following definition of such play in a mathematical context:

> The following features of mathematical play have been suggested: (a) it is a solver-centered activity with the solver in charge of the process; (b) it uses the solver's current knowledge; (c) it develops links between the solver's current schemes while the play is occurring; (d) it will, via "c", reinforce current knowledge; (e) as well as assist future problem-solving/mathematical activity as it enhances future access to knowledge; and (f) these behaviors and advantages are irrespective of the solver's age.

The authors note, however, that teachers need professional training to recognize the teachable moments within children's mathematical play and to know how to engage with the children mathematically at those times. This book is an attempt to support you in making sure the children's play is the children's work.

Paradoxically, it is because we want to give children the freedom to learn math on their own that we have to place some restrictions on how they use the math materials. The children are expected to use the materials respectfully and for exploration of mathematical ideas. There is nothing wrong with you approaching children who are abusing materials and saying

> I'm sorry. If you're not going to take care of our classroom materials, you should not be using them. Please put them away for now.

Or if children are using pieces of activities as part of nonmathematical pretend play, you can say:

> Those are our *math* materials. If you don't want to do a math activity with them, you should put them away.

Learner-Centered Instruction

How We Tend to Teach . . . and Why

Much of the math instruction I witness in classrooms follows a pattern that is pedagogically disastrous: The teacher

1. Notices that the children are not very good at a particular skill,
2. Finds an activity that requires them to use that skill,
3. Explains the activity,
4. Has the children start the activity,
5. Notices that most of the children can't do the activity,
6. Frantically runs around assisting the children (i.e., showing them step by step how to come up with the answers), and
7. Concludes that, because most of the children have now written down the right answers, they learned something.

One definition of insanity is to keep doing the same thing that hasn't worked in the past over and over again and expect a different result. I tell my pre-service college students that "activity is not instruction." You must either give the children a task that is do-able or teach them enough to make it do-able. If children lack a certain skill, don't throw them another task you already know they can't do and hope this time it will click.

So what's the alternative to this deflating and ineffectual teaching paradigm? There are two very different schools of thought on how lessons should be taught, and as the National Mathematics Advisory Panel (2008) noted, neither side can make a strong case that all instruction should be done one way or the other. The National Association for the Education of Young Children (Bredekamp & Copple, 1997) argues in its definition of developmentally appropriate practices that we should engage in *both-and* thinking rather than *either-or* thinking—meaning there are times and places where each approach makes sense. What are these two approaches? Although they go by different names, I shall call the two paradigms the direct instruction and the inquiry models:

1. **The Direct Instruction Model.** This model calls for information to be modeled and taught to the children in a clear, concise, linear fashion, followed by guided practice, which in turn is followed by individual practice. In this paradigm, assessments and reviews should occur regularly to make sure the information has been retained and is being used in an error-free fashion.

   This type of instruction has its place. There are times when we want to impart a particular piece of knowledge to a child, a small group, or the whole class, and we should know how to do this well. The technique can be used at any point in the activity cycle; for example:

   a. *Before the children begin an activity.* Sometimes we want to introduce a particular technique or strategy and have all the children practice it to help them become aware of its potential and comfortable enough with it that they can use it. We then look to see if the children start using the strategy spontaneously in their subsequent activity.

   b. *While an activity is in process.* Sometimes as the children are working, we see that many of them are making a similar mistake. We may decide to have the whole class pause so we can do a mini-lesson to clear up the point of confusion before having the children resume their work.

   c. *After the activity has been completed.* It is good practice, after the children have engaged in a problem-solving exercise, to lead a discussion in which they share results. Sometimes during those discussions, we choose to highlight a certain technique that was used because we want to make sure the whole class understands what that child did and how much it simplified the problem. Again, our goal is to increase the likelihood that other children will use that strategy on future occasions when it would prove useful.

2. **The Inquiry Model.** This model calls for children to find their own way to solve a problem. When we teach this way, we simply pose a problem clearly to the child or group of children and specify any limits on what is allowed and all criteria the solution must satisfy. We then let the children work. While the children work, we circulate and observe, occasionally commenting or posing a question but limiting the amount we correct or redirect. These problem-posing, problem-solving sessions often conclude with a share-and-compare session.

This type of teaching also has its place—and, in fact, you probably realize by now that I find this approach has much power. It is a good approach to use if you want to

a. Find out what the children know or are capable of or how typical certain types of errors are in their reasoning.

b. Find out whether children recognize which tools in their repertoire work best on which problems. Learning theory teaches us that children need *mixed practice* if we want skills to become fully functional. In this less directive format, children have to decide for themselves which circumstances call for which techniques.

c. Find out what strategies the children are comfortable enough with to use spontaneously.

d. Have the children teach each other alternative strategies that can be used to tackle the same problem. This drives home the very important point that there is seldom only one way to solve the problem—and that I as a teacher am not fishing for any particular type of solution. In fact, it encourages the more precocious mathematicians in the group to not settle for the most obvious strategy but to challenge themselves to come up with something not everyone else is doing.

As I said, either one of these models can be done well, and both have their place in a fine-tuned mathematical classroom. I must caution, however, that they must be mixed carefully. In too many classrooms, I see children being given a preliminary opportunity to explore and invent strategies, followed by a teacher presentation of the "right" way to solve such problems, followed by a series of drills to help them remember the steps in doing it the teacher's way. Under such conditions, the children take no pride in their accomplishments; in fact, they feel duped into exposing their ignorance before being shown the "right" way to approach such problems. Risk-taking and mental sense-making go down, and reliance on poorly understood algorithms goes up. Ultimately, mathematical progress suffers.

The correct approach? Give children opportunities to put their skills to work so you can figure out where they are on the teaching-learning path (i.e., what they *can* currently do). Use that information to mindfully and strategically insert instruction designed to teach them (or remind them of) techniques that will move them from where they are to where you hope they will go next, and then select activities that will allow them to put their newfound skills (along with their preexisting ones) to work. That's master teaching.

Creating the Learning Community You Want

Eighty percent of the benefits of a learning event in the classroom come not from the activity itself but from how the children as a group process the experience—and *you* fashion the mind-set of your students as a learning community. In a vibrant learning community, children

- Trust each other.
- Respect each other.
- Listen to each other.
- *Respond* to each other.
- Learn how to communicate their thoughts in ways others can understand and how to explain using different words if their audience doesn't "get" it the first time.

- Disagree with ideas rather than with people.
- Have the courage to ask questions.
- Dare to disagree when everyone else seems to agree.
- Dare to be wrong.
- Value multiple points of view, not settling too quickly on one "right" answer or one right way of doing things.
- Value elegant solutions over easy ones.
- Believe they as a group can decide whether they "got it right" without deferring to the teacher/textbook/internet.

That's a tough list of personality traits and learning dispositions to expect of children still in the early childhood stage of social and intellectual development, but you can mold a learning community where these attitudes and patterns of interaction blossom and thrive. The following are among the strategies that will get you there:

- Be neutral to responses, whether you agree or not. Continue to ask for other ideas even after you've heard the one you were listening for, and do not conclude by providing the answer you were hoping to hear.
- Have the group finish exploring one idea before moving on to another. Children tend to be competitive and want to immediately give a different answer rather than exploring the one already given. Increase the value of each contribution by holding the class's attention on it before moving on. How?

  1. **Probe for group consensus.** "How many of you agree with that?" Call on someone who agrees and ask him to state why or restate the solution. Call on someone who does not agree to explain why.
  2. **Probe for explanation.** Ask children to explain how they came up with their answer.
  3. **Probe for understanding.** Call on someone else in the class to explain what she thinks the person did in her own words.
  4. **Probe for attentiveness.** Call on individuals randomly to repeat what the previous person said.
  5. **Probe for questions.** "Raise your hand if you understand what ____ did. Raise your hand if you would like to ask ____ a question."

- Discourage the tyranny of the majority and the dominance of alpha personalities in the group. Encourage divergent thinking. Say: "That's what they think. What are some other ideas?" Or: "I know you have an idea, ____, but let's hear what some other people think."
- Enforce wait time. Value insight rather than speed. Give reflective thinkers time to get up to speed. Children panic and give up if they see a sea of frantically waving hands when they're still trying to think of an answer. Say: "Put your hands down; some children are still thinking." Or: "I'm going to ask you a question, and I don't want to see any hands right away. I want you to think about it. When I'm ready to hear some of your answers, I'll signal you."
- Encourage looking out for each other and using each other as resources. If children are stumped coming up with an answer, allow them to "phone a friend" (i.e., call on another child to advise them) and then respond. Or use the Think-Pair-Share technique:

1. Have the children think silently how they would answer the question.
2. Ask them to discuss their idea with a peer.
3. Open up the floor to questions. By this point, all the children feel a little more confident in their own ideas and, if they were stumped, have had the benefit of someone else's perspective to help them relate to the discussion that follows.

- Teach children the lesson it took *you* as an educator a while to learn: Rescue is robbery. If a classmate is struggling, the class's role is to help him work through the solution himself, not to provide the answer. Have children practice the skills of scaffolding. We do this in the social arena, encouraging children to become peer mediators in conflict resolution situations. Why don't we also encourage the same strategies in the *intellectual* arena?

Teacher-Led Lessons

The math materials you put in the classroom are not meant to be open-ended props for the children to use in whatever way they fancy. They have a purpose, and in choosing them, the children are choosing to use them for their intended purposes. But the children do not automatically know what to do with materials when they first appear on the shelf. They need to have the purposes and appropriate ways of using the materials shown to them. This can be done by

- Demonstrating the activity as part of group time.
- Presenting the activity to an individual child or small group of children who are showing an interest or readiness.
- Partnering the child with a child who already knows how to do the activity.
- Supervising two or more children as they go through the steps the first time.
- Setting out the materials in workstation format with simple written or orally delivered instructions.

But remember: The main learning will likely occur after you leave or on their subsequent returns to the same activity. Set the children up for independence, and don't hover or settle in.

In addition to the core design of an activity, extensions and variations can help adjust the difficulty level up or down, change the skills or strategies being practiced, or rekindle interest. Often the children will come up with their own alternatives to the procedures or rules you have developed. In many cases, these are better suited to their current abilities and interests than the ones you developed, and they should be allowed. And be careful about always trying to show the children *new* ways to use the materials. Again, it takes multiple returns to an activity for its value to be truly realized by the children, and if you are constantly changing it or moving on to more complex levels, you don't allow them to assimilate the concepts. If they're bored or frustrated by the task at hand, they will let you know!

The Perils of Group Work

It should be clear by now that I consider mathematics to be a very social enterprise. Children should be constantly sharing their understandings, comparing their problem-solving strategies, debating, disagreeing, questioning, and so on. In many cases, mathematical activities work better in a social context, both as a motivator and as a vehicle for children to learn from one another.

As advantageous a group work is, however, there are drawbacks. I will discuss two of them here:

1. When working with peers, it is very easy for a child whose understanding is shaky to sit back and let those with more confidence do the work. If the gap between their understanding and the work others are generating is too great, they will not benefit from observing the problem-solving process. In educational jargon, they are *outside their zone of proximal development*. Care should be taken to monitor group processes to make sure everyone is engaged. Whenever possible, structure group activities so each child's participation is required for the task to be completed.

2. When problems are solved by a group, it is much more difficult to judge the abilities of the individual participants. In part, you can overcome this by carefully observing as the group works and by questioning individual members. If an activity is going to be used for assessment purposes, it is important to build components into the task that will require the individual children to share not just their solution, but also their explanation of the process or to have children work individually on a follow-up problem and share their results with you in a journal entry.

When you want children to be working independently, you want to take steps to make sure this happens. The first step is to clearly communicate that, on this particular task, children are to answer as best they can without consulting with their peers or looking at someone else's work. If children trust that you are doing this only so you can develop a clearer understanding of how to help them learn, they will not try to circumvent your request. You might want to create some freestanding "cubicle" dividers for children to put around their desktop workspace on these occasions or teach them how to quickly and quietly turn their desks into individual work formations when you signal them to do so.

The Role of the Teacher as the Children Work

Even though the children are essentially teaching themselves (and each other) through these activities, you still play a vital role in turning their experiences into broad and rich learning. For example, you can

- Use what you know about children to influence their activity choices.
- Help children adjust the way they use the materials to better fit their individual abilities or to re-spark their interest.
- Provide additional materials that help children be more successful or explore a mathematical concept in a different way.
- Provide hints that help children think about a problem in a new way so they can experience greater success and greater learning. For example, you might say:

  - *"Would it help to line them up side by side?"*
  - *"Maybe if you got some counters you could figure it out."*
  - *"Would counting them help?"*
  - *"Here's a number line. See if that helps you."*

- Partner with children in their activity. This gives you the opportunity, when it is your turn, to talk out loud about what you are doing, or use a strategy that the children haven't thought of, or intentionally make an error and let the children catch you at it. This is a variation on what educators call *indirect correction.*

- Join in their excitement and celebrate their accomplishments. Help them realize how smart they are and what they have accomplished. From their perspective, they've just been playing! However, be careful not to praise the children with empty phrases like these:

  - *"Good job!"*
  - *"Nice work!"*
  - *"I like that!"*

Instead, encourage them by using more meaningful phrases, like the following, that focus on the children and the specific way they approached the task:

  - *"I like the way you organized the materials. That made counting them a lot easier."*
  - *"I've never seen it done that way. That's amazing! Do you mind if I take a picture of it?"*
  - *"That's interesting how you figured that out. Tell me about it."*
  - *"That was a hard problem, but you figured it out! You must be pretty proud of yourself!"*
  - *"You're so smart! Can you explain to Alexa how you did that?"*
  - *"Look at that! You both did it a different way, and you both came up with the same answer!"*

Keeping Everyone Safe

For children to learn, they must take risks, and for children to take risks, they must feel safe. Through both your actions and your effect on peer interactions, you have primary responsibility for maintaining the social, psychological, and intellectual safety of the environment.

Let's start by examining how we interact with the children as they share their ideas, insights, and confusions. In our desire to support children grappling with difficult tasks, we are tempted to bury the children under an endless stream of comments like "Good job!" and "Nice work! and "Very good!" (see above). Educators need to know the difference between *encouragement* and *praise.* Our goal is to *en-courage* (which, taken literally, means to fill the children with courage). Courage does not come when we make children dependent on our praise or have them look to us to judge their work. We want to say things that get them examining their own work and how they feel about it. We want them to understand that it is through their continued efforts that they will make progress. Yes, we want to celebrate their successes and help them survive their failures, but there are better ways to do this than by using a limited repertoire of verbal tics that are devoid of meaning. I heard the behavioral therapist Janine Fitzgerald tell an audience what she tells children: "There's no such thing as 'I can't.' There is only 'I can't . . . yet.'" I like that. It acknowledges the reality of the present but spotlights the future, and it places ultimate success under the children's control. It encourages them.

We are obviously not the only people in the classroom who affect whether children feel safe. Children do much of their mathematical problem solving in small groups rather than alone, and we often ask children to share their solutions with the rest of the class. Even a child working alone often has other children around who are curious about what she is doing, are eavesdropping on your conversations with her, or have opinions about what they see and hear. You need to help the children learn the rules of polite discourse in a learning community and insist that the children practice them. These rules include the following:

- Mistakes are an important part of learning, and seeing others' mistakes helps us clarify our own thinking.
- There is often more than one approach to the right answer, and there is often more than one solution.
- It is as important to carefully listen to your peers as it is to share your own thoughts.
- If you disagree or are confused, you should ask the person to explain what he did rather than assuming he is wrong.
- We should debate ideas without making personal judgments or remarks.
- It is not the teacher's job to decide what is correct. It is the class's collective responsibility to make those judgments.

Let me emphasize this last point. The quickest way for a teacher to get the class to stop thinking is to provide the right answer. If you jump in, you take away the opportunity for the child's peers to react and respond. If the children in your class feel you are the person with the Correct-o-Meter, they will defer to your judgment. I often say one of the key skills teachers need to develop is how to not have what gamblers call a *tell*—some verbal or behavioral cue that signals what you are thinking. The tell might be in your facial expression, your tone of voice, or your cadence in calling on children. It may be a phrase you reserve for wrong answers—such as "That's an interesting idea" or "Did anybody else come up with a different answer?"—rather than your customary "Good job!" If you avoid tipping your hand, the children will continue comparing their own sense-making with that of their peers and can join the conversation—politely, of course—if they disagree. And at the end of the conversation, they feel smart because the truth came from their thinking and their consensus rather than from the teacher or the answer key in the back of the book.

There are other ways we work to keep children safe. In Montessori circles, they have a phrase called *making the match*, which refers to matching a child up with the materials and activities that are appropriate for her at this time. In part, we control this by choosing what lesson we introduce to a particular child or small group or by encouraging them to work at certain activities. Some teachers help children make appropriate choices by negotiating weekly contracts with them that cover the types of math activities they will include in their choices that week. Sometimes we see children have made poor choices and are in over their head. Nothing good can come from allowing them to become frustrated and disillusioned. At those times, it is important to gently step in and suggest that the children put that activity away for now and direct them to one that will be a better match. In an environment where the children know you have their best interests at heart, they accept these gentle interventions as being for their benefit.

Authentic Assessment

The word *assessment* comes from the Latin *ad sedere*, meaning "to sit alongside." Assessment, in its purest form, is an attempt to experience the world through another's eyes—to "walk a mile in their moccasins," as they used to say when I was young. Achieving this level of intimate connection requires getting close, in a relaxed and trusting atmosphere, with no pressure or preconceptions. It is not how we typically think of assessment, and it is about as far from standardized testing as you can get, but it is what we need to do. Why? Because this deep, quiet, intimate, and interactive level of information gathering generates the richest and most true portrait of what the child currently knows and can do. No other system can come close.

Why assess? Well, the statement above pretty much answers that question. A long-standing mantra in education is "Assessment informs instruction"; in other words, to teach, you need to build on what children already know—hence the need to know what they know. The subtitle of this book, *Turning Math Inside Out*, implies that we use what's already inside the child as the foundation for our instructional decisions. If we don't know where a child is, we don't know where to take him.

When and how do we assess? Again, within this paradigm the answer should be obvious. We assess *constantly*. Teaching in this new paradigm requires spending less time telling and more time observing, asking probing questions, and having children explain their reasoning. When you do that, you are assessing. The act of teaching and the act of assessing are two sides of the same coin. The interactive skill sets that serve both functions are indistinguishable.[4]

When you teach in the style advocated in this book, children *make their learning visible*, meaning their individual strategies, concepts, and misconceptions are on display. And since you are increasingly freeing yourself from the responsibilities of holding the entire class's attention, you have more time to look at individual children's work and ask follow-up questions. These are the hallmarks of what is now called *authentic assessment*. You become a better teacher by shifting your attention to becoming a better assessor.

As educators, most of us eventually have to produce report cards and grades. Sadly, in the current age of accountability, standardized assessment instruments and high-stakes testing are the norm for generating these reports, even though teachers on the front lines lament that the results don't accurately reflect what their children know and are able to do. I am appalled at how teachers who have developed a rich sense of their children's current abilities are forced to use standardized end-of-unit tests from far-off publishers to generate their official "grades." We as an educational establishment have tricked ourselves into believing that the hard numbers these instruments generate are more real than the nuanced understandings available to the skillful and aware classroom teacher. I am here to tell you that is simply not true. More to the point, for those educators reading this book, even if you do use those instruments to generate grades and reports, they do not provide the information you need to go back into the

---

[4] One caveat: We need to keep clear in our mind when we are providing information and when we are asking the children to share their own impressions. If we seesaw back and forth too rapidly, jumping in to correct mistakes every time we notice one, we destroy the atmosphere of relaxed trust and respect that is needed for children to open up and share freely.

classroom and teach the next day. To get that information, you must yourself become a skilled assessor.

How do you capture and preserve your assessment information? A full treatment of this question goes beyond the scope of this book. But it should be obvious that, if this form of data gathering yields the richest and truest information available to you, it is worth capturing and preserving. Many of the detailed, individualized insights we form as we move about the classroom fade over time into vague impressions of how the children did. And children change so rapidly at this age that we forget what they were doing and were capable of two months ago if we have not taken steps to capture it in some authentic way.

A side benefit of going to the trouble of documenting children's learning is realized when it comes time to share information with families. Parents are probably used to seeing stacks of worksheets and homework assignments coming home as evidence that their children are learning math. In the absence of those artifacts, they may conclude that math is being neglected in your classroom. Give them a chance to see and understand what their children are doing and accomplishing in your classroom, and your parent group will become your biggest fan club. Your storehouse of well-chronicled, well-analyzed moments communicates the true nature of these budding mathematicians better than anything else you can offer. It rings true, and it allows you and the child's family to pause for a moment and "sit alongside" the child you all care about.

 ## Teaching Tips

Helping Children Talk about What They Know

In our effort to have children learn from experience rather than instruction, we sometimes go overboard by not having children reflect on what they have just done through conversation. What we want is not hands-on learning, but hands-on, *minds*-on learning. Putting what they have just done into words helps them process the information in a new way and consolidate their insights. It also allows

1. You to better understand what they are thinking.
2. Their peers to compare their own ways of approaching the problem to that being shared.

When you have conversations with children, use open-ended questions that encourage them to think about what they are doing and why they are doing it that way. For example, you could say:

- "I don't understand what you just did. Can you explain it to me?"
- "Is there any other way you could do that?"
- "You said they are both 'four,' but they don't match. I wonder why that is."
- "How can this one be a bigger number than that one? That one is more full."
- "Is nine more than seven? How can we find out for sure?"
- "Somebody showed me another way to do this problem. What they did was ____. What do you think about that?"

There are other ways to have children share their thoughts besides conversation, such as *journaling*. When having children journal their math solutions, it's a good idea to structure the writing prompt so the children are not using just one way of capturing their thinking. For example, suppose the children have just been working on the problem "How much is 23 tens and 23 units?"—you could say: "For your journal entry, write the number you decided is the same as 23 tens and 23 units. Also draw a picture of how you solved the problem, and use two or three sentences to describe why your solution is correct."

Also practice *wait time*. It is a consistent research finding that we tend not to wait nearly long enough after we ask a question for the children to respond. Wait time results in more responses and more complex responses. Also practice wait time *after* a child has responded. This gives the other students time to process the answer they have heard and also allows the child to elaborate if she thinks of something else. Classrooms where wait time is practiced consistently have better conversations. Sometimes you have to take steps to enforce wait time because the children tend to compete to get your attention. It is a good idea to let the children know that you will signal when you are ready for them to start sharing their thoughts and that, until then, they should keep their hands down. Hard questions require time to answer. Make sure children are given that gift of time.

Three Levels of Vocabulary Acquisition

Children need to be exposed to and eventually master the vocabulary of mathematics. Be sure to adjust your verbal prompts to their current level of vocabulary mastery. For example, if the children are beginning to associate number games with quantity:

- **Level 1.** At level 1, you are modeling the proper terminology. In other words, this is the vocabulary *teaching* phase:

  - *"This is the eleven . . . this is the twelve . . . this is the thirteen."*
  - *If the child is having difficulty coming up with the name or has just named something incorrectly, repeat the names of all the items, with the one they missed named last and asked first: "Very good. So the thirteen is here, the eleven is here, and the twelve is here. Now can you tell me which one is the twelve? . . . The thirteen? . . ."*

- **Level 2.** At level 2, children can recognize the name and know what it means (known as *receptive language*), but you are not forcing them to try to come up with the name themselves (known as *expressive* or *productive language*):

  - *"Point to 74."*
  - *"Who has 14 beans?"*
  - *"Make 24 for me."*
  - *"Which one is the 13?"*
  - *"Show me how to write 47."*
  - *"Bring me 19 beans."*

If a child hesitates or makes errors at this level, return to the first level.

- **Level 3.** At level 3, the child must come up with the name himself (*expressive language*):

  - *"What's this?"*
  - *"What quantity did you make?"*
  - *"And this one is called what?"*
  - *"Which one is missing?"*
  - *"What do you call that?"*

This is the hardest of the three types. If the child is struggling at this level, return to the second or first level.

Concrete before Abstract

When we are teaching, we often make the mistake of naming a concept before we teach the concept. Worse yet, we believe that, if children can say the name back to us in appropriate contexts, they have mastered the concept. Children learn early on the words we use to discuss concepts and parrot them back to us. Vygotsky (1934/1936) talked about children forming *pseudo-concepts*, meaning they can talk about events using the vocabulary we have provided them without understanding the concepts those events signify. When children use the vocabulary of mathematics, we assume they understand those words the same way we do. Quite often they don't.

A mantra within mathematics education, especially in the early childhood years, is concrete before abstract—hands-on learning. Children need to be able to act upon things in the world in order to experience how they work. That's why early childhood programs have dramatic play areas. Children can much better understand roles and social relationships if they can act them out rather than just seeing them or hearing about them.

As an example, the teens and tens boards (see Chapter 3) are critical pieces of apparatus in helping children sort out the base-10 system. In manipulating the concrete materials, children actually transform the numeral 10 into a teen number by first covering the zero with a digit; then they count the teen quantity by first counting a 10 bar and continuing to the target number using loose units. They then see the two visible digits of the teen numeral correspond to the two sets of counted objects in front of them, a ten and loose units. All this happens through their actions and their transformations.

We sometimes feel we can be more efficient and have fewer "things" cluttering up our room by showing objects and their transformations in picture form. But children aren't able to actually move the objects in the pictures around to create the new relationships, and, therefore, they don't experience them the same way. Nor can they make mistakes and find ways to correct them. There is a time to move on to the picture stage, but it's not the earliest stage. That's why having numeral tiles for children to physically place on a hundreds board is better than handing the children a blank hundreds board and having them write the numerals on it.

This brings us to another point: Numerals are much more abstract than the quantities they represent. A wise math educator (I wish I could remember who) once told me we should keep numbers adjectives as long as possible rather than treating them as nouns. By that, she meant that children can relate much better to having 7 apples, eating 2 apples, and having 5 apples left than they can to $7 - 2 = 5$. Yet we are so anxious to get on to the "real" math that we tend to use the concrete (or a picture representation of an event) only as a brief introduction to a task and

Go to the PDToolkit to find the online template referenced to here.

then have the children do a whole series of examples just with written numerals. Even in classroom discussions, we tend to slip into treating numbers as nouns, answering the question "How many days have we been in school?" with "29" rather than "29 days." In measurement, we insist on answers including the unit being used ("19 inches," not simply "19"). We should follow the same advice with all our discourse concerning quantities of objects in the world.

The Same Thing Many Ways

As you will note, many activities in a particular chapter revisit the same skill. This is not redundancy for redundancy's sake. As teachers, we are too quick to check off that children "have" a particular skill or idea when we see evidence of it once. Children's mathematical development is not nearly so black and white. For an awareness, skill, or concept to be firmly in place, it needs to be practiced in a wide variety of contexts and over an extended period of time.[5] It is boredom, not familiarity, that indicates children are working below their appropriate level.

Errors Are Information

Our knee-jerk reaction to mistakes is to correct, to model the correct solution, or to ask a set of leading questions to pull the right answer out of a child's mouth. None of these end up being very useful—or very empowering. Mistakes should impel you to assess and plan, not to correct.

Take a tip from the reading people: If children are making occasional errors at a task, they are probably operating at the appropriate level of difficulty. If they are making too many errors, you probably need to restructure the activity or move them to a different activity that is do-able. For that matter, if children are coming up with right answers effortlessly, it might be time to ratchet up the difficulty so they once again have to apply effort and attention in order to succeed—with the occasional error.

Competition

Many of us in the early childhood field have been taught to downplay competition in our classrooms in favor of cooperative games. You might wonder, then, why many of the suggested activities in this book involve competition. Personally, I don't feel it benefits children to eliminate competition from their lives. It's the same way I treat other touchy subjects, like what to do when children use swear words or refuse to share. I would much rather have these things happen in my presence—which allows me to influence how children feel about them—than to ban them entirely from my classroom. In its best form, competition is a means by which people seek to do their best work in a social context. Children engage in more interesting mathematical thinking when they do these activities with other children rather than by themselves, and competitive games encourage focused attention and maximum effort.

If you look closely at the activities, you will see that the emphasis isn't on winning but on doing something enjoyable with others. Once a round is over, the children quickly shift into playing again rather than dwelling on who won and who lost. It's fairly easy to monitor the interactions—and talk with individual children, if necessary—to make sure the "winners" are being gracious and the "losers" are not getting discouraged.

---

[5] The mantra I picked up from my Montessori training is "The same thing many ways, and many things the same way." That simple premise has served me well over the years.

Answer Keys or No Answer Keys?

I have mixed feelings about having children use answer keys to check their work.[6] Yes, keyed solutions allow children to self-check rather than relying upon the teacher to tell them whether they got everything right. But it is precisely that emphasis on "getting everything right" that is the problem. I want children to turn inward to evaluate their work, not rely upon an outside authority. It's not that I'm against right answers, but I want the rightness to be a conclusion reached by the child's logical-mathematical mind. There are at least three things that happen when children have the right answers at their fingertips to check their work, all of them bad:

- Children who made a lot of errors feel badly about themselves and avoid the activity in the future, even though it might be the perfect activity to help them develop a new concept or skill.
- Children peek at the answer key when they are uncertain of the answer rather than make their own best guesses and risk being wrong.
- Children who got all the answers right decide there's no point in doing that activity again.

Children get better by continuing to engage in challenging and intriguing work, not by getting all the answers right. Constantly checking to see "Is this right?" inhibits their initiative, ownership, and enjoyment.

So does this mean teachers should retire their red pencils, not marking errors on children's submitted work even when it is riddled with errors? Not at all. For one thing, parents would be appalled to see error-filled work coming home with no indication the teacher noticed anything wrong with it. But those papers usually are more part of your assessment system than your primary teaching tools. Here we are talking about the hands-on activities children use to hone the skills that will eventually result in error-free performance. *Error-free practice is not the path to error-free performance.* In the skill-building phase, children need to be thinking, reexamining, comparing, questioning, hypothesizing, debating, and deciding. Errors disappear as understanding and confidence advance. That comes from mindful activity, not constant correction.

A similar logic applies to the situation where children come up to us and ask: "Is this right?" By answering that question, we do a lot of harmful things:

1. We signal that getting the right answer is more important than how the answer was arrived at.
2. *We* now own the problem, not the child.
3. We miss an opportunity to learn from the child how she approached the problem.
4. We stop the thinking process.

That's why our response to that question should most often be "What do you think?" or "Show me how you came up with that." That way mathematics continues.

[6] Variations on answer keys, common in making early childhood materials, include using puzzle cuts or matching colors or symbols on the backs of pieces and color-coding correct matches to show which ones go together.

Study Group Discussion Starters: Turning Math Inside Out

Given the choice, will children voluntarily choose math?

What attempts have you made to make math activities part of the choice time in your environment? Have you devoted more shelf space to math materials and labeled the area as such? What math-rich materials have you added to the environment, and how have they been received? What ground rules have you had to lay down so the children use those materials for their intended purposes?

Have you tried designating a certain time of the day as math time but not specified which math activities the children should use during that time? If so, what do you think of the choices they've made? What ground rules have you had to lay down so they use that time profitably?

If you have tried moving away from teacher-designated whole-group activities, have you seen any changes in the way children engage in their mathematical tasks? Would you say their level of engagement or interest was higher or lower? Did they seem to be thinking more or less? Was there a change in their conversations or what they shared with their peers or with you?

How much teaching is required for children to progress mathematically?

To what extent can children practice and perfect mathematical activities through their own activity and their interaction with their fellow learners? At what times do you find it important to teach a concept, and how much guided practice is needed before the children are ready to proceed independently?

Does there come a point where gentle encouragement and scaffolding should give way to firm insistence and direct modeling? Discuss cases of children for whom a more child-centered approach hasn't seemed to work. Did a more teacher-directed approach better help those children develop understanding and flexibility, or did they stay dependent on the modeled algorithms?

How can children of differing abilities engage in mathematics simultaneously?

Share your experiences of having mathematical activities of varying difficulty going on simultaneously in the classroom. Have you experimented with letting children self-select which activities to do and for how long? If so, how satisfied have you been with the result? Would you say the children gravitate to the activities that are easiest or to the ones that they find challenging? Do you find them spontaneously adjusting the difficulty of the task to make it harder or easier? If so, what do you think they are trying to accomplish? What role have you played in helping them make their selections or modify the activities?

What has been your experience when children of differing abilities pair up in a shared activity? How have they resolved the disparity? What has been your role in negotiating the interactions or the difficulty of the task? Do you think they have both ended up benefiting from the experience?

How do you respond when children make mathematical errors?

In your experience, what happens if children's mathematical errors go unchallenged? Have you found the result is persistent error, confusion, or frustration? If so, how do you intervene? Do children often turn to you to verify whether they have done their math correctly? If so, how do you respond?

What is your role if children disagree on a mathematical procedure or result? What techniques have worked to get children to share their thinking processes with you and each other? How do you respond when you see a flaw in their reasoning? Do you have an example to share of a really great classroom discussion that emerged from a mathematical disagreement?

PLACE-VALUE AWARENESS LAUNCH POINTS

What This Is—And Why It Is Important

Early on, children take pride it showing how high they can count (the counting numbers are also called *cardinal* numbers). Children quickly notice the pattern of the decades, which allows them to repeat the familiar sequence of one through nine with a different prefix. The most frequent mistakes they make are continuing the units count past the decade shift point ("... thirty-nine, thirty-ten, thirty-eleven ... ") and forgetting what decade name comes next ("... thirty-nine ... FIFTY!").

Parents often come up to their young child's teacher proudly proclaiming that their child can count from 1 to 100. In many cases, they're right, but oral counting from 1 to 100 is actually a fairly minor accomplishment in terms of mathematical development. The critical piece that children have not yet figured out is how these new numbers are constructed from combinations of tens and ones.

Nor should we expect them to figure this out on their own. Consider how cleverly we disguise this critical feature by the way we name the teen and tens numbers in English. How can we expect a child to discover that the number after 10 adds 1 to a base number of 10 when we call it *eleven*? Better yet, consider how cleverly we disguise the fact that *fifteen* is 10 and 5 more: The 10 is encoded as -*teen* and the 5 as *fif*-, and the two parts of the word are *inverted* (i.e., logically, 15 should read *teenfif*). And why would anyone in their right mind call 20 *twenty* rather than *two-ten*?[1] Not surprisingly, research shows that in language communities where the early counting numbers are more rationally named—where, for example, 13 is called *ten three*

---

[1] There are, of course, historical reasons for these naming conventions, but that doesn't help the poor child trying to make sense of this system.

and 57 *five-ten seven*—children move much more quickly and comfortably into place-value awareness.

Since we are not likely to change the English language, we must provide many classroom experiences to help children see the underlying base-10 aspect of numbers beyond 10. Unfortunately, many math curricula, in their headlong rush to get to the "real" mathematical stuff like addition and subtraction, spend little time on the types of mathematical experiences described in this chapter. One of the great things about the recent report from the National Research Council (NRC) on early childhood mathematics (NRC, 2009) and the Common Core standards that emerged from it (National Governors Association Center & Council of Chief State School Officers, 2010) is that place-value awareness is emphasized much earlier than it has been in the past. I believe there is no such thing as spending too much time helping children develop a secure and intimate understanding of base-10. Children who do not develop a deep and strong place-value awareness are at high risk of failing to thrive mathematically in subsequent years.

Not that there aren't those who say we are jumping the gun. Piagetians warn that young children lack *hierarchical classification*. In number sense terms, this means that children treat both tens and ones simply as objects to be counted. For example, if you give them three tens and two ones and ask them how many they have all together, they are likely to say, "Five." Mathematicians would say they do not differentiate between *place value* (treating the *3* in *32* as *30*) and *face value* (treating the *3* in *32* as *3*).

But plenty of personal experience and research evidence has convinced me that young children can maneuver meaningfully in the world of bigger numbers if we give them learning materials that continuously ground them to the true magnitude of the numbers they are manipulating. It's not so much that they can't develop number sense at this more sophisticated level; it's that we can't assume it will just appear spontaneously, without meaningful physical experiences and our own strategic and sustained assistance.

What Comes Before—And How to Get There

One of my maxims is that we cannot teach the children we wish we had in our classrooms; we have to teach the ones that are actually there. There are skills that precede the ones discussed in this chapter, and if children have not yet developed those foundational skills, we must provide opportunities to get them up to speed. Very briefly, here are the foundational concepts children should have developed by the time they reach kindergarten age and a few suggestions for activities that help them master these concepts. (For a more extensive look at these earlier developmental levels, see the number sense findings of the NRC, 2009 in Appendix A.) If children need more work at this level, you might try activities such as these, which were originally published in greater detail in *Math at Their Own Pace*, published by Redleaf Press.[2]

---

[2] *Math at Their Own Pace: Child-Directed Activities for Developing Early Number Sense* by Greg Nelson. Copyright © 2007 by Greg Nelson. Reprinted with permission of Redleaf Press, St. Paul, MN; www.redleafpress.org.

(For those of you who might need a brief review of the Common Core standards, which the codes below refer to, please see the Preface.)

Logical Quantification

K.CC.4b *The number of objects is the same regardless of their arrangement or the order in which they are counted.*

Logical quantification is the ability to make judgments of "how many" and compare quantities. Children are able to make these judgments long before they know how to count. Gradually, they learn to base these judgments on the actual number of items that make up the set and not on other factors such as how close together the pieces are, how long they are, or how much they fill up a container.

If children need more work at this level, you might try activities such as these:

- **Quantity Concentration.** Hide objects under opaque bowls and have the children find matching quantities. Use different objects under the matching bowls (e.g., two beads and a Unifix cube under one bowl and a bead, a button, and a counting bear under the matching bowl). The goal is for children to remember not what objects are under the bowl but how *many* objects are under the bowl. Not as easy as it sounds, especially for a young child.

- **The Store Game.** This game requires "a store" (shelf with interesting objects where children can "shop"), a small "shopping basket," and a set of "shopping lists" that have from 1 to 10 images on them (e.g., playing cards ace through 10, with the numerals whited out). Children look at a shopping list and then go to the store to pick up exactly that number of objects. The key is that the children must leave the shopping list behind and *remember* how many things to bring back.

- **Quantity Sorting.** Create sets of containers, picture cards, or dot plates showing from one to six objects of different types, sizes, and arrangements. The children's task is to sort them into sets that have the same quantity.

- **Showdown.** This is the game of War played with a deck of cards similar to those used for The Store Game above. Pairs of children simultaneously turn over a card and then decide whether they have the same amount or whether one of them has more (can be played with either "more" or "less" taking the trick).

- **Graphing Activities.** Even pre-counting children can make judgments of more, less, and the same by comparing length. Supplying the children with graphing mats, egg cartons, or ice-cube trays allows them to take sets they have created themselves and make comparisons of relative quantity because the containers ensure that all the objects in each category are equally spaced.

Accurate Counting to 10

K.CC.1 *Count to 100 by ones and by tens.*

K.CC.4 *Understand the relationship between numbers and quantities; connect counting to cardinality.*

K.CC.5 *Count to answer "how many?" questions about as many as 20 things arranged in a line, a rectangular array, or a circle, or as many as 10 things in a scattered configuration; given a number from 1–20, count out that many objects.*

It takes not just practice but also a series of cognitive "aha" moments before children begin counting small quantities accurately. Counting requires, among other things, using the number names in the right order, counting all the objects once and only once, stopping the number chant when the last object is counted, and knowing the last number name said is how many there are (Gelman & Gallistel, 1978).

As logical quantification and accurate counting come together, children gradually convince themselves that rearranging objects may make a quantity *appear* to increase or decrease but in fact it stays constant. In other words, children begin to realize that once they have counted a set, they know how many are in the set as long as no items are taken away or added (this awareness is known as *conservation of number*). This in turn allows children to develop the skill of *counting-on*, meaning that, as more items are added to an already counted set, you can continue the count from that point rather than starting over at one and counting the whole set. For example, if children have already counted seven items and they see three more added, they count: "seven . . . eight, nine, ten."

If children need more work at this level, you might try activities such as these, which were originally published in greater detail in *Math at Their Own Pace*, published by Redleaf Press[3]:

- **Toothpick Patterns.** All you need is a supply of toothpicks (or cotton swabs, craft sticks, etc.). Children take a specified number of toothpicks—say, six—and arrange them in a design of their own choosing, then they take six more and make a different design, and so on. If they wish, they can glue each design down on a separate sheet of paper and make a "Book of 6," or the class can make a wall mural of all their designs. This simple activity provides striking visual proof that six can look many different ways and still remain six.

- **Number Rods, Decimeter Rods, and Tabletop Rods.** Make two-colored rods of incremental lengths from one decimeter to one meter (*number rods*) or one centimeter to one decimeter (*tabletop rods*), with alternating segments of the same color (i.e., all the odd segments end in one color, all the even in the other).[4] Children can practice identifying which rods are which quantities by sight and then count to verify. They can also practice putting the rods in sequential order or do "Which Is Larger?" games. If you supply loose tiles to go with the number rods, children can place them on the rod segments as they count, to verify the quantity. If you make a pile of decimeter rods to match the segments on the number rods, children can re-create the number rods from loose parts—on top, in front, as a reflection, or at a distance. Children can also practice counting-on when they count one rod and add another to it—though their tendency is to count the total quantity.

- **Cuisenaire Rods.** These are similar to the number rods, but each of the 10 rods is color-coded, and multiple sets are used. Children become acquainted with which colors represent which quantities, which makes the rods useful for number sense activities to come. I prefer the connecting Cuisenaire rods

---

[3] *Math at Their Own Pace: Child-Directed Activities for Developing Early Number Sense* by Greg Nelson. Copyright © 2007 by Greg Nelson. Reprinted with permission of Redleaf Press, St. Paul, MN; *www.redleafpress.org*.

[4] I have made these out of wood or stiff cardboard wrapped with tape. Most recently, I have used the linking counting squares sold by Cuisenaire, which work quite well.

because they have the incremental units marked on one face of the rod, so children can count and verify the quantities.[5] If you have children connect a rod with the increments showing to one not showing the increments, you have a perfect tool for encouraging them to count on from the first number rather than counting the whole quantity.

- **Ten Frames.** You need a mat or container displaying two rows of five squares, one row above the other.[6] Children place objects in the frames, one object per square, first filling the top row from left to right and then filling the bottom row from left to right, counting as they go. Ten frames are a perfect tool for using 5 and 10 as *anchor numbers* from which to count on or count back in recognizing the quantities; for example, 4 is seen as 1 less than a full row of 5, 7 as 2 more than 5 and 3 less than 10, and so on. Later, children do quantity recognition games, instantly identifying a quantity just by seeing a partially filled frame.

Connecting Numerals to Quantities up to 10

K.CC.3 *Write numbers from 0 to 20. Represent a number of objects with a written numeral 0–20 (with 0 representing a count of no objects).*

Obviously, learning to recognize and name the symbols 0, 1, 2, and so on is a separate skill from counting. We can help children work at this with a variety of memory games. After they recognize the numerals, they must practice associating the numerals with the quantities they represent, which gives added confirmation that counted quantities can be named. The numeral gives finality to the count and visually suggests that two quantities may differ in appearance but are the same in a mathematical sense.

If children need more work at this level, you might try activities such as these:

- **1–10 Pencil Box.** This is a tray with 10 compartments. Each compartment is wide enough and long enough for five pencils to fit side by side and tall enough to hold two layers of pencils. On the back wall, the compartments are labeled with the numerals 1 to 10 (include 0 if you like). Children count pencils into their hands and then place them in the appropriate compartments.[7] They can also bundle the pencils with rubber bands and play "Who Has?" games, play greater than/less than games, or arrange the bundles in numerical order.
- **Unifix Stairs.** Unifix makes a 1–10 tray in which to place Unifix towers. Typically, the set of Unifix cubes used with the tray have only one of one color, two of another, and so on for children to connect into same-colored towers. They then have to count the cubes in the towers and decide which compartment each belongs in. The color aspect lends itself to games of greater than/ less than and quantity estimation (e.g., look at a collection of loose cubes,

---

[5] Until these came along, I marked off the unit increments on one face of my Cuisenaire rods with pencil.

[6] I take egg cartons or ice-cube trays and cut them down to size.

[7] I like to use clear acetate for the front wall of the compartments so the children can see the arrangement of the erasers from the front. That way they can see that seven, for example, is five and two more.

estimate how many there are, and then connect them and find which tray they fit in).

- **Numeral Tiles on Tabletop Rods.** You can write numerals 1–10 on counting tiles (ten 1's, nine 2's, etc.); then the numerals can be placed in sequential order on each of the 1–10 tabletop rods. Many discoveries regarding the tiles and the numerals can be made by arranging the rods and tiles in different ways.

- **Number-Numeral Bingo.** The easier version—and the one that gives the most practice with numeral recognition—uses quantity cards for the caller and numerals on the bingo cards. The caller can either name the quantity or simply show it. If the calling cards have numerals on them and the bingo cards have different pictured quantities, the children get more practice with quantity estimation as they estimate which ones might match the shown numeral. I advise against putting the quantity icons in any standard format or always using the same image for the same quantity so children get added practice in separating quantity from color, image, or arrangement cues (e.g., the 2 might be shown as two elephants side by side on one card and two monkeys in opposite corners on another).

Concepts and Skills Being Reinforced at This Developmental Stage

Children will not understand place value by being told about it. As researcher Constance Kamii (1985) noted, children have to reinvent arithmetic for themselves, in their own time and in their own minds, before they will own it and understand it. Children will truly "know" this different way of visualizing numbers at the point they excitedly run up to you and describe what they have just discovered.

There is much to be learned. Here is a summary of the place-value number concepts children will gain mastery of though experiences such as those described in this chapter, along with the Common Core benchmarks associated with each.

Teen Numbers Have 10 as a Base

K.NBT.1 *Work with numbers 11–19 to gain foundations for place value.*

As children learn to count, there is nothing that makes ten-eleven-twelve seem any different from one-two-three. It's just counting. They need to take a step back and reexperience these larger numbers as something more than simply a continuation of one-to-one counting. They represent the beginning point of packaging numbers into bundles of tens and ones.

The Use of Zero as a Placeholder

1.NBT.2c *The numbers 10, 20, 30, 40, 50, 60, 70, 80, 90 refer to one, two, three, four, five, six, seven, eight, or nine tens (and 0 ones).*

Suddenly, zero means more than "nothing." The *decades* (10, 20, 30 . . .) all have a zero at the end. The zero tells you that the quantity is made up of tens with no leftover units. If the numeral 30 did not include a zero, you would not know that the 3 means 3 tens instead of 3 units.

The Part-Whole Concept Extended to the Place-Value System

K.NBT.1 *Compose and decompose numbers from 11 to 19 into ten ones and some further ones, e.g., by using objects or drawings, and record each composition or decomposition by a drawing or equation (e.g., 18 = 10 + 8); understand that these numbers are composed of ten ones and one, two, three, four, five, six, seven, eight, or nine ones.*

1.NBT.2 *Understand that the two digits of a two-digit number represent amounts of tens and ones. Understand the following as special cases:*

    a. *10 can be thought of as a bundle of ten ones—called a "ten."*
    b. *The numbers from 11 to 19 are composed of a ten and one, two, three, four, five, six, seven, eight, or nine ones.*
    c. *The numbers 10, 20, 30, 40, 50, 60, 70, 80, 90 refer to one, two, three, four, five, six, seven, eight, or nine tens (and 0 ones).*

We want children to apply their budding part-whole awareness to see the 10 embedded in the teen numbers and the multiple sets of tens embedded in 20, 30, 40, and so on. We want them to automatically think of 13 as "ten and three more" and 37 as "three tens and seven more."

Place Value versus Face Value

1.NBT.2 *Understand that the two digits of a two-digit number represent amounts of tens and ones.*

It is the position of a digit in a numeral that tells us what the quantity is; for example, the 2 in 27 represents 20, not 2. In mathematical terms, we say the 2's *face value* is 2, but its *place value* is 20. The right-most digit always tells how many units there are, the digit to its left tells how many tens there are, and so on. That is why we call it a *place*-value system.

The 10:1 Relationship between Tens and Units

1.NBT.2a *10 can be thought of as a bundle of ten ones—called a "ten."*

Children need to gradually convince themselves that turning 10 units into 1 ten or turning 1 ten into 10 units does not change the quantity. This is the next big step in their ability to conserve quantity. As a corollary, they need to realize that, if they have more than 9 in any place-value category, they can't easily name the number. So if a child has 4 ten-bars and 23 unit cubes and wants to name how many he has, he needs to

1. Pare down his units pile by counting out 10 units and trading them for a ten-bar,
2. Continue to pare down his units pile by counting out another 10 units and trading them for another ten-bar,
3. See that the units pile is now less than 10, and
4. Name the quantity—6 tens and 3 units, or 63.

Directionality in Reading Multidigit Numerals

1.NBT.1 *In this range [1–120], read and write numerals and represent a number of objects with a written numeral.*

In our culture, we read from left to right, and we do so when we read numerals as well. But the bundling of ever-increasing place-value groupings proceeds from right to left. This discrepancy is not without consequence—it is one of the main reasons children confuse 37 and 73. It makes sense for our naming system to state the largest quantity first, but when asked to count, rearrange quantities into place-value groups, or add and subtract, we work in the other direction, from smallest to largest. It takes some time for children to get comfortable with which direction goes with which task.

Counting-On Using Place-Value Categories

K.CC.1 *Count to 100 by ones and by tens.*

K.CC.2 *Count forward beginning from a given number within the known sequence (instead of having to begin at 1).*

1.NBT.1 *Count to 120, starting at any number less than 120.*

One of the greatest "aha" moments for children is when they realize that, when given materials organized in sets of 10, they don't have to count every item, starting with 1. They can count the tens first and count on from there ("One ten, two tens, three tens—that's thirty . . . thirty-one, thirty-two" or "Ten, twenty, thirty . . . thirty-one, thirty-two"). To do this, however, requires adding a new skill to their repertoire. Anyone who has worked at teaching young children how to count money or read time on an analog clock knows children have a hard time switching their skip counts in midstream. For example, if I give a child five nickels and five pennies and ask her to count how much money she has, she would need to start by skip counting "five, ten, fifteen, twenty, twenty-five" and then *stop* counting by fives and switch to counting by ones: "twenty-six, twenty-seven, twenty-eight, twenty-nine, thirty." Children have a hard time making that switch. The same applies to counting five ten-bars and three unit cubes—"ten, twenty, thirty, forty, fifty . . . fifty-one, fifty-two, fifty-three."

Counting Backward through the Decades

Just as children find it difficult to count backward from 10 to 1 even after they have mastered the forward counting sequence, they find it difficult to count backward through the decades. It is well documented that children counting backward through the early twenties will pause at 21 or 20 and often say the next number is 31 or 30. The skill of moving flexibly both forward and backward within the place-value system is vital to children's soon-to-be-needed strategic approach to two-digit addition and subtraction.

Estimating Large Quantities

As children's ability to count higher races forward, their sense of how big those numbers are lags behind. For a long time, children most frequently name a large pile of counters as being either 20 or 100. A child who can count to 100 but doesn't know whether the group of objects in front of him is more likely in the 30 range than 70-something has a long way to go in the number sense department.

Greater than/Less than in the Place-Value System

1.NBT.3 *Compare two two-digit numbers based on meanings of the tens and ones digits, recording the results of comparisons with the symbols >, =, and <.*

When numbers are large, children don't necessarily know which is larger. For example, if asked, "Is 42 larger than 37?" face value confuses their sense of place value—since 37 has a 7 in it, they instinctively think 37 must be the larger number. It takes a great deal of practice before children comfortably process the relative importance of the tens place and units place in making greater than/less than judgments.

The Relationship between Hundreds and Tens

2.NBT.1 *Understand that the three digits of a three-digit number represent amounts of hundreds, tens, and ones; e.g., 706 equals 7 hundreds, 0 tens, and 6 ones.*

When children's count reaches that magic number 100, they are suddenly in new territory—the numeral is now *three* digits long, and it contains *two* zeroes. Children cannot truly appreciate the place-value system until they are confronted with the fact that the left-most digit is not automatically tens or that the number after one hundred is not two hundred but one hundred one—and it is written 101, not 1001. In the numerals 101 to 109, children get a new appreciation for zero as a placeholder!

L/aunch Points

The Launch Points are described in simple terms, as they would be introduced to the children. But there are many ways to vary the activities to keep them fresh. If you simply put the materials out and have all the children use them the same way every time, they will soon be gathering dust, and you will not be using them to maximal effect.

Sometimes the materials themselves can be altered to allow different mathematical activity. For that matter, children have a remarkable ability to come up with their *own* variations, and when they do, they provide a useful window on what math currently makes sense to them. Contrary to popular belief, children are not always looking for the easy way out. Left to their own devices, children tend to adjust the activities so they find them challenging enough to still be interesting.

Still, it is good to have some ideas for how to simplify a task, add new layers of complexity, or simply have the children practice the same skill in a novel way. Following are some further insights into what skills are being developed in each of the Launch Point activities and some ways to vary them.

PD **pd** TOOLKIT™

Go to the PDToolkit to find the online templates referenced in the following activities.

Launch Point

TEEN BOARDS WITH BASE-10 MATERIALS

MATERIALS AND SET-UP

- Two 10 cm × 26 cm boards.[8] When the boards are oriented vertically with one right below the other, the boards display the numeral 10 nine times (five on the first board and four on the second, with the lowest space left blank). The 0 digit in the units place is green, and the 1 digit in the tens place is blue. Stuck to the middle of the 0's on the boards are nine transparent Velcro buttons.
- 4 cm × 5 cm numeral cards, 1 through 9, all green. The cards all have a transparent Velcro button on the back so they can stick to the boards in the units place.
- A supply of at least 45 units and 9 tens manipulatives (blocks, straws, bean sticks, etc.).
- The numeral 20 from the place-value card set and two more tens manipulatives.

Figure 3.1 Teen Boards with Bean Sticks

LAUNCH POINTS

Part A. Introduce Quantities Only (i.e., leave boards on the shelf)

1. Pull out a ten-bar: "How much is this?" Let the child count if necessary. Ask the same question after you place a single loose unit next to the ten-bar. Emphasize the connection between the teen number and the tens-and-ones: "Ten and one more is eleven."
2. Have the child recognize 12 through 19 in a similar fashion, letting the child participate in forming and naming the numbers. Pause periodically to see if the child is remembering the names of earlier combinations by asking various three-level vocabulary questions (see Chapter 2, "Three Levels of Vocabulary Acquisition").
3. After 11–19, have the child add one more unit to the tens-and-ones arrangement of 19: "Now how many do you have?" After the child answers, "Twenty," hold up two ten-bars and look confused: "But I thought *this* was twenty." Have the child help you figure out that the 10 loose units are equivalent to the second ten-bar you are holding.

Part B. Introduce Boards Only (i.e., leave quantity materials on the shelf)

1. On the first teen board, point to the first printed 10: "What numeral is this?" (*Note*: If the child does not know 10, the child is not ready for a teens lesson, and you should put the boards away).
2. Pull out the 1 numeral card: "Ten (point to the 10) and one more (attach the 1, covering the 0) is . . . ?" Pause to let the child look at the numeral and respond. If the child does not know, finish the sentence: " . . . eleven."
3. Proceed down the board, making 12 through 19 in a similar fashion, letting the child participate in forming and naming the numerals. Pause every once in a while to go back and see if the child is remembering the names of earlier teens by asking various three-level vocabulary questions (see Chapter 2, "Three Levels of Vocabulary Acquisition").

[8] All measurements in this book are given in metric units—it's time for the United States to join the rest of the world! Just remember that 2.5 centimeters is about 1 inch; therefore, these boards are approximately 4" × 10".

4. Get the 20 from the place-value numeral cards, and place it in the empty slot at the bottom of the second board: "What numeral do you think this is?" If child does not know, provide the name: "This is twenty. Twenty has two tens (point to the 2) and zero units (point to the 0)."

<u>Part C.</u> <u>Boards and Quantity Materials Together</u>

1. Have the child make and name one of the teen quantities using tens and units next to the first teen board.
2. Point to the first 10 on the teen board: "So now you have fourteen, but this doesn't say fourteen. How

can you change it so it shows fourteen?" The child finds the 4 and uses it to cover the 0.

3. *Drum roll please—because here is where the key concept is driven home*: "That's interesting because over here (point to the quantity materials) you have *one* ten and *four* units and over here the numeral fourteen has a *1* and a *4*."
4. Take all the quantity materials away, and move all the 1–9 numeral cards to random positions on the two teen boards. Have the child name the numerals and construct the appropriate quantities to the left of each.

Launch Point

TENS BOARDS WITH BASE-10 MATERIALS

MATERIALS AND SET-UP

- Boards and numeral cards similar to those used for the teen boards.
- A supply of at least 45 units and 45 tens manipulatives (blocks, straws, bean sticks, etc.).
- The numeral 100 from the place-value card set, another 10 tens, and a hundred square.

LAUNCH POINTS

<u>Part A.</u> <u>Quantities Only</u> (i.e., leave boards on the shelf)

1. Use the same basic sequence as with the teen boards. The first round should not involve units. Work first on learning the names of the *decades*, using the ten-bars; for example: "Now you have three tens. Ten, twenty, thirty. Three tens is thirty."
2. Once children have become comfortable with naming the decades, proceed to demonstrate combining tens with units, laying out a quantity of ten-bars and some loose units to the right: "Now we have how many tens?" "Four." "And how many units?" "Three." "So how many is that all together?" "Forty-three." This should be a fairly easy step for the children to master. If not, do the skip counts, pointing to the materials as you count them together: "Ten, twenty, thirty, forty . . . forty-one, forty-two, forty-three. Four tens and three units is forty (point to the ten-bars) three (point to the loose units)."
3. Lay out 10 tens: "What number do you say after ninety when you count by tens?" "Ten, twenty . . . eighty, ninety, one *hundred*!" "That's right. Ten tens is one hundred. And when we want to show one hundred, we use one of these"—pull out a hundred

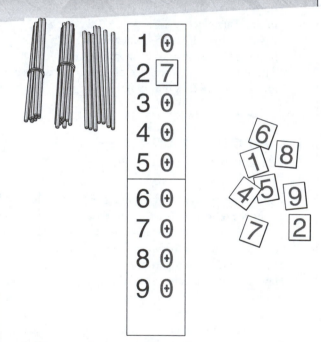

Figure 3.2 Tens Boards with Bundled Straws

square. "This is one hundred." Show that the 10 tens laid side by side make a square the same size as the hundred square.

<u>Part B.</u> <u>Boards Only</u> (i.e., leave quantity materials on the shelf)

1. The 10 and 20 on the tens boards should already be well known from the teen exercises above. However,

focus on the place-value parts of the numerals by emphasizing: "Yes, one ten (point to the 1) and zero units (point to the 0) is ten. Two tens (point to the 2) and zero units (point to the 0) is called twenty."

2. Continue reviewing the numerals 30 through 90, which the child will probably know in sequence from the familiar oral sequence of counting by tens. But now you are emphasizing *reading* the numeral by reading the place values: "Three tens (point to the 3) and zero units (point to the 0) is called thirty," and so on.

3. Place the units numeral cards randomly in the different decades positions, and have the child identify the numeral.

4. Get the 100 from the place-value numeral cards, and place it in the empty slot at the bottom of the second board, with the 1 digit extending off the left side of the board: "If I have ten tens, it's not called tens any more. We call it one (point to the 1) . . . ." Pause to let the child finish the sentence; if she does not, say:

". . . *hundred*. See? I have one hundred (point to the 1), zero tens (point to the middle zero), and zero units (point to the last digit)."

5. Lay the 100 place-value card under any of the other numerals made on the board, and read the result; for example, if you place the 100 under the 40 and attach the 5, you would say: "Now you have one hundred (point to the 1) forty- (point to the 4) five (point to the 5)." Point out how the numerals on each card are covering up zeroes on the card underneath.

Part C. Boards and Quantity Materials Together

1. Have the child make different quantities with the ten-bars and place them next to the appropriate decades numerals on the tens boards.

2. Have the child place units numeral cards in random positions on the two boards, name the numerals, and construct the appropriate quantities to the left of each.

At first glance, the use of the teens and tens boards to explore numerals and quantities may seem dry, teacher-directed, and unidimensional, but the boards serve to translate the sequential counting that children have been doing up to this point into a mental map organized around tens and units better than any other tool I know.

Every educator should experience at least once the moment when children discover that the 1 and 3 in the numeral 13 correspond to the one ten and three units it takes to make the quantity. As mentioned earlier, there are three different masking codes in the word *thirteen* to keep children from knowing it is one ten and three ones:

a. It says *thir-* rather than *three*.

b. It says *-teen* rather than *ten*.

c. The order is inverted. Rather than the *-teen* coming first, as the 1 does in the numeral, it comes last!

How much easier our children's lives would be if it were called *ten-three*! But because it is not, we must reteach children the cardinal numbers they already know, this time focusing on their place-value structure.

Here are some ways to vary how children use these valuable tools so they will revisit them often enough to master the concepts they embody:

1. One child makes a random number on the board. Another child makes the quantity out of place-value materials.

2. Use the boards with a mystery bag.[9] One child places a mystery quantity in the bag. Another child reaches in, feels the tens and units, and indicates what he thinks the quantity is by making the numeral on the board. The children then

---

[9] This is an opaque bag or box open at one or both ends, so a child can reach in and feel objects placed inside without seeing them. An oatmeal carton with a sock pulled over it makes a good mystery bag.

dump the mystery bag to check the answer. It's amazing how using the tactile sense rather than sight adds depth to their understanding of the materials.

3. Play "Who Has?" games. Make several numerals on the board and their associated quantities. Have children each pick up one of the quantities and hide them behind their backs. Caller says: "Who has ____ ?" or "Who has this one?" pointing to one of the spaces on the board. The child who thinks she has it reveals the quantity, saying "I have ____ ," and places the quantity next to the appropriate numeral.

4. Use other base-10 materials in the room to make the quantities.

The next group activity, Hands Up #1, takes what the children are most familiar with as counting tools—their fingers—and puts them to good use. You might think of this as the ultimate in hands-on learning! Notice that this activity and ones later in this book are not having children use their fingers to count. Counting answers on fingers is in fact one of the habits we are desperately seeking to overcome. But it is foolish to ignore the set of place-value manipulatives children were born with. In this activity, we are having children use their fingers to represent quantities in a place-value fashion, using 5 and 10 as anchor numbers.

Go to the PDToolkit to find the online templates referenced in the following activity.

Launch Point

HANDS UP #1   THIS IS A WHOLE-CLASS ACTIVITY

MATERIALS

- The main manipulatives are children's fingers![10] A quantity is displayed by a child (or several children) holding their hands up in front of them, palms outward, and raising the appropriate number of fingers: the pinkie finger on the right hand for one, the pinkie finger and ring finger for two, and so on. For six, the child raises the thumb on the left hand, and so on, up to 10. In other words, fingers are raised so that, *to the viewing audience*, counting progresses from left to right.
- Optional: Place-value numeral cards or a wipe-off board to display numerals 1–99.
- Optional: Picture cards showing from 1 to 10 fingers raised.

LAUNCH POINT

- Children take turns leading the activity. They can select assistants as needed.
- Start by asking the child to hold up a certain number of fingers between 1 and 10. (Alternately, draw a numeral card from the deck to indicate what quantity to make, or write the numeral on a wipe-off board.)
- Begin asking the child to display teen numbers, which will force the child to select another child to join him at the front of the class. The child instructs his assistant to hold up all 10 fingers; the child stands to his assistant's right (from the audience's perspective) and holds up the number of additional fingers needed to make the teen quantity. Ask the class members if they agree. Occasionally, request that another child come up and count the fingers to verify the count.
- Proceed to two-digit numbers, up to 99. The child selects the number of children needed, arranges them, and gives them instructions to create the linear display of the desired number of fingers. Ask the class members if they agree the appropriate number of fingers is being displayed, and ask them how they know.

---

[10] I was first introduced to the power of this type of finger math in a workshop by the Australian educator Brian Tickle, creator of *decacards* (teaching kits available at *www.origoeducation.com/decacards/*).

Children develop a number of useful insights and habits as a result of this first Hands Up activity:

a. They have to display the tens to the left of the units.

b. They see that the 2 in 27 represents a larger quantity than the 7 does. Not only are 20 fingers up, but also it takes two children to do so, whereas the 7 units can be represented by a single child.

c. They use five as an anchor number (e.g., each time they make seven, they do so by holding up five fingers and two more).

d. They must communicate their mathematical thinking to others, since they cannot display the total amount themselves but must tell their peers how to help them do so.

Here are some ways to vary or extend the activity:

1. Keep the group active and engaged by always asking the group members to decide if the display is correct, and ask one of the children who respond to explain her reasoning.

2. Before representing the quantity, ask the leader or one of the children in the audience to tell you how many children it will take to form the quantity. Do the children realize that to make 37 they will need *four* children, whereas to make 73 they will need *eight*?

3. Display two or more two-digit numbers, and have the children discuss their relative magnitude. The children can first predict which will be more and explain their reasoning. Once the quantities are displayed on fingers, they can check their predictions.

   A much more advanced question would be to ask how *much* bigger one displayed quantity is than another. Sit back and watch how creatively and intelligently they prove their answers.

4. *Secret Number Game.* The leader looks at a control card that tells her what quantity to display. The children in the audience then use response cards (e.g., place-value cards, wipe-off boards) or place-value response wheels to display what numeral they think is being represented.

5. Once a quantity has been displayed, ask a child to find the corresponding numeral on the class hundreds board or on the class "How Many Days We've Been in School" display.

PD **pd** TOOLKIT™

Go to the PDToolkit to find the online templates referenced in this and the following activities.

Children have been told how old their parents and grandparents are, but they have no real sense of how big these numbers are or how they compare. By converting these numbers to lengths, children can visually compare the relative sizes of numbers that are important to them. By representing these numbers as composed of tens and ones, they see these numbers in a new way. It is an eye-opener for a child to look at his 6 page next to his mother's 27 or his grandfather's 51. Children also like to compare their pages to those going into their friends' books.

Here are a few additional things you can do to extend this activity:

1. Teachers can make books of their own and share them with the children. Not only will the children be fascinated with your pages, but also they will be amazed at how old *your* parents, grandparents, and children are.

Launch Point

"HOW OLD ARE WE?" BOOKS

MATERIALS AND SET-UP

- Construction paper strips 2.5 cm wide:
  1. Green unit strips 1.8 cm (3/4") long.
  2. Blue tens strips 18 cm long, segmented with lines at 1.8 cm intervals. [*Design note*: It's easier to draw the lines on the blue construction paper sheet *before* cutting it into strips!]
- "How Old Are We?" blank pages. See Figure 3.3.
- Cellophane tape.
- Information sheets from home.
- Stapler, or hole-punch and yarn.

Store the strips in bowls or trays and the "How Old Are We?" blank pages where the children can access as many of them as they need.

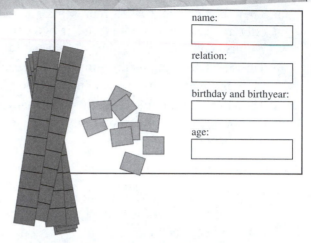

Figure 3.3   "How Old Are We?" Page Materials

LAUNCH POINT

1. Send home a letter explaining that the children want to make a book containing the names of significant individuals in their lives, and to do so, they need some simple biographical information, printed neatly so the children can copy it. For each potential entry, the individual should write down *Name*, *Relation* (i.e., how this individual is related to the child—children can include family members, friends, neighbors, pets, or whomever the child wants), *Birthday and Birth Year*, and *Age* (i.e., how old the individual is currently[11]).

2. Starting with a blank "How Old Are We?" page, the children write the information on the page about the individual they want to add to their book.

3. Children go to the supply shelf and get the number of green unit rectangles and blue tens strips they need for the age they have written down.

4. Children tape the strips together end to end, starting with the blue tens and ending with the green units.

5. Children tape the bottom tens strip vertically on the left side of the "How Old Are We? page and fold the remaining sections accordion-fashion onto the page (see Figure 3.4). A small piece of tape can be used to anchor the last folded section of the strip to the page so the folded age strip stays

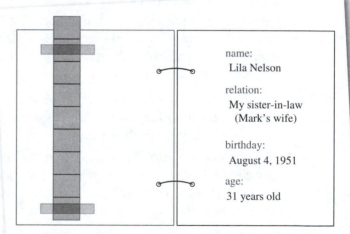

Figure 3.4   "How Old Are We?" Assembled Page

in place (obviously, if the age is 10 or less, no folding is necessary).

6. Children fold their pages at the center crease and save them until they have made as many pages as they wish.

7. When all the pages are complete, the children can wrap a construction paper cover around their finished pages, use the stapler or hole-punch and yarn to complete the book, and take it home.

---

[11] Older children could calculate the age themselves, but it's probably better for the purposes of this activity to have the information provided.

2. Ask children to keep their books in the classroom library for a time. Other children in the class will get a great deal of enjoyment out of examining the pages and asking the authors for more information on the people and pets that are included.

3. Children can represent the ages by making Unifix towers or using tens and units from the place-value blocks.

4. You can place a pile of counters in front of the child that corresponds to the age of one of the people in her book and challenge her to find which entry it represents.

We don't encourage children to estimate nearly often enough. When you think about it, most of the math we do in our everyday lives is actually estimation rather than exact calculation.

Launch Point

ESTIMATION ACTIVITIES

MATERIALS AND SET-UP

- Large supply of Unifix cubes (commercial product) or any other materials that snap together.
- Large supply of connecting Cuisenaire rods (commercial product).
- Estimation containers: baggies or jars filled with small, countable objects.
- Cuisenaire 1–100 rack (commercial product).
- Ten-frame tag-board or vinyl mats (i.e., rectangles divided into two rows of squares, each row five squares long). Alternatively, you can make ten frames out of egg cartons or ice-cube trays cut to form two rows of five.[12]
- Small cut-out versions of ten frames showing quantities 1–10 filled in with dots (1–9 on green laminated card stock, 10 on blue).

LAUNCH POINTS

Unifix Cubes

1. Children make a big pile of Unifix cubes and estimate how many there are (or each child makes his own pile and estimate).

2. Children snap the cubes together in sets of 10, leaving the remainder as loose cubes.

3. Children count the tens and units, say the number, and compare their estimate to the actual amount.

4. Optional: Children use the place-value numeral cards to show the amount they have or find the numeral on a number line or a hundreds chart.

Connecting Cuisenaire Rods

1. Children make a long train, design, or construction using the Cuisenaire rods and then estimate how many units there are all together.

2. Children place a marker next to the numeral corresponding to their estimate on the Cuisenaire 1–100 rack.

3. Children reconstruct what they have built in the Cuisenaire 1–100 rack. If their number goes past 100, they can start building a second layer of rods on top of the first.

---

[12] My rule with ten frames is to fill them from left to right and top to bottom (e.g., seven is always shown with the top row and the two left-most squares on the bottom row filled. Sticking with this routine rather than letting the children fill the frames randomly makes quantities recognizable by sight, without counting (a process known as *subitizing*). Children should have had plenty of experience making and recognizing quantities on a ten frame before doing this activity.

4. Children read the total and compare their estimate to the actual amount (if they wish, they can use place-value materials to build the difference next to the rack, to see how much they missed by).
5. Optional: Children use the place-value numeral cards to show the amount they have, or they find the numeral on a number line or a hundreds chart.

2. Children fill ten frames with the items.
3. Children count the full ten frames and the partially filled frame, say the number, and compare their estimate to the actual amount.
4. Optional: Children use the place-value numeral cards to show the amount they have, or they find the numeral on a number line or a hundreds chart.

Ten Frames

1. Children select an estimation container and guess how many items are inside.

Children do not understand how large a number is simply because they can count that high. An important part of children developing a sense of place value is developing a visceral sense of how quickly quantities expand when they are increasing by tens compared to when they are increasing one at a time—4 looks like only slightly more than 2, but 40 looks like quite a bit more than 20.

Here are some additional ways that estimation of quantity can be encouraged:

1. Children can each make their own piles of counters and guess whose is more. Children convert their piles into tens and units and compare.

2. The number of cubes can be the result of some other meaningful activity. For example, the children might have been using Unifix cubes to

   - Keep track of points earned in a game.
   - See how tall a Unifix tower they could make before it breaks.
   - Build a fence around their block construction.

3. Children can estimate how long or how heavy something is, using a nonstandard unit (e.g., pennies or washers), and then measure and count the actual amount.

4. Children can select several estimation containers and arrange them in order, from the container they think contains the fewest items to the one they think contains the most. After doing all the counting, children can compare the actual counts and decide whether they arranged the containers in the correct order.

5. Wipe-off picture cards can be made showing three collections of quantities visibly different in amount—for instance, 15, 26, and 41 buttons. Print the three numerals below the images in random order. Children draw a line connecting each numeral and the collection they think it goes with; then they count to see if they are correct.

6. Children can start to develop mental strategies for determining how close their estimates are to the actual quantity. For example, if they guessed 65 and the actual count was 51, they could say: "Well, 51 plus 10 is 61, so 61, 62, 63, 64, 65—that's 4 more, so I was off by 14."

7. Have children use response boards to record their amounts or show their answers to a posed estimation question. A response board can be as simple as a wipe-off board or chalkboard. For displaying answers up to four digits, it is

PD **pd** TOOLKIT™

Go to the PDToolkit to find the online templates referenced in this activity.

useful to make place-value response wheels. These are cards that have four notches in the top and four wheels that can rotate to show chosen digits 0–9 in the notches, allowing the children to display any numeral up to 9,999[13] (see Figure 3.5). Having children all hold up their answers at once when you say, "Reveal," is a great way to get a quick read on each child's ability to do the problem rather than just the child you call on. Used at this level, it is also a good way to remind children that the units place is furthest to the right and the tens place is to the left of it (and that there are more places yet to come!).

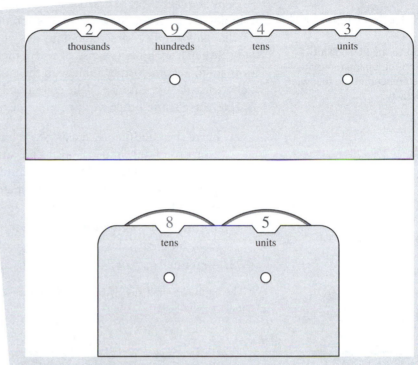

Figure 3.5 Place-Value Response Wheels

[13] If you wish, you can make a two-digit version of the response wheel to use at this developmental stage.

Launch Point

RACE TO 100

MATERIALS AND SET-UP

- Place-value blocks (commercial product): 1 hundred square and at least 20 ten-bars and 30 unit cubes (more if more than two children are playing).
- Eight large lima beans or some other flat, two-sided manipulative. Use a permanent marker to draw a dot on one side of each bean (representing units) and a line on the other side (representing tens).
- Shaker cup.

LAUNCH POINT

1. All the place-value blocks are placed in a supply pile in the middle.
2. Children take turns shaking the lima beans, dumping them out, and collecting the indicated number of tens and unit blocks. For example, if three of the beans show a line and five show a dot, they collect three ten-bars and five unit cubes.
3. When the supply of units gets low, children can trade 10 unit blocks from their piles for one of the ten-bars in the supply pile.
4. When one of the children has 10 tens, that child can trade them in for the hundred square, and that round of the game ends.

Go to the PDToolkit to find the online template referenced in the following activity.

Children need lots of practice understanding the 10:1 ratio of units to tens and tens to hundreds. By seeing how many tens and units they have accumulated, they see that (1) changing piles of loose units into sets of 10 makes their collection more coherent and (2) they have a better sense of where they are relative to their goal. It is important for them to become comfortable with the idea that this process of trading ones for tens is changing the appearance of the collection but not the quantity.

Here are some other ways to practice the same skill:

1. Have the children use a classroom bank of place-value materials.[14] If children go to the bank and "deposit" an amount equal to their "withdrawal," they have made a fair trade. So if a child brings 30 units to the bank and takes away 3 tens, that was a fair exchange—the quantity the child has in her possession has not been changed.

2. To make the game go more quickly, you could draw a line (representing tens) on both sides of one or more of the beans.

3. A spinner or pair of dice can be used to choose quantities to collect.

[14] The bank is a shelf supply of unit, ten, hundred, and thousand blocks where the child can go to make exchanges.

 Launch Point

HUNDREDS BOARD

MATERIALS AND SET-UP

- 100 2.5 cm × 2.5 cm numeral tiles with numerals 1–100 printed on them. The units digits on the tiles are green, the tens digits are blue, and the hundreds digit is red.[15]
- 25 cm × 25 cm wood or tag-board puzzle frame divided into 10 rows and 10 columns of 2.5 cm × 2.5 cm squares. The square in the top left-hand corner has the numeral 1 printed on it, and the square in the bottom right-hand corner has the numeral 100 printed on it (see Figure 3.6).

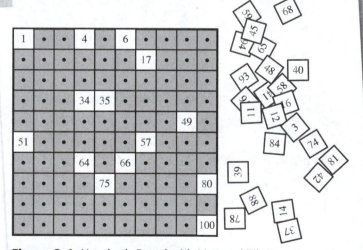

Figure 3.6 Hundreds Board with Numeral Tiles

LAUNCH POINT

1. Children find the tile with the numeral 1 printed on it and place it in the top left-hand corner. They then find the 2, the 3, and so on.

2. Make sure the children realize that each new row starts in the left-most position, under the 1.

3. Children continue to fill the hundreds board, row by row.

[15] To make the numeral tiles, I use the red and blue counting tiles that are sold by many educational suppliers as red-blue-green-yellow counting sets. The reason I use these two colors is to continue the red-blue, odd-even theme that is present in the earlier counting materials such as the number rods (Nelson, 2007) and in the metric measuring materials presented later in this book (see Chapter 7). I print the numerals—with their green-blue-red digits—on glossy photo paper, cut them out, and tape them to the tiles; the odd numbers go on the red tiles and the even numbers on the blue tiles. The result is an extremely durable and attractive set of tiles that is easy for young hands to manipulate.

4. *Race to Zero.* Each child starts out with a hundred square. Children toss the beans to determine how many units they must give away (on their first roll, the children will need to convert their hundred square into 10 tens and turn one of the tens into 10 units). The goal of the game is to get rid of your entire hundred square as quickly as possible. *Note*: Just as subtraction is harder than addition, Race to Zero is a harder game than Race to a Hundred.

5. *Race to a Dollar.* This game is played the same way as Race to a Hundred, but the supply is pennies, dimes, and a dollar bill, and the dots on the beans represent pennies and the lines represent dimes. The object of the game is to collect the dollar bill.

As discussed in the Hundreds Board activity shown on the previous page, a hundreds board emphasizes the place-value pattern of our number system by arranging the numerals in sets of 10. Children quickly notice that, in each column, the units digits are the same and the tens digits go up by one.

Educators debate whether children should use a 1–100 board or should instead use a 0–99 board. The 1–100 board has the decades numerals (10, 20, 30, etc.) in the right-most column. The 0–99 board has the decades in the left-most column. The advantage of the 0–99 board is that it consistently shows all the same decade numerals on the same line; for example, the fourth line starts with 30 and ends with 39. But for me, the 1–100 board wins out. It corresponds more to the rhythm of how we count: The decade number is the accent at the end of a counting sequence ("thirty-eight, thirty-nine, forty! . . ."), and then the next vocal sequence begins (". . . forty-one, forty-two . . ."). The same applies to the measurement of historical time: 1980 marks the end of a decade, not the beginning. Besides, it's frustrating for a child to count all the way to 99 and not be able to say, "One *hundred*."

Let children catch their own errors, such as mistakenly counting past the decade marker ("thirty-eight, thirty-nine, thirty-ten, thirty-eleven . . .") or placing a numeral in the wrong location. The materials are designed to provide visual feed-back that something is amiss. Even reversals (putting the 73 where the 37 belongs) become apparent when the visual pattern is broken. The hundreds board is really just a fancy puzzle with the "fit" being determined by logic rather than by shape. We love puzzles in early childhood precisely *because* they are self-correcting. Children much prefer catching their own errors to having them pointed out to them.

Here are some ways to keep children engaged as they work with the hundreds board:

1. Children put all the numeral tiles in a mystery bag and draw them out one at a time, placing them as they go. Note that this task requires the children to use the board and the tiles already on it in a far more sophisticated manner,[16] demonstrating strategic knowledge such as

    - The teen numbers are on the second row, the twenties on the third, and so on.
    - If a new tile has the same tens digit as a tile already on the board, the child needs to look at the units digit and:
        - if it is smaller move the new tile to the left and count backward ("thirty-seven, thirty-six, thirty-five");
        - if it is bigger move the new tile to the right and count forward ("thirty-seven, thirty-eight, thirty-nine").

---

[16] See Hundreds Board Magic Windows (Chapter 4) for another example of practicing this skill.

- If the new tile has the same units digit as a tile already on the board, the child needs to look at the tens digit and:
  - if it is smaller move the new tile upward and counts backward by tens ("thirty-seven, twenty-seven");
  - if it is bigger move the new tile downward and count forward by tens ("thirty-seven, forty-seven").
- The units digits in the hundreds board columns should match, as should the tens digits in the hundreds board rows. If they don't, something is wrong.

2. The children can turn the hundreds board upside down. Now they count backwards from 100 to 1, finding the appropriate numeral tiles as they go. Note that in this set-up the numbers get smaller as you progress from left to right and top to bottom.

3. Provide a hundreds board that does not arrange the numerals by decades. Some children are so gifted spatially that they rely *too* much on their visual sense to solve mathematical puzzles. That's why it's important to occasionally provide them with alternative materials where the visual cues are removed, to see if their number sense is strong enough to meet the challenge. For example, you could put out a 7 × 14 board that goes from 1 to 98. If you wish, you could print one numeral on each line of the board to serve as anchors to help them get started.

4. Provide a board that only goes partway to 100 or that doesn't start at 1. For example, you could set out a 5 × 5 board that goes from 1 and 25 or from 36 to 60, or a 7 × 7 board that goes from 1 to 49 or from 22 to 70. Have some scattered anchor numerals already printed on the board (but don't include the starting and stopping numerals). Provide the necessary numeral tiles to fill all the blanks.

PLACE-VALUE AWARENESS CHECKPOINTS

These assessment probes provide good opportunities for you to observe the children's typical solution strategies and realize what comes easily and naturally to them and what is still difficult or unclear. When used as assessments, they work best

1. The first time you present them to a child and
2. If you do them away from the rest of the group because you want to

    a. Concentrate fully on the child's approach and
    b. Make sure the child is not distracted by others' approaches to the task.

It is hard for us as adults and teachers to not fall into the trap of thinking that just because we have set out activities and the children have done them, another step on the child's mathematical journey is now complete. These assessment probes are a reality check—not for the child, but for you. Checking one's assumptions is particularly important in this chapter's focus area, place-value awareness. As Piagetians warn us, hierarchical classification (of which our place-value number system is an example) does not come easily to the young child. Children are prone to treat objects as objects, so tens and ones are both just things—which makes 4 tens and 3 units look more like 7 than 43 to them.

In a classic Piagetian task, Constance Kamii (1985) had children draw 16 dots on a page and then write the numeral 16. When they were done, she pointed to the digit 6 in the 16 and asked: "Can you draw a circle around the dots that this part of the 16 describes?" After they had done so, she pointed to the digit 1 and asked: "And can you draw another circle around the dots this part of the 16 describes?" The majority of first and second graders got this last part wrong, circling only one dot, at which point she asked: "So what part of the 16 describes all these dots that don't have a circle around them?" The children stared, bewildered. They had no explanation. Try it on your own children. You might be surprised that what you thought you had adequately covered has not yet *un*-covered what place value is really all about.

Resist the temptation to teach the answers to these questions! There are at least two good reasons to hold back:

1. This is a testing moment, not a teaching one. One of the most common mistakes made by teachers is to jump in immediately after children give a wrong answer to a question and correct it. This violates what I consider an unwritten contract between the children and the teacher, which states:

   > I am asking you questions because I am genuinely curious how you will answer them. Whatever your answer, you will have given me what I wanted to know.

   Children will not take risks if they fear you will pounce on their errors. Yes, their response tells you that more teaching is needed, but wait to start doing that until after the questioning is over. To haphazardly mix teaching and testing is the kiss of death for the free-ranging exchange of ideas in a learning community. Remember: It is the children's continuing work with the activities you set out for them that will solidify their place-value understanding, not answers supplied by you.

2. As Piaget noted, teaching children the answers to such probes does little to change their overall level of understanding. The whole idea is to present children with a situation they have never encountered before and have them make sense of it. Once they've been told the right answer, the task is worthless for assessment purposes. That's why you do these probes in a one-on-one format, without other children looking on.

So here are several activities that work well to check how the children are doing, along with some suggestions for what specific concepts and skills you can monitor as they do them. This is followed by a discussion of several key aspects of our own educational assumptions and habitual response patterns that all teachers need to reconsider if they wish to maximize the mathematical learning outcomes in their classrooms.

Launch Points

Assessment Probe

CUISENAIRE TENS

MATERIALS AND SET-UP

- A set of 1–10 connecting Cuisenaire rods (commercial product with the unit increments marked on one face of each rod).

ASSESSMENT PROBE

1. Place the Cuisenaire 10-rod on the rug, segmented side down.
2. Add one of the other rods to the end of the 10-rod, segmented side down.
3. Have the child guess the new quantity. Ask the child how he came up with that answer.
4. The child turns each rod so the marked side is up and then counts the quantity to verify the total.

5. Continue to make other teen combinations, always starting with the 10-rod.

VARIATION

1. Do the same activity vertically with a number rod set (ranging in length from 1 decimeter to 1 meter) inserted in a vertical rod holder (see Nelson, 2007).

● What you are looking for

Does the child count on from 10 to determine the teen quantity?

With the Cuisenaire rods, the child knows the 1–10 increments by color, so he knows that the orange rod is 10. Counting the whole quantity would indicate that the child is not comfortable using 10 as an anchor number from which to count on and is very shaky on thinking of the teens in place-value terms.

Does the child automatically translate "ten plus a certain number of units" to its teen equivalent?

Counting on from 10, either visibly or silently, indicates the child is not comfortable with the shortcut that place-value awareness affords. Even hesitation would signal the child is not automatically translating the teen numbers he knows well in a counting sense into their place-value counterparts ("Ten plus five—that's fifteen").

Assessment Probe

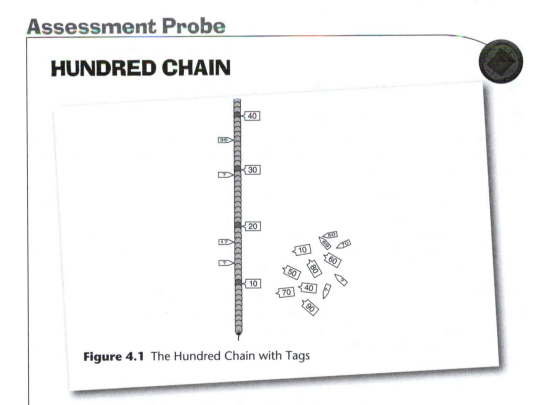

Figure 4.1 The Hundred Chain with Tags

MATERIALS AND SET-UP

- Two colors of stringing beads, 90 of one color and 10 of the other. I have found the wooden beads from an old car seat massager cushion work well.
- Numeral arrows on which are written random numerals between 1 and 100.
- Question mark arrows.

String the beads on a strong string or cord to make the hundred chain, with every 10th bead in the contrasting color. Tie the ends of the cord so the beads stay on the chain.

ASSESSMENT PROBES

Introduction

"This chain has one hundred beads on it. This is bead #1, and this is bead #100." Have the child count the entire chain from 1 to 100, pointing out that at the decades she is pointing to the beads of a contrasting color.

Assessment Probe #1

Point out that the hundred chain is made up of tens. Let the child verify. Have the child use the contrasting color beads to skip count to 100 by tens: "10, 20, 30. . . ."

Assessment Probe #2

Have the child try doing it in reverse: "100, 90, 80. . . ." Have the child count the entire chain from 100 to 1.

Assessment Probe #3

Pull out several numeral arrows and ask the child to show you which bead each should be pointing at.

VARIATIONS

1. Point question mark arrows at several different beads along the chain and ask the child to identify which beads are being pointed to.
2. Challenge the child to start with the 100 bead rather than the 1 bead to locate the target bead.
3. Put out a 200 chain on which the child locates target beads.

● What you are looking for

Can the child accurately read two-digit numerals?

At the most basic level, you want the child to be able to read the numeral accurately, using the appropriate decade and unit terminology. You are specifically on the lookout for reversals (e.g., the child reads 79 as 97).

Can the child accurately count in the 1–100 range, both forward and backward?

When a child has a manual task, even a task as simple as pointing at beads on a string, she can be distracted enough to have difficulty remembering the decades transitions. Pay careful attention to how comfortable she is at the transition points: ". . . 58, 59. . . ." This task is considerably more difficult if you have the child count backward from 100 to 1: ". . . 62, 61. . . ."

Does the child use the decade anchor points to quickly locate two-digit quantities?

The arrows tasks provide an excellent opportunity for you to observe not just whether the child can answer correctly but also *how* she answers correctly. For example, if the numeral is 38, here is a rank ordering of strategies the successful child might be using, from least to most sophisticated:

1. The child counts from the beginning, from 1 to 38.
2. The child counts by tens to 30 and then counts individual beads up to 38.
3. The child counts by tens to 40 and then counts backward to 38.

You want the child to be comfortable enough with the place-value structure of our number system that she intuitively sees that counting large quantities is slow and wasteful when place-value clues are available.

Assessment Probe

PAGE WALK

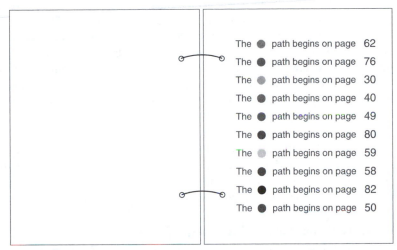

The ● path begins on page 62
The ● path begins on page 76
The ● path begins on page 30
The ● path begins on page 40
The ● path begins on page 49
The ● path begins on page 80
The ● path begins on page 59
The ● path begins on page 58
The ● path begins on page 82
The ● path begins on page 50

Figure 4.2 Table-of-Contents Page from Page Walk Book

PD **pd** TOOLKIT™

Go to the PDToolkit to find the online template referenced in this activity.

MATERIALS AND SET-UP

- Book with a table-of-contents page followed by 100 pages numbered 1–100 in the upper right-hand corner.
- The table-of-contents page lists the starting pages for 10 color-coded "paths" that can be taken though the book. See Figure 4.2.
- The first nine pages of each path have the page number color-coded to the path and in the middle of the page is the phrase "Go to _____," listing the page number of the next stopping point on the path. Also printed on the page is the next clue of a 10-part mystery message to be assembled.
- The tenth page on the path simply says, "The end of the _____ path," with the color code indicated. The page also provides the final piece of the mystery message.

The puzzle is typically a 10-letter phrase ("M-a-t-h-I-s-C-o-o-l"), a 10-syllable phrase ("You-are-my-sun-shine-my-on-ly-sun-shine"), or a familiar 10-word phrase ("Simple-Simon-met-a-Pie-man-going-to-the-fair").

It's easy to create new books. Simply take a list of all the numbers 1–100 and start randomly crossing out numbers and assigning them to one of 10 columns. Voila! You have the 10 paths for a new book!

ASSESSMENT PROBE

1. The child chooses a path on the table-of-contents page and navigates to the first page on the path.
2. Upon reaching each page on the path, the child writes down the mystery message clue that appears on that page.
3. At the end of each path, the child solves the puzzle and decides which path to go down next.

● What you are looking for

Does the child understand the relative magnitude of two-digit numbers?

The idea for the Page Walk book came to me when I remembered how lost I was when I was first asked to look up a word in the dictionary. I considered myself an ABC's expert, but suddenly I was faced with navigating from random starting points: If I were looking for a word that started with H and I opened the dictionary to K, I had no idea whether I had gone too far or not far enough. I had only mastered the alphabet sequentially, so I was forced to go "ABCDEFGHIJK . . . aha, I've gone too far." In other words, the alphabet was for me a rote list, not a flexible navigation tool ("K is a couple letters past H in the alphabet. I need to go back.").

Children need the same practice navigating the counting numbers 1–100, intuitively judging where those numbers fall on an imaginary 1–100 number line (or hundred chain, as in the previous probe). Each time the child turns pages, you get new clues as to whether he has a meaningful grasp of relative quantity at the symbolic level, using two-digit numbers he doesn't routinely encounter in his everyday counting world.

Does the child confuse the units and tens digits?

It is particularly telling if the child sees a numeral such as 62 and starts navigating to the twenties section of the book. Even if he doesn't say anything, you know he is not easily interpreting which is the tens place and which is the units place. If he arrives at page 26 and is perplexed why he is suddenly on the wrong path, you know he needs more work with the activities in this chapter of the book.

Does the child estimate where in the book to start the search?

If the child is trying to find page 51, does he intuitively know it should be near the middle of the book? If not, his sense of where that two-digit number falls on an imaginary number line is off.

Does the child know which direction to turn pages to adjust his latest estimate?

When looking for page 51, if he initially turns to page 39 does he easily decide that 39 is smaller than 51, not bigger? This is not as easy a choice as you might think. After all, 39 has a 9 in it, whereas the largest digit in 51 is 5.

Does the child know approximately how many pages to turn to adjust his latest estimate?

If he is looking for page 51 and lands on page 39, does he have a sense of how much bigger 51 is than 39? In other words, does he adjust page by page, or does he jump several pages ahead? If he lands on page 49, does he confidently turn two pages, expecting to have landed at his destination?

Does the child treat tens-place information differently from units-place information in terms of relative magnitude?

The child may have a vague sense that differences in the tens digit mean he turns a lot of pages and differences in the units digit mean he turns just a few pages. But in two-digit numbers, using this knowledge becomes more complicated. What if I'm on page 59 and I'm looking for page 64? The tens digit hints to jump forward 10, but the units digit indicates to jump *back* 5. How does the child incorporate both those pieces of information to make a judgment of relative magnitude? What if I'm on page 71 and I'm looking for 59? I sense I should go back, but how many pages? Without a firm grounding in place value, the digits start swimming in front of your eyes.

Assessment Probe

HUNDREDS BOARD MAGIC WINDOWS

Figure 4.3 Hundreds Board Magic Windows

PD **pd** TOOLKIT™

Go to the PDToolkit to find the online template referenced in this activity.

MATERIALS AND SET-UP

- Laminated tag-board frames cut in odd shapes. On the frames are drawn a collection of 2.5 cm × 2.5 cm connected squares (i.e., matching the size of the squares on the hundreds board). Squares either share an edge or share a corner.
- Wipe-off marking pens.

The same frame becomes a different experience each time because you can write any starter number in any square—even turning it sideways or upside down transforms it into a new puzzle.

ASSESSMENT PROBE

1. Make sure the child is familiar with the hundreds board and realizes that the squares on this frame are meant to be "magic windows" to an invisible hundreds board hidden beneath (it can even be laid on top of a hundreds chart to make the point).
2. Let the child decide which window frame to use and which direction to turn it.
3. Choose one of the squares near the middle of the frame as the starter square, and write a numeral such as 45 in that square.
4. The child then proceeds to write numerals in the remaining empty squares that match "the invisible hundreds board" beneath.

V A R I A T I O N S

1. Take a sheet of construction paper that fits on top of a printed hundreds board, laminate it, and carefully cut out flaps that can be folded forward to reveal the hundreds board numerals underneath. The child opens any flap to reveal a starting number and then predicts what numeral she will see when she opens another flap. Now there is no need to *imagine* a hundreds board beneath—it's there!

2. Use windows with starter numerals already printed on them, and provide numeral tiles that match the empty squares.

3. Provide a printed hundreds board and sticky notes. Place sticky notes over several numerals on the board. Say to the child: "Show me ____." The child then removes the appropriate sticky note.

● What you are looking for

Can the child mentally navigate place-value space within the frame when moving up (10 less), down (10 more), left (1 less), right (1 more) and diagonally (changing by either 9 or 11, depending on the direction)?

A child familiar with the hundreds board has noticed relationships among numerals sharing a row or sharing a column. Have these patterns translated to a mental map of how changing by 10 differs from changing by 1? A child who is less secure with place-value notation will tend to lock into one type of transformation rather than comfortably shifting. The most difficult transformation is to combine changes of units and tens in the same move (e.g., moving diagonally from 57 to 48). Going up and to the right within the frame requires subtracting 10 and then adding 1, resulting in a net change of 9. Keeping track of which digit needs to go up by 1 and which needs to go down by 1 is a complex mental exercise.

What does the child do if an open window forces her to leave the borders of the imaginary hundreds board beneath?

The task suddenly becomes much more complex if you write a starter number on the frame such that the edges of the frame extend beyond the edges of an imaginary hundreds board underneath. This often happens by accident when the child writes the starter numeral on her own. Interesting things happen when empty squares extend

1. To the left of the ones column or to the right of the decades column. If the child decides to write 60 to the left of the 61 or 91 to the right of the 90, her choice might not correspond to a true hundreds board, but it does signal solid place-value awareness.

2. Below the 90's line. Maybe she will realize that the number right below 94 is 104. If she does, she's brilliant! But don't be surprised if she writes it as 1004—that signals yet another place-value mystery she has yet to solve.

3. Above the units line. Is it possible for numbers to be less than zero? Mathematicians say yes, and the dilemma may initiate a fierce discussion amongst the children and, perhaps, the discovery of negative numbers. If it does, so much the better!

In any of these scenarios, the child might decide, as did the ancient mariners, "There's nothing out there." If so, she simply leaves the illegitimate squares blank, which also signifies she is aware of the physical layout of a hundreds board.

Assessment Probe

DECADE TRANSITION BOARDS

?	30	?
?	60	?
?	10	?
?	80	?
?	40	?

?	70	?
?	20	?
?	100	?
?	50	?
?	90	?

9	?	11
49	?	51
99	?	101
69	?	71
39	?	41

19	?	21
79	?	81
29	?	31
89	?	91
59	?	61

Go to the PDToolkit to find the online template referenced in this activity.

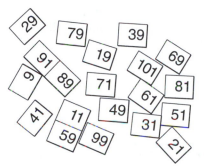 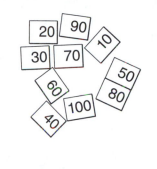

Figure 4.4 Decade Transition Boards with Numeral Tiles

MATERIALS AND SET-UP

- Two tag-board boards with short "slices" of a number line displayed. Each slice shows three complete 2.5 cm × 2.5 cm squares and portions of the squares on either side. The two boards contain number-line slices of different types (see Figure 4.4):
  Board #1 The center square contains a decades numeral (e.g., 40) and the bracketing squares contain question marks.
  Board #2 The bracketing squares have printed numerals in them (e.g., 39 and 41), and the center square contains a question mark. The printed numerals always bracket a decade numeral (in this case, 40).
- Thirty 2.5 cm × 2.5 cm tiles (10 to go with the first board, 20 to go with the second) with numerals written on them corresponding to the missing numerals on the number-line slices.

Color-coding the two sets helps keep the pieces from getting mixed together.

ASSESSMENT PROBE

1. Place the tiles for the chosen board face up. The child looks at each number-line slice and decides what numeral tiles are needed to complete the segment.
2. Harder version: Place the tiles for the chosen board face down. The child turns over a numeral tile and has to place it where it belongs before choosing a new tile.

VARIATION

1. Boards can be made for transition points in the hundreds (e.g., 149 __?__ 151; __?__ 380 __?__ ; or 499 __?__ 501).

● What you are looking for

Can the child easily transition across the decade marks?

We know that the transition points between decades are where children struggle. Once they hit 40, using the standard pattern of 41, 42, 43, and so on gets them to 49, but then

1. They must remember to *stop* the rhythmic pattern. In other words, they have to not say, "Forty-ten."
2. They must remember the name of the next decade.

This is particularly evident if the child hesitates when using the first board, where the decade numeral is provided. He needs to know that, of the two numerals bracketing 50, it is the numeral to the right that signals the new patterned count ("51"). The numeral to the left ends the count from the previous decade ("49").

Children are much more likely to have problems with the second board, where the decade numeral is the one that is missing, because it requires them to count backward through the decade transition point. Children are much more confident that 51 goes after 50 than they are that 49 precedes it.

Assessment Probe

HOW MANY NOW? VARIATION #1[1]

MATERIALS AND SET-UP

- Collection of counters (at least 25).

ASSESSMENT PROBE

1. Give the child a quantity of counters in the high teens to count.
2. Give her one additional counter at a time and ask her what the new quantity is, into the low twenties.
3. Now start taking one away at a time, and ask her what the new quantity is, into the midteens.

VARIATION

1. Start with a larger set of cubes so she has to count up through a higher decade transition point and back again.

---

[1] Examples of diagnostic interviews such as these can be found in Richardson (2002) and Burns (2003).

● What you are looking for

Can the child count upward through the decade transition point?

Hopefully, the child is comfortable enough with counting that transitioning from the teens to the twenties comes easily. But notice you have introduced a time lag to disrupt her count. This forces her to recover each time you hand her a new cube ("Let's see . . . the last cube was number 18, so this will be number 19"). This makes the task more difficult than just asking her to count from 1 to 25.

Can the child count downward through the decade transition point?

If the child has 22 cubes and you take one way, she can probably tell you she now has 21. Remove one more, and she can probably tell you she now has 20—but some children will hesitate. Remove one more, and you'll be surprised how many children cannot tell you, "19." You'll likely get a long pause and then a hesitant, "21?" This can really be an eye-opener for you, as their teacher, in terms of what they know about numbers and what they do not.

Assessment Probe

HOW MANY NOW? VARIATION #2

MATERIALS AND SET-UP

- Collection of counters (at least 40).

ASSESSMENT PROBE

1. Place a pile of counters (between 30 and 40) in front of the child. Let's say there are 34 counters.
2. Ask the child to estimate how many counters there are. Ask the child to write down that numeral on a piece of paper.
3. Ask the child: "Do you think there are enough for you to make a pile of 10 over here?" (Point to a spot off to the side.) Have the child make the set. Then ask: "Do you think there are enough left to make another pile of 10 over here?" (Point to a different spot on the table.) The child does so again. Repeat the same question until the child can't make another 10.
4. "So here you didn't have enough to make 10? How many did you have?" The child answers. Now comes the key question: "So you have a pile of 10 here . . . a pile of 10 here . . . a pile of 10 here . . . and 4 extra ones over here. In a moment, I'm going to ask you to count them all so we can know how many there are all together, but before I do, let me ask you a question: You guessed that there were _____ counters. Do you still think that is a good guess, or do you want to change your guess?" If the child decides to change, ask for a reason; then have the child count them all, keeping the piles intact.
5. As a final question, ask: "So there are actually 34 counters. Can you write that number?" The child does so. "Is there any way you could have looked at your piles and known there were 34 counters before you counted them?"

● What you are looking for

Does the child automatically take advantage of the place-value arrangement of quantities to identify the total amount?

This is a great diagnostic activity to see if children are connecting linear counting with place-value thinking. It takes a long time for children to automatically interpret quantities they count one by one in terms of tens and units. Because the probe is structured as an estimation activity and you are telling children they will soon count the total quantity, you are not alerting them to the fact that they can use what they know about place value to know the answer *without* counting.

This is a good probe to do after children have worked a lot with larger numbers and you suspect that place-value thinking is starting to crystallize. Be prepared to be disappointed. This interview is a great way to reveal how precarious children's early understanding of the place-value system truly is.

Don't put a band-aid on the problem (i.e., provide the correct answer) in a vain attempt to make it go away. Your results simply tell you that what you've been assuming they know is not actually what they know. Math is such a great area to teach because the right answers will reveal *themselves* over time. These children need more practice with the types of activities provided in this chapter to deepen their understanding, fill in the gaps, and eliminate their faulty assumptions. That's why this book is filled with so many different ways of addressing the same skills.

Assessment Probe

HOW MANY NOW? VARIATION #3

MATERIALS AND SET-UP

- Collection of counters (at least 40).

ASSESSMENT PROBE

1. Have the child count out a given number of counters and write down the numeral. Let's say again the number is 34.
2. Tell the child: "I'm going to ask you to separate your 34 counters into piles of 10, but before you do that, how many piles of 10 do you think you'll be able to make?" The child guesses. "And do you think there will be any counters left over? . . . How many?" Ask for reasons for the guesses.
3. Have the child make the piles.
4. "So you were able to make 3 piles of 10, with 4 left over. You said all together you have 34 counters, which is the number that you wrote down over here (point). Is there anything about the number you wrote down that could have helped you figure out how many piles you were going to be able to make?"

● What you are looking for

Does the child automatically take advantage of place-value digits to anticipate how many tens and units he has?

This is similar to the previous probe, but reversed. In this case, you identify the total quantity in advance and are asking the child to anticipate what the place-value arrangements will look like. Harken to the first launch point in Chapter 3, the teen and tens boards, where we introduced children to the fact that the two digits in a two-digit number signal the number of tens and the number of units in the total. Did the children really internalize this? Here is your chance to find out by presenting them with a loose collection of objects.

Assessment Probe

HOW MANY NOW? VARIATION #4

MATERIALS AND SET-UP

- Collection of counters (at least 40).

ASSESSMENT PROBE

1. Place a large number of counters in front of the child—let's say, in this case, 43 counters.
2. Have the child count the total.
3. Have the child arrange the counters in piles of tens and loose units—in this case, 4 piles of 10 with 3 left over.
4. Ask the child to remove a number of counters (e.g., remove 7), starting with the loose counters. In this case, the child would remove the 3 loose counters and 4 from one of the groups of 10.
5. Then say: "You had 43, and now you've taken 7 away from that. How many do you think you have now?" Ask for a reason for her guess.

● What you are looking for

Can the child use place-value arrangements to interpret quantities that were not originally presented in place-value terms?

This is yet another example of misdirection, where the original action does not clue the child to solve the problem using place value. In this case, we have had the child subtract amounts past the decade marker, which interferes with her ability to know the answer by counting backward from the starting quantity. Will she abandon that strategy and instead use the place-value arrangement to know the answer? Here's a chance to find out!

● Study Group Discussion Starters: Secure Place-Value Awareness

At what age do children develop the skills covered in this section?

Share your impressions of what you've seen your children doing and struggling with to date. How do you know what your children are and are not ready for?

Are the children you work with ready for these place-value awareness activities? If not, what stage are they at, and what will it take them to get to a level where they can profit from working with these place-value concepts?

Conversely, have your children already mastered these understandings to a point where the tasks outlined in this chapter are pointless and boring for them? How do you know? What do you do if some of your children seem to have a firm understanding of place value but others are still struggling?

How well do your children understand teen numbers?

Discuss your experiences with children's ability to interpret teen numbers in terms of tens and units. Have you tried giving them a teen quantity and asking them to tell you how many tens they could make out of it and how many they would have left over or to predict what filled ten frames would look like if the materials were placed in them? If so, how did they explain their answers? Conversely, have you tried showing them a teen numeral and asking them what the two digits stand for? Is it important that children know the teen numbers in place-value terms, or is it enough that they know them well as counting numbers?

How well do your children transition through the decade numbers?

Discuss your experiences with children counting forward and backward through the decade transition points. Do they count both forward (38, 39, 40, 41, 42 . . .) and backward (42, 41, 40, 39, 38 . . .) with confidence? Is backward harder than forward? What types of errors do they make, and what do those errors signify? What explanations or materials have you tried to help them resolve their difficulties?

How good are your children at estimating loose collections with up to 100 objects?

Do your children have a sense of how much quantities between 20 and 100 look like? If you display 70 objects, how close are their estimates? When given a large quantity, what are their most common guesses? If you count part of the quantity and let them change their estimates, do they make a more accurate estimate, and what reason do they give for the change? What role do you think estimation of quantities plays in children's emerging number sense?

How comfortable are your children navigating in hundreds space?

Have you tried some of the activities where children use a base-10 organization to quickly zero in on particular numbers or numerals (e.g., Hundred Chain, Page Walk, or Hundreds Board Magic Windows)? How quick are children to distinguish changes signaled by the tens digit from changes signaled by the units digit?

A related issue: Can your children instantly make greater than/less than judgments when comparing two-digit numerals, even if the smaller numeral has a greater number of units (e.g., 27 compared to 41)? Can they estimate how close the two numerals are to each other?

ADDITION/ SUBTRACTION FLUENCY LAUNCH POINTS

What This Is—And Why It Is Important

Mastering addition and subtraction is more than memorizing facts. Mindless flash-card drills and Mad Minute speed tests will eventually result in children knowing their basic math facts, but at what cost? How many children do we still see in fourth and fifth grades who have forgotten a math fact and are secretly counting the answer on their fingers under the table, having no better strategy available to them? Children who routinely work with the types of tasks laid out in this chapter will have their basic addition and subtraction facts memorized, but they will also

- Be experts at using powerful and flexible mental math strategies to solve math problems (which, among other things, allows them to quickly reconstruct a forgotten math fact without finger counting).
- Be confident in their ability to untangle difficult math problems without being given step-by-step directions how to proceed.[1]
- Think that math is fun—and can't wait to do more of it!

Both *Curriculum Focus Points* (NCTM [National Council of Teachers of Mathematics], 2007) and *Common Core State Standards for Mathematics* (Council of Chief State School Officers & National Governors Association Center, 2010) emphasize that children in the early grades should be spending much less time memorizing math facts and more time

---

[1] Polya's (1957) classic four-step model of problem solving starts with (1) clearly understand the problem and (2) brainstorm strategies for tackling the problem. Children who routinely work with activities such as those in this chapter will be good problem solvers.

developing deep number sense and flexible problem-solving strategies, but accountability measures have led many teachers to adopt wrong-headed short-term fixes to boost test scores. The research community has a pretty good handle on the teaching-learning paths that lead to long-term mathematical fluency (NRC [National Research Council], 2009); we simply have to trust that children will learn well if allowed to exercise their natural intelligence and curiosity. Given a proper learning environment, children will confidently abandon counting the answers on their fingers, first because they have developed faster and more foolproof ways of generating answers than finger counting and later because they simply *know* the answers. More significantly, when they *do* reach automaticity on their math facts, they will do so without believing they must rely on arbitrary rules and gimmicks to come up with the answers to problems. Instead, they will believe that math makes sense and that they are mathematicians.

What Comes Before—And How to Get There

Basic Part-Whole Awareness

K.OA.3 *Decompose numbers less than or equal to 10 into pairs in more than one way, e.g., by using objects or drawings, and record each decomposition by a drawing or equation (e.g., 5 = 2 + 3 and 5 = 4 + 1).*

As children become convinced that quantities stay the same even when the pieces are arranged differently (known as *conservation of number*), they are free to make a further discovery: Not only does the total quantity remain the same but also the parts show regularities and patterns of their own. Let's consider some of the discoveries children can make with the quantity 7; for example:

- They can see that every time they separate 2 from the 7, the other part is predictably and invariably 5.
- They can realize that, if they reversed the process and started by separating the 5 from the 7, they would end up with the 2. In other words, they can invent the *commutative property*.
- Having earlier discovered that 6 can be divided into two 3's, they might now be amazed to notice that they can divide the number that is 1 more than 6 into two 3's with 1 left over.

As these examples illustrate, once children have acquired number conservation, a whole world of fascinating patterns opens up for their discovery and invention. The message to us, as teachers, is that long before children are expected to start memorizing their addition and subtraction facts, they should have had endless opportunities to explore and discover these relationships on their own and excitedly share them with you and each other.

In this chapter, the basic part-whole awareness described above is extended to larger numbers, and children in this set of launch point activities are expected increasingly to notice, predict, and remember the parts into which wholes can be broken. If you find that your children haven't had enough preparatory experiences with smaller numbers to confidently move to this next level, here is a short list of the kinds of activities that can get them ready, taken from my earlier work published by Redleaf Press (Nelson, 2007):[2]

- **Hand Game.** Hold a known quantity of objects in one hand; put both hands behind your back and transfer some of the quantity to the other hand. Reveal the contents of one hand and ask the children to guess what's in the missing hand before revealing.

- **Cover Up.** Display a known quantity; have the children close their eyes while a portion of the quantity is covered up; ask them to guess the covered quantity.

- **Bears in a Cave.** This is a variation on hide-and-seek. A given number of bears ask their "guests" to hide their eyes, while some of the bears go hide in a cave; other bears remain where they can be seen. The objective is to guess how many bears are hiding in the cave.

- **Shaker Boxes.** A given number of pennies is placed in an opaque box. One child shakes the box, opens the box, sorts the pennies, and announces how many heads there are. The objective is to guess how many tails are showing in the box.

- **Toothpick Designs.** Every child is given the same number of toothpicks (or cotton swabs, craft sticks, etc.) and asked to arrange them in a design. All the inventive ways that the same number of toothpicks can be arranged are then compared.

Concepts and Skills Being Reinforced in This Chapter

The activities presented here have children apply their budding awareness of part-whole to work on problems with numbers up to 20—an organic start to what will eventually be their memorized addition and subtraction facts. Special emphasis is placed on children being able to break apart and put together tens, since tens are such useful anchor numbers in many mental math strategies.

Here is a summary of the part-whole number concepts children will gain mastery of though experiences such as those described in this chapter.

Part-Whole Patterns for Numbers Up to 20

K.OA.3 *Decompose numbers less than or equal to 10 into pairs in more than one way, e.g., by using objects or drawings, and record each decomposition by a drawing or equation (e.g., 5 = 2 + 3 and 5 = 4 + 1).*

K.OA.4 *For any number from 1 to 9, find the number that makes 10 when added to the given number, e.g., by using objects or drawings, and record the answer with a drawing or equation.*

---

[2] For a more extensive discussion of the activities suggested in this list, see *Math at Their Own Pace: Child-Directed Activities for Developing Early Number Sense* by Greg Nelson. Copyright © 2007 by Greg Nelson. Reprinted with permission of Redleaf Press, St. Paul, MN; *www.redleafpress.org*.

Children's ability to conceptualize larger numbers in terms of tens and units is related to an even more basic concept: Quantities can be subdivided and rearranged in different ways without changing the quantity. For example, 7 can be laid out as 5 and 2, or it can just as easily be configured as 3 and 4. Children begin to develop this concept as they re-count sets that they have rearranged, discovering they still have the same quantity. Children's secure acceptance of this attribute of numbers is essential for them to confidently move away from counting complete sets and more closely examine patterns and regularities in their parts.

Decomposition and Composition of Numbers

K.OA.3 *Decompose numbers less than or equal to 10 into pairs in more than one way, e.g., by using objects or drawings, and record each decomposition by a drawing or equation (e.g., 5 = 2 + 3 and 5 = 4 + 1).*

K.NBT.1 *Compose and decompose numbers from 11 to 19 into ten ones and some further ones, e.g., by using objects or drawings, and record each composition or decomposition by a drawing or equation (e.g., 18 = 10 + 8); understand that these numbers are composed of ten ones and one, two, three, four, five, six, seven, eight, or nine ones.*

1.OA.1 *Use addition and subtraction within 20 to solve word problems involving situations of adding to, taking from, putting together, taking apart, and comparing, with unknowns in all positions, e.g., by using objects, drawings, and equations with a symbol for the unknown number to represent the problem.*

1.OA.6 *Add and subtract within 20, demonstrating fluency for addition and subtraction within 10. Use strategies such as counting on; making ten (e.g., 8 + 6 = 8 + 2 + 4 = 10 + 4 = 14); decomposing a number leading to a ten (e.g., 13 − 4 = 13 − 3 − 1 = 10 − 1 = 9); using the relationship between addition and subtraction (e.g., knowing that 8 + 4 = 12, one knows 12 − 8 = 4); and creating equivalent but easier or known sums (e.g., adding 6 + 7 by creating the known equivalent 6 + 6 + 1 = 12 + 1 = 13).*

Being comfortable with taking numbers apart (known as *decomposition*) and making larger parts out of smaller pieces (called *composition*) is the key to the next stage of numeracy. Children who know, when confronted with the problem 9 + 7, that they can pull one of the numbers apart strategically (making the problem 9 + [1 + 6]),[3] and then change which pieces are connected to one another (making the problem [9 + 1] + 6),[4] which leaves them with the much easier problem 10 + 6, or 16, are well on their way to mastering addition and subtraction.

The Commutative Property of Addition

1.OA.3 *Apply properties of operations as strategies to add and subtract. Examples: If 8 + 3 = 11 is known, then 3 + 8 = 11 is also known (Commutative property of addition). To add 2 + 6 + 4, the second two numbers can be added to make a ten, so 2 + 6 + 4 = 2 + 10 = 12 (Associative property of addition).*

2.NBT.5 *Fluently add and subtract within 100 using strategies based on place value, properties of operations, and/or the relationship between addition and subtraction.*

---

[3] Believe it or not, this simple transformation involves both the *multiplicative property of 1* and the *distributive property*: $7 = 1*7 = 1*[1 + 6] = [1*1] + [1*6] = 1 + 6$. See how intelligent children's intuitions are!

[4] Known as the *associative property*.

2.NBT.6 *Add up to four two-digit numbers using strategies based on place value and properties of operations.*

The commutative property is also known in many classrooms as *the turn-around facts*; the simple discovery that 3 + 5 is equivalent to 5 + 3 cuts the number of facts to be memorized almost in half. In the meantime, it allows children still at the counting on stage to count on from the larger of the two addends. In other words, if they are asked to solve the problem 3 + 9, they can think: "nine . . . ten, eleven, *twelve*."

Addition and Subtraction as Inverse Operations

1.OA.1 *Use addition and subtraction within 20 to solve word problems involving situations of adding to, taking from, putting together, taking apart, and comparing, with unknowns in all positions, e.g., by using objects, drawings, and equations with a symbol for the unknown number to represent the problem.*

1.OA.4 *Understand subtraction as an unknown-addend problem. For example, subtract 10 – 8 by finding the number that makes 10 when added to 8.*

1.OA.6 *Add and subtract within 20, demonstrating fluency for addition and subtraction within 10. Use strategies such as . . . using the relationship between addition and subtraction (e.g., knowing that 8 + 4 = 12, one knows 12 – 8 = 4).*

1.NBT.4 *Add within 100, including adding a two-digit number and a one-digit number, and adding a two-digit number and a multiple of 10, using concrete models or drawings and strategies based on place value, properties of operations, and/or the relationship between addition and subtraction.*

2.NBT.9 *Explain why addition and subtraction strategies work, using place value and the properties of operations.*

Children who see numbers not just in their entirety but as composites do not see addition and subtraction as any great mystery. When a child knows that, if 3 and 6 are the parts, then 9 is the whole, it is no great leap for the child to know that, if 9 is the whole and 3 is one of the parts, then the other part is 6. In other words, if the child understands the part-whole relationship, then the child simultaneously understands that

$$3 + 6 = 9$$
$$6 + 3 = 9$$
$$9 - 3 = 6$$
$$9 - 6 = 3$$

These four facts are so intimately related to one another that they are rightly known as a *fact family*.

Fact families graphically illustrate why it makes no sense to teach children addition and subtraction separately and why we should not arbitrarily describe a real-world situation as being either an addition or a subtraction problem, since in most cases the situation could rightfully be thought of as either one (more on this in the section "The Real Scoop on Those Dreaded Word Problems" in Chapter 6).

PD pd TOOLKIT™

Go to the PDToolkit to find the online templates referenced in the following activity.

HANDS UP #2 ADDITION/SUBTRACTION

MATERIALS AND SET-UP

- The children's fingers!
- Optional: Place-value numeral cards 1–20.
- Optional: 1–10 finger cards. The 1–9 finger cards are on a green background, and the 10 finger card is on a blue background (see Figure 5.1).

LAUNCH POINT

Addition (Join model[5])

- Have two children stand side by side, facing the class. Give each a single-digit number to display with his fingers: The pinkie finger on the right hand is raised for one, the pinkie finger and ring finger for two, and so on. For six, the child raises the thumb on the left hand, and so on, up to 10. In other words, fingers are raised so that, *to the viewing audience*, counting progresses from left to right.
- Ask the children in the class how many fingers are showing all together and how they know.

Subtraction (Separate model)

- Have a child or children display a quantity up to 20.
- Ask them to lower a quantity of fingers up to 10. Ask the children in the class if they did it correctly and how they know.

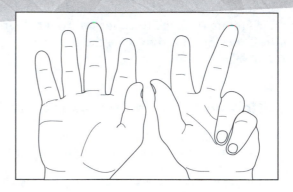

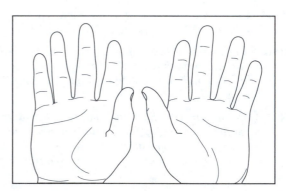

Figure 5.1

Variation

- Set up the problems using finger cards.

---

[5] See "The Real Scoop on Those Dreaded Word Problems" in Chapter 6 for an explanation of the various addition-subtraction word problem models.

In simple but powerful ways, children solving these problems are being encouraged to use 5 and 10 as anchor numbers to solve addition and subtraction problems. For example, in the Join problem, if both children had up 4 fingers, the class might say the first 4 is almost 5. To make it 5, the class would take 1 from the other child, and the children know that a hand with 5 fingers plus 3 more fingers is 8. Or the class may say that the combined fingers are 2 less than 10, or 8. If more fingers are displayed—for example, if one child displays 8 fingers and another 4—the class is likely to say that if the second child lowers 2 fingers and the first child raises 2, then there will be a full set of 10 and 2 more, or 12.

Separate problems are a bit trickier, but children will still tend to solve them using their number sense rather than simply counting the answer. For example, if

12 fingers are on display and the task is to lower 5 fingers, one strategy might be to break the 5 into 2 and 3, lowering the 2 isolated fingers and 3 more from the set of 10. Or someone is likely to suggest that they simply drop one of their hands (with its 5 fingers), leaving 8 fingers showing.

As can be seen in these types of problems, a hallmark of the solution is that multiple ways of approaching the problem are possible, and they are not being posed as "This is an addition problem" or "This is a subtraction problem." It's a problem, period. Although Join and Separate models are the most common formats for practicing addition and subtraction, it is possible to pose others. For example:

- **Comparison Model.** Have a child or children display a quantity up to 20. Have another child display a quantity up to 10. Ask the children in the class how much larger the one number is than the other and how they know.
- **Part-Whole Model.** Have a child or children display a quantity up to 20. Have two more children come to the front, one displaying a quantity up to 10 and the other just standing there. Ask the children in the class how many fingers the last child should hold up so their combined fingers equal those displayed by the first set of children. Ask how they know.

Once children get good at these kinds of problems, they quickly and easily move on to applying the same reasoning to larger numbers. For example, if given the problem 23 + 38, the solver would invite three children up to model the 23 (two children holding up all their fingers, one to their left[6] holding up 3) and then four more children to display 38 (three holding up all their fingers, the child to their left holding up 8); then the solver would ask all the children holding up 10 fingers to move to the right and the two children holding up 3 and 8 to move to the right. It is then obvious that the answer is 50 + 11, or 61. So simple! Children can practice these kinds of problems on their own using the picture version of units and tens hands.

Go to the PDToolkit to find the online templates referenced in this activity.

___
[6] The audience's right.

Launch Point

TEN-BAR IN A CAVE GAME

MATERIALS AND SET-UP

- 1 ten-bar and 10 unit place-value blocks.
- Bowl or small, opaque stacking bin to serve as the "cave."

Note: This game is an extension of Bears in a Cave, explained earlier in "What Comes Before—and How to Get

There." The story involves a variation on hide-and-seek, where the person who hides her eyes needs to decide how many bears are hiding, not where they are.

LAUNCH POINT

1. The ten-bar is set on top of the "cave" (the over-turned bowl or bin) by the child who will be the hider. The supply of 10 unit blocks is temporarily hidden from view.
2. Seekers all close their eyes while the hider replaces the ten-bar with the 10 unit blocks, placing some of the unit blocks inside the cave and leaving the remaining blocks on top.
3. Seekers open their eyes and try to guess how many blocks are hiding in the cave.
4. After all the guesses are in, the cave is lifted to reveal the actual number of blocks hidden.

5. Hider and seekers switch roles. Unit blocks are secreted away, and the ten-bar is placed back on top of the cave.

Variations

- The same game can be played with the whole class using an overhead and an opaque circle or cave silhouette.
- A variation on the Hand Game (described earlier in "What Comes Before—and How to Get There") can also be done. Here the 10 unit blocks are "secretly" held in one closed hand while the ten-bar is displayed in the other. The hider puts

both hands behind her back, slips the ten-bar into a waistband or back pocket, switches some of the units to the now-empty hand, brings both hands to the front with her fists closed, and then opens one hand. Seekers guess how many units are in the closed hand. Then both hands are moved behind the back, units transferred to a single hand, the ten-bar retrieved, and both hands brought to the front to show the ten-bar once again (the hand holding the units stays closed). The cycle then repeats.

- Can start with two ten-bars to extend parts-of to 20.

The children won't be fooled by the switch from the ten-bar to 10 units, but they love the theatrical element of pretending this is some awesome magic trick. Obviously, any materials could be used as the collection of 10. But it is particularly important to do this with the ten-bar because it is a fixed place-value representation. Unlike a stack of Unifix cubes or a bundle of 10 straws, it is a single object that is being called "ten." Don't underestimate the lingering effects of preoperational thinking—what we want the children to think of as ten can easily slip into being thought of as one. By having the ten "magically" decompose into 10 movable objects, we hope to dismantle this misconception.

Launch Point

ADDITION/SUBTRACTION USING AN EQUAL-ARM BALANCE SCALE

MATERIALS AND SET-UP

- Balance scale or equal-arm balance.
- A supply of uniform weights: pennies, ceramic tiles, counting bears, or washers. The weights should be heavy enough that a single one is enough to make the balance tilt noticeably.
- Scratch paper or a visual representation of a balance scale, to help children remember what went into the two sides of the scale or what was taken out.

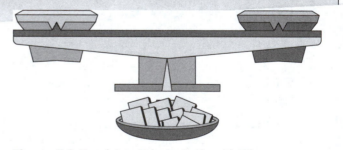

Figure 5.2 Equal-Arm Balance Scale with Tiles

Sturdy classroom scales are available from most educational suppliers. You can also make a serviceable one quite easily; for example, suspend two baskets from the ends of an old broom handle using cup hooks. Screw a third cup hook into the midpoint of the handle to suspend the balance from a plant hanger or the ceiling.

Whittle or sand the ends of the broom handle until perfect balance is achieved. Small adjustments can be made by taping paper clips to the handle.

LAUNCH POINT

Join Problem (Addition)

- One child places two quantities into one side of the scale: "Okay, I'm putting in five tiles—one, two, three, four, five. And now I'm putting in four more tiles—one, two, three, four."
- The child then asks: "How many should I put in the other side to make it balance?"
- Other children make their guesses, and then tiles are added one at a time until the scale balances.

Separate Problem (Subtraction)

- Same as addition, except the child sets up the problem by counting a number of tiles into one side of the balance scale and then takes out a certain number of those tiles: "I'm putting 12 tiles on this side . . . now I'm taking out 5 of those tiles. How many do you think I should put in the other side to make it balance?"

Compare Problem

- The child counts a number of tiles into one side of the balance scale and then counts a different number of tiles into the other side of the scale: "I'm putting 13 tiles on this side. And now I'm putting 9 tiles on this side. Which side do you think I should add more tiles to to make the scale balance, and how many should I add?"

This activity is incredibly versatile in terms of having children move forward and backward in mental number space. Besides, what better metaphor can you have for balancing an equation than actually bringing a balance scale into balance!

If you are working with a group or observing a group in action, occasionally ask the children to share out loud how they are coming up with their solutions. This is particularly important if there is a difference of opinion regarding the answer. But even when the children agree, it is important for them to realize they might be arriving at the same solution using different strategies.

Be careful of rushing too quickly to the abstract (i.e., using number sentences to record the solutions to balance-scale problems). Although such is certainly a valuable transition activity, the beauty of this activity is how it lets children solve mathematical problems in the concrete world rather than on paper. As I mentioned earlier, one of the best pieces of advice I've been given in recent years is this: "We should have children treat numbers as adjectives rather than as nouns as long as possible." It is much easier for a child to think about the difference between the 13 tiles on one side of a scale and the 9 tiles on the other than it is to compare 13 to 9. With the balance scale, numbers are adjectives describing objects the child can manipulate using mental imagery (during the prediction phase) and then physically (during the checking phase). On paper, $13 - 9$ treats numbers as the objects themselves, without referents or a story context. Besides, we can't anticipate in advance what number sentence will best capture how a particular child solves the above problem. Which of these might it be?

$$13 - 9 = ?$$
$$13 = ? + 9$$
$$13 - ? = 9$$

Several years later, children will solve the exact same problem, now written in algebraic terms:

$$13 - 9 = x. \quad \text{Solve for x.}$$
$$13 = a + 9. \quad \text{Solve for a.}$$
$$13 - p = 9. \quad \text{Solve for p.}$$

We don't know how to write the problem until we know how the child solved it. The worst thing we can do is chastise a child for using an addition strategy for what we considered a subtraction problem.

The variations on how to add things to or take things away from a balance scale or which part of the problem to leave unknown are virtually endless, but here are a couple of other ways to vary and extend the scale's use as a mathematical tool:

1. Do multiple additive and subtractive steps before calling for a solution. For example, a tricky problem would be this: "I'm putting 4 tiles on the left side . . . and I'm putting 9 tiles on the right side . . . and I'm adding 7 more to the left side . . . and I'm taking 2 out of the right side. All done! *Now*, which side do you think I should add more tiles to, and how many should I add?"

2. Do mystery addition or subtraction. In this case, a child puts a quantity on one side and then has the other children hide their eyes while he adds a quantity to or subtracts a quantity from that side. Then everyone counts as weights are added to the other side until the scale balances. The children must guess how much the child added or took out while their eyes were closed.

3. Have children draw cards from a 1–10 deck one at a time, placing the indicated number of weights on each. After each new card is added, they try to re-arrange the cards to make two equivalent groups of weights. If they can't do it, they draw another card and try again. When they think they have it, they place one set of cards on one side of the scale and put the weights in that basket and then do the same with the other set on the right side of the scale. If the scale balances, they got it right.

   • Or multiple children can each draw four cards and arrange them into two piles they think are as equivalent as possible. Children take turns putting the indicated amounts on each side of the scale and seeing how many additional weights they need to add to make it balance. The child who has to add the fewest weights wins that round.

   • Or the same game can be played as a difference game: Children arrange their four cards so they think the differences between the paired cards are as similar as possible. Children take turns putting the larger quantity from each set on the two sides of the scale and then taking out the equivalent of the smaller quantity in each set from their respective sides. The child who has to add the fewest weights to bring the scale into balance wins that round.

   • Practice simple multiplication and division as successive addition or successive subtraction. For example, a child could say:

      • **Multiplication:** "I'm putting 4 tiles on this side 3 times. How many tiles do you think I should add to the other side to make it balance?"

      • **Division:** "I'm putting 15 tiles on this side and no tiles on the other side. I'm going to pull out 3 tiles at a time. How many times do you think I can remove 3 before the scale is balanced again?"

Go to the PDToolkit to find the online templates referenced in the following activity.

The best way I know to wean children from counting addition and subtraction problems on their fingers is to use ten frames. If children visualize numbers in terms of their parts relative to 5 and 10, they can easily "see" ways to combine the parts to make "recognizable" numbers, even when the frames are not physically

Launch Point

ADDITION/SUBTRACTION USING TEN FRAMES

MATERIALS AND SET-UP

- Ten frames.
- Manipulatives to put on the frames (lima beans, Unifix cubes, etc.).
- Optional: Printed tabletop ten frames.

I prefer using ten-frame containers to mats (see Figure 5.3). I also prefer to position the ten frames horizontally and fill them from left to right and top to bottom (which parallels the directionality of reading). However, many practitioners like to orient the ten frames vertically and fill them from bottom to top and left to right. Either way works.

LAUNCH POINT

Addition (Join problem)

- Have the children position two ten frames one above the other. Have them put between 1 and 9 manipulatives in each of the ten frames.
- Ask the children to predict how many manipulatives there are all together. Ask how they know.
- Have the children move the manipulatives to check their answer.

Subtraction (Separate problem)

- Have the children make a quantity between 2 and 20 in a double ten frame.
- Ask them how many they think they will have left if they take out _____ (select a number where the answer will be 10 or less). Ask them how they know.
- Have them remove the quantity to check their answer.

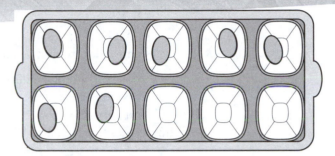

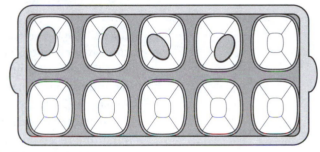

Figure 5.3 Addition with Egg Carton Ten Frames

Variations

- Have preprinted cards with numerals between 2 and 20 on both sides, where the difference between the numbers on the two sides is 10 or less. Children make the larger quantity in a double ten frame and predict how many they will have left if they take out the quantity on the flip side.
- Let the children create problems with the printed ten frames. The printed versions lack the hands-on advantages of children constructing the quantities themselves, but they are much more compact and allow children to set up problems much more quickly.

present.[7] Confronted with the problem 8 + 6, if children visualize 8 as a full row of 5 and 3 more and 6 as a full row of 5 and 1 more, fewer children will resort to the slow and error-prone finger-counting method of

- "Eight, then nine, ten, eleven, twelve, thirteen, fourteen—14!" and more children will use strategies such as these:

---

[7] There is a system called TouchMath that has children visualize counting dots on the written numerals themselves. However, this system tends to prolong children's dependence on counting strategies rather than weaning them from them. Ten frames provide a much better path to powerful mental math strategies.

- "If I take 2 from the 6 to make the 8 a 10, that will take away the 1 from the bottom row of the 6 plus 1 from the top row. That's 10 and 4—14!"
- "I have two full 5's, with 3 left over from the 8 and 1 left over from the 6. The 3 and the 1 make 4—14!"

Occasionally, you'll have even more creative solutions shared, such as this:

- "Hey, if I take 1 away from the 8 and give it to the 6, now they're both 7's, and I know that 7 plus 7 is 14!"

Any of these signals children on their way to becoming powerful mathematicians. Finger counting does not get them there, even though it does yield right answers.

You can also model other types of addition/subtraction problems on the ten frames besides Join and Separate problems. For example:

- **Compare Problem.** Set up a ten frame with a quantity 1–9 next to a double ten frame with a quantity 11–20, and ask the children how much more the one is than the other. Ask how they know. Or if you want to do simpler quantities in a competitive game, each child gets three ten frames, one for playing and two for keeping score. Have the children draw cards from a 1–10 card deck and make that quantity in their game frames. The child who has the most (or least) scores points equal to the difference between his frame and the next largest quantity, which he keeps track of in his double scoring frame. First one to 20 wins.
- **Part-Whole Problem, with Missing Part.** Set up a double ten frame with a quantity 2–20 and a single frame with a quantity 1–10. Ask how many would have to be added to the single frame to make the quantity in the double frame (make sure to choose a sum where the missing addend is 10 or less). Or set up a *series* of double ten frames with sets of addend frames to match them. Mix up the addend frames, have each child select one, and then ask the children to find a partner with whom they can equal one of the double frame quantities. Note that, when you play this way, there might be multiple partners standing next to the same frame. Ask the children how that is possible. You could follow up by asking if they can find a different partner with whom to stand next to a different frame. Or you could hold up a particular frame and ask how many pairs of children can make a quantity equivalent to that frame . . . or ask if any trios can equal the frame. The possibilities are only as limited as your imagination!

Go to the PDToolkit to find the online templates referenced in the following activity.

The next step in the ten frames is to use them to model two-digit addition and subtraction. For example, when given the problem 37 + 26, the children would first fill 3 ten frames and put 7 in another and then fill 2 more frames and put 6 in another. Visual inspection will quickly lead them to conclude: "Well, I have 5 full ten frames plus 7 + 6, which is 13. So that's 63." To cut down on the amount of time spent filling frames, these problems are better used with the tabletop picture sets. Note that the mental process by which the children solve this problem parallels their natural tendency to solve place-value addition and subtraction problems from left to right rather than in the right-to-left fashion we teach them in the standard algorithm (Kamii, 1985).

Double-sixes are the standard dominoes, of course, and can be used. I like the 18-dot sets because they extend the addition facts that can be modeled to 9 + 9. There are also 24-dot sets that allow you to go up to 12 + 12 (or take out a few

DOUBLE-NINES DOMINOES SORTING

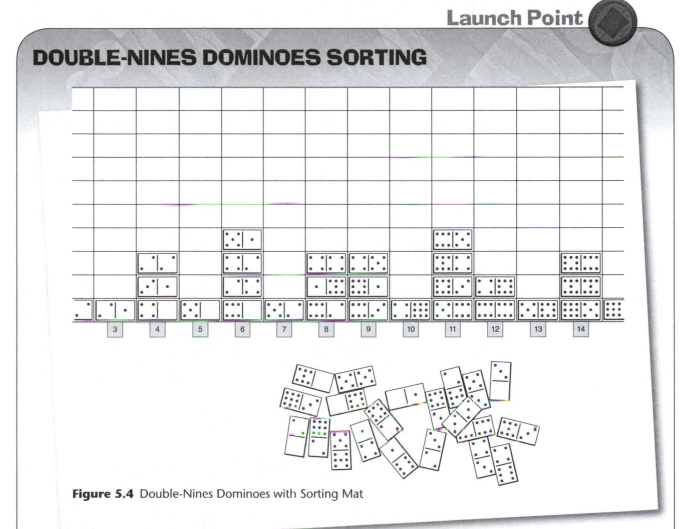

Figure 5.4 Double-Nines Dominoes with Sorting Mat

MATERIALS AND SET-UP

- Commercial set of dominoes that go up to nine dots on each section (i.e., totals range from 0 to 18).
- Sorting mat with horizontal rectangles slightly larger than the dominoes. The mat is 19 rectangles wide and 10 rectangles tall. Printed below each of the columns of rectangles are numerals, starting on the left with 0 and ending on the right with 18 (see Figure 5.4).

LAUNCH POINT

- Children pick up any domino, decide how many dots it has on it, and place it in the appropriate column.

Variations

- **Addition or Subtraction War.** Children each have an opaque container or bag of dominoes. They each set out a domino and decide who has the largest sum (or difference).

- **Make-the-Decade Game.** Dominoes are all in a central pile. Children take turns pulling out a domino and having the second child add a domino so the total sum is 10, 20, or 30. For example, if the first child plays a [5,8], the second child needs to add either 7 or 17. They have lots of options. For example, [3,4], [0,7], and [8,9] would all work. Children continue making pairs until no more are possible.

and stop at $10 + 10$). The one thing I don't like about the extended sets is that they tend to have color-coded dots (e.g., the six-dot configuration is a different color than the seven-dot). But that's really only a problem with matching games, where you want to make sure children are matching quantities, not colors. You can always take a permanent marker and make all the dots black.

Finding different dominoes that add up to the same sum is a great way for children to discover part-whole relationships. For example, all the combinations that add up to 8 are collected in the same column. This is also a good opportunity for children to notice the turn-around facts (i.e., the commutative property of addition), when, for example, they see that $4 + 8$ is in the same column as $8 + 4$. They might even say: "Hey, why are there two of each?!" That would be a good thing—it would mean they see the inverted addition fact as redundant.

When all the dominoes are properly placed, they form an approximation of a bell-shaped curve, with a single domino on both ends and a central column that is 9 dominoes high. For a couple of reasons, I intentionally don't make the mat match this arrangement because

- I want this pattern to be discovered, not provided. It's much more satisfying to the children to inform *me* of the surprising result of their sorting activity.
- I want to allow children to make errors in their placements without feeling they've messed up. It's more important that they concentrate on the activity than that they concentrate on being right.

There are ways to vary the uses of the dominoes, to keep the children interested and to expand and extend their thinking:

- Children can rearrange the dominoes in the columns to form an ascending pattern. For example, in the 8 column the dominoes could be arranged $0 + 8$, $1 + 7, 2 + 6, 3 + 5, 4 + 4, 5 + 3, 6 + 2, 7 + 1$, and $8 + 0$.
- Children can use the dominoes to play games like Dominoes War (where the player with the largest sum takes the trick) or Dominoes Concentration (where pairs of dominoes with the same sum are mixed in an array of upside-down dominoes and players have to try to remember the location of certain sums to make a match).
- Children can sort the dominoes by differences between the two sides, which can range between 0 and 9. This will require a taller, narrower mat.
- Children can record the addition or subtraction fact that each domino represents. For example, in the 15 column are dominoes representing:

$$6 + 9 = 15 \quad \text{or} \quad 15 - 6 = 9$$
$$7 + 8 = 15 \quad \text{or} \quad 15 - 7 = 8$$
$$8 + 7 = 15 \quad \text{or} \quad 15 - 8 = 7$$
$$9 + 6 = 15 \quad \text{or} \quad 15 - 9 = 6$$

- Older children can be given a set of addition facts or addition flash cards and asked to sort them in a similar fashion.

In too many classrooms, children practice only their basic addition facts. Stringing together three or more numbers gives children the opportunity to practice

DOMINO TRAINS

MATERIALS AND SET-UP

- Large collection of double-six dominoes.
- Numeral cards indicating target sums from 8 to 20.

Figure 5.5 Domino Trains—Making Tens

LAUNCH POINT

- Children select the numeral for their target sum.
- Children find dominoes that add up to the target number and place them end-to-end.
- Children see if any other domino combinations add up to the same sum.

more nimble number manipulation. For example, if children lay down dominoes [3,4][6,1][3,3] to make 20, one child might say:

"Well, the first two dominoes are both 7, and that's a doubles fact so that's 14. And the last domino is 6. 6 and 4 make 10, so I've got 2 tens. Yup, I've got 20."

while another child might be thinking:

"I see 4 and 6 together, so that's 10. Then there are three 3's, so that's 9, and 1 more is 10. Yup, I've got 20."

Those are much more sophisticated strategies than that of the child who proceeds mechanically down the line, saying:

"3 and 4 is 7 . . . and 7 plus 6 is 13 . . . and 1 more is 14 . . . and 3 more is, let's see, 4 and 3 is 7, so 17 . . . and 3 more, hmmm, 18, 19, 20. Yup, that's 20."

More basic still would be the child who says:

"Three . . . four, five, six, seven . . . eight, nine, ten, eleven, twelve, thirteen . . . ."

That child is still stuck at the counting-on stage and needs more work with materials that will encourage more sophisticated mental math strategies.

Making the sum in multiple ways makes children check whether they've already made a certain combination, only with dominoes in a different order or turned in the other direction. For example, making the sum of 16 with [5,4][3,4] is equivalent to making it with [4,3][4,5]. If children make it both ways, don't correct them; just notice that they are doing so. They aren't wrong, after all: 5 + 4 + 3 + 4 is a different expression than 4 + 3 + 4 + 5.

Here are some ways to extend the children's work with the dominoes:

- Provide mats with drawn outlines of blank dominoes in train, snake, triangle, square, or rectangle configurations. Children fit dominoes into the spaces to create the specified sums. Note that shape versions offer an interesting feature: The end pieces on each side have to work for *two* sets of running sums.
- Children can record their solutions, either as drawn dominoes or as number sentences with long strings of addends. Drawn solutions can be put together

DIRECTIONAL RODS WITH ADDITION/SUBTRACTION RACK

MATERIALS AND SET-UP

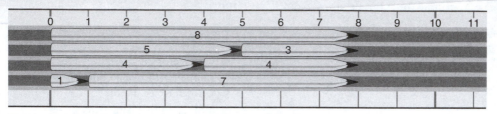

Figure 5.6 Directional Rods with Addition/Subtraction Rack

- Several sets of directional rods, 1–10, with numerals written on their sides indicating their length. I make mine out of doweling in 2.5 cm increments. The rods are sharpened to a dull point on one end, with the tip colored red to indicate it is the front (see Figure 5.6).

- A thin board 75 cm long, marked off and numbered from −5 to 25 in 2.5 cm increments. The board has four to six grooves running horizontally from end to end, which the directional rods can fit in. I used a short piece of grooved molding from the hardware to make mine (see Figure 5.6).

LAUNCH POINT

- Pose an addition or subtraction problem or, better yet, a word problem that involves addition or subtraction. Have children place directional rods on the rack in the following manner to solve the problems.

Join Problems (e.g., 6 and 8 more)

- Place the 6-rod on the upper groove, starting at the 0 and pointing to the right (i.e., pointing to the 6).
- Place the 8-rod on the groove below, lined up with the tip of the rod above (i.e., starting at the 6) and pointing to the right.
- The tip of the lower rod is pointing to the answer (i.e., 14).

Separate Problems (e.g., 14 take away 8)

- Place the 10- and 4-rods on the upper groove, starting at the 0 and pointing to the right (i.e., pointing to the 14).
- Place the 8-rod on the groove below, lined up with the right-most tip of the rods above (i.e., starting at the 14) and pointing to the left.
- The tip of the lower rod is pointing to the answer (i.e., 6).

Compare Problems (e.g., 14 is how much more than 8, or 8 is how much less than 14)

- Place rods on the two upper grooves corresponding to the two numbers, both starting at the 0 and pointing to the right (i.e., on the upper groove rods pointing to the 14, and below it a rod pointing to the 8).
- Find a rod to put in the third groove that starts at the tip of one of the numbers and stops at the tip of the other.
- The rod on the third groove is the answer.[8]

Part-Whole Problems (e.g., 6 boys and 8 girls are on the playground. How many total?)

- Place the two quantities on the two upper grooves, both starting at the 0 and pointing to the right (i.e., the top rod pointing to the 6, and the rod below it pointing to the 8).
- Ask how many that is all together.
- Move the bottom rod to the top groove to check the answer (i.e., the second rod starts at the tip of the 6-rod and points to the right, ending at the 14).

---

[8] *Note*: Missing-part problems (e.g., the total is 14 and one of the parts is 5) are modeled in similar fashion: Put the known part and the known whole on the board, and find a directional rod that will stretch from the end of the known part to the end of the known whole.

on a master classroom chart. For a new solution to be added to the chart, the children must agree it is not a repeat of one already on the chart—a source of interesting conversations. Children can also debate whether they think the class has found all possible solutions and why.

- Larger sums and more complex problems can be practiced using 18-dot or 24-dot domino sets.

The directional rods and rack are an improvement on the standard number line taped to the top of children's desks to assist them in solving problems. Use of those number lines has fallen out of favor with the math community, mainly because research has shown children tend to stagnate in their mathematical development when they use them. Why? Because they use them to count the answers to posed problems. In other words, the number lines are serving as a crutch, just like their fingers—a simple counting tool.

But just as fingers can be used as a powerful tool for encouraging mental strategies (as illustrated in the Hands Up activities in this book), so, too, can the number line be used as a powerful tool for supporting and modeling advanced mathematical reasoning. To be fair, those taped number lines can be and sometimes are used in a manner similar to the rods and rack to model solution strategies more advanced than counting. For example, when a Separate problem such as $14 - 8$ is first introduced on the number line, we often draw a long arch over the number line from the 0 to the 14, then draw a series of 8 little "hops" back to the left, after which we draw a large arch over the 8 little hops to combine them into one operation. But again, this method basically models a counting backward strategy rather than taking away the second quantity as a single motion, and that's what the children do when they use them to solve subtraction problems. The rods don't model counting; they model the steps in the problem. In the early stages of using the rods, the children can use the rack to generate the solution. But the rods and rack are most useful to children if they are asked to predict the answer to the problem before modeling it on the rack. The manipulatives then become a checking and confirming device rather than a means of coming up with the answer. This is hands-on, *minds*-on learning.

I debated whether to have the rack start at 0 rather than extending into negative space, but I think I like it the way it is. It is initially a source of puzzlement to the children as they wonder why there are numbers to the left of the zero, and we have some interesting conversations around that, including a look at how similar numbers appear if we keep subtracting 1 on a calculator after we have reached 0. Occasionally, a child will propose a solution to a missing-part problem as a Separate problem, where those numbers come in handy. For example, if we're making decorations to put in the 8 classroom windows and we've made 6 so far, some child will say "so we're missing 2" and show it on the rack as $6 - 8 = -2$—another reason we shouldn't teach children this mindless crutch: "In subtraction problems, always write the bigger number first."[9]

---

[9] In fact, this is a precursor to what older children do when they strategically solve more complex problems in their head. For example, when subtracting 19 from 37 they might say: "Well, I took 20 away from 37, which gave me 17, but I took away 1 too many, so the answer is 18." If they wrote it down, they might show a "save" box with a -1 in it. Or they might say: "Well, 30 minus 10 is 20, and 7 minus 9 is negative 2. 20 minus 2 is 18, so the answer is 18." In either case, by temporarily going into negative space they were able to easily solve a problem in their head rather than resorting to the more cumbersome exchanging method.

Here are some ways to extend the use of the directional rods:

- **Pose Multipart Problems.** For example, you could ask what $8 - 4 + 6$ would be. Again, ask for the children to solve the problems in their heads and share their solution strategies before modeling the solutions on the rack.
- **Pose Parts-of Problems.** (See Figure 5.6.) Place a rod in the top groove (e.g., 9), and ask the children to suggest combinations of rods that will make the same sum. Start with two-part addends (e.g., $2 + 7$ and $4 + 5$), but the children

Launch Point

ADDITION/SUBTRACTION USING SEGMENTED CUISENAIRE RODS AND 1-100 RACK

MATERIALS AND SET-UP

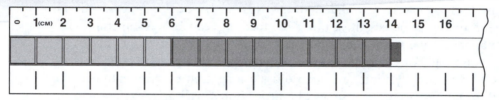

Figure 5.7 Segmented Cuisenaire Rods on 1–100 Rack

- Multiple sets of plastic connecting Cuisenaire rods (commercial product), 1–10. Each length of Cuisenaire rod has its own color code. This version has the unit increments etched on one face. If you use the traditional sets, I suggest using a pen or pencil to mark the units on one face.

- 0–100 Cuisenaire rack (commercial product). The rack is like a grooved meter stick. The Cuisenaire rods fit in the rack's groove (see Figure 5.7).

LAUNCH POINT

Join Problem, without the Rack

- Have children connect two Cuisenaire rods, with the grooved sides down.
- Ask how many they think there are all together. Ask how they know.
- If the sum is 10 or fewer, lay the Cuisenaire rod of that length below the connected rods to check the answer. If sum is more than 10, use a connected 10-rod plus the rod for the unit quantity to check the answer.

Join Problem, with the Rack

- Place the combined rods in the rack to check the answer.

Compare Problem, without the Rack

- Have children make any quantity up to 19 (if the quantity is a teen number, use the 10-rod plus the rod for the unit quantity).

- Pick up any rod of 10 or less that is less than the original quantity: "If you were to remove this many from that number, how many do you think you would have left?" Ask for their reasons.
- Lay the shorter rod on top of the original quantity, aligned on the right-hand side. Count the uncovered amount to check the answer.

Compare Problem, with the Rack

- Make the original quantity in the rack. Lay the shorter rod on top of the rod(s) in the groove, aligned on the right-hand side. The answer is the uncovered portion of the rod(s) in the groove.

will soon probably start sprinkling in multipart sums (e.g., 3 + 3 + 3) and subtraction problems (e.g., 11 − 2), and they may even start suggesting ways to mix and match addition and subtraction (e.g., 8 + 5 − 4). A particularly good variation is to put a teen number in the top groove so children focus on the place-value representation of sums.

- **Go Large!** Place a giant number line in the hallway or on the playground, and provide giant directional rods for checking the answers to word problems you or the children make up.

The Cuisenaire 1–100 rack is a nice addition to your collection of math manipulatives. Not only is it metric, it is yet another way to model solutions to addition-subtraction problems on a number line that does not encourage counting to check one's answers. As an added benefit, the rack can be used with the place-value materials, since the place-value units and tens blocks are scaled to the same dimensions as the Cuisenaire rods.

The rack lends itself particularly well to modeling the Compare model of addition-subtraction. These are problems where the difference between two quantities is questioned; for example: "Mary has 8 apples. John has 4 apples. How many more apples does Mary have than John?" These are particularly problematic for children, not only because the phrasing is more complex but also because the word *more* is being used for what is mostly likely solved as a subtraction problem ("How many apples would Mary have to lose to have the same number as John?") or a missing-addend problem ("How many more apples would John need to have the same number as Mary?"). All the more reason not to teach children the key-word method to decide whether to add or subtract.

To get more use out of the 1–100 rack, consider some of the following:

- Have the children combine multiple rods and estimate how many they have all together; then have them put the rods in the rack to see how close their estimate was.
- Give the children two sets of rods 1–9, along with two extra 5-rods. Have them pair them up to make tens and then connect the pairs in the rack. Each pair should end at a decade mark, and the total set should equal 100.
- Include missing-addend problems in the card deck, such as " ____ + 7 = 15." Children place the 7 in the rack and predict what they need to add to it to hit the 15.
- Have children solve problems where they are adding or subtracting a single-digit quantity from a quantity larger than 20. Start with problems that don't involve exchanging, such as "47 − 5" or "33 + 4." Let them discover that solving these problems is no harder than solving "7 − 5" or "3 + 4." After they get their feet wet, they can tackle problems like "45 − 8" or "36 + 7," where they will either

  1. Bridge past 10 (i.e., exchange), thinking: "Well, 45 minus 5 would be 40, and 3 less than that is 37" or
  2. Think addition-subtraction facts: "Well, that's just like adding 6 + 7, but starting at 30 rather than zero. So it's 30 + 13. That's 43."

These both parallel the algorithms we teach for multidigit addition and subtraction, but they represent the children's own making sense of the problem rather than a memorized procedure, and their thinking can be modeled on the rack.

ADDITION/SUBTRACTION USING DOUBLE-FIVES ABACUS

MATERIALS AND SET-UP

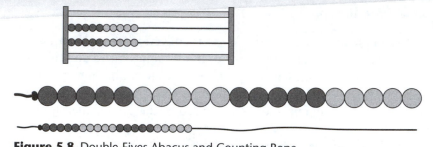

Figure 5.8 Double-Fives Abacus and Counting Rope

- Abacus with two rows of 10 beads. On each row, the first five beads are white and the second five red (commercial product—see Figure 5.8).

- Card deck with Join and Separate expressions on them.

LAUNCH POINT

- Position all the beads on the abacus to the right.
- Have children pick a card, predict what they think the answer will be, and then model the problem on the abacus. Encourage the children to form each of the numbers in a single motion rather than moving beads one at a time. For example, if the card says 8 + 5 they should slide the 8 beads (5 white, 3 red) to the left in a single motion and then simultaneously shift the remaining 2 beads on the top row and 3 beads on the bottom row (i.e., a total of 5 beads) to the left, making the sum 13. If they were doing the difference 13 − 5, they would perform these motions in reverse.

Variation

- Use a 20-bead counting rope where the beads alternate white and red in groups of five (commercial product—see Figure 5.8). It has the same advantage of modeling addition and subtraction with 5 and 10 as anchor numbers.

The abacus has been around a long time, of course. The standard model, I believe, has 5 counters in a frame on the left, to represent single counts, and 2 counters in their own frame on the right, to represent 5's. Counting would then proceed on the left up to 5, at which point 1 bead on the right would be moved over to the zero position so 6 through 10 could be counted. In other words, the abacus was designed to use both 5 and 10 as anchor numbers.

In early childhood classrooms, the simplified abacus has usually been just 10 beads per bar. I think this is a mistake because numbers beyond 5 are too hard to recognize visually and it doesn't support the early modeling of part-whole, bridging strategies. The two-color abacus brings those features back. I haven't used either the abacus or the counting ropes very much, but I think if I had a first- or second-grade classroom today, I might have one or the other on each child's table rather than a number-line strip. Not only are the quantities movable, but also the color segmentation encourages noncounting solution strategies.

ADDITION/ SUBTRACTION FLUENCY CHECKPOINTS

The shift to having children use a range of number sense strategies to intuit sums and differences rather than spending a great deal of time having them memorize addition and subtraction facts does not alter the end game: fluency. Increasingly, children's responses to addition and subtraction problems should come confidently and quickly, and their reliance on counting on or counting back should decrease. Over time, their use of mental strategies will become indistinguishable from memorized responses in terms of speed and accuracy.

It is also important to start giving children tasks where the materials do not provide the answer. This way you can tell how comfortable they are with solving the problem in their heads rather than using manipulatives. It is also important to continue to monitor how they come up with their solutions by periodically requiring them to reveal their strategies out loud to you and to each other.

The materials that follow allow you to monitor how much children rely on materials to solve addition and subtraction problems, while still encouraging use of a deep understanding of part-whole and base-10 as they move toward automaticity.

Assessment Probe

PD **pd** TOOLKIT™

Go to the PDToolkit to find the online templates referenced in this activity.

PURSUIT GAME

M A T E R I A L S   A N D   S E T - U P

- Large, durable numeral mats 0−9 arranged in a circle.
- Deck of 0−9 cards (such as those in the place-value card set) to determine moves (or use a 0−9 die or spinner).

A S S E S S M E N T   P R O B E

1. Children playing all start at the 0 mat. Each takes a turn drawing a card and moving forward that many spaces.
2. Each time a child pulls a card, he has to predict whether he will land on a mat occupied by one of his peers. If so, he names that person. If he ends up being correct, he earns a point. Periodically, ask the children to explain how they are deciding.
3. The first child to get 10 points wins that round.

V A R I A T I O N

1. Have the children carry 1−100 place-value flip cards with them as they go around the circle, continuing their count into the subsequent decades. The first child to reach 100 in the flip cards wins.

● What you are looking for

Are the children using base-10 knowledge to relate to numbers larger than 10?

Note that the children have to interpret the teen numbers in terms of their unit values, since the largest number on the circle is 9. By this, I mean that, if a child is standing on the 7 and she rolls a 6, she needs to see if anyone is standing on the 3, since 7 plus 6 is 13. Children who are shaky on knowing their teen numbers as 10 plus a certain amount will not easily read the mats this way and hence will have a hard time tapping their addition fact knowledge to make their predictions. Listen to their explanations of how they solve the problem. If a child says: "Well, 3 more gets you to the zero, and 3 more gets you to the 3," you know the child is staying in the 0−9 range.

But even children who are staying in the 0−9 range can use place-value knowledge to anticipate their moves. For example, a child standing on 5 and rolling a 9 might confidently predict he will land on the 4. When asked how he knew, he might say: "Nine is 1 less than 10, so I have to move back 1."

If children do the place-value cards variation, they continue to make their predictions into the decades. For example, the child standing on the 5 might be up to 45. When he rolls a 9, he will move to the 4 and should change his place-value cards to 54. Look for children to realize that adding 9 to 45 is no different than adding 9 to 5; they are just doing it from a higher base-10 starting point.

Are the children counting to make their predictions, or are they figuring out where they will land by other means?

This is a good activity for getting the children up and moving while they practice their math facts. Since it is possible to silently count on to figure out the landing mat, even children who are not yet fluent with addition and subtraction can make accurate predictions. Watch their eyes. Certainly, if they are looking mat by mat, it would be a clear sign that they are counting the answer. But even if the eyes are rolled upward and the head is bouncing up and down slightly, it probably means they are counting forward on a mental number line. Sometimes it's the fingers that give them away. But to truly know, you'll probably have to ask. See if they are breaking numbers down strategically to come up with an answer.

Assessment Probe

TEN-FRAME FLASH CARDS

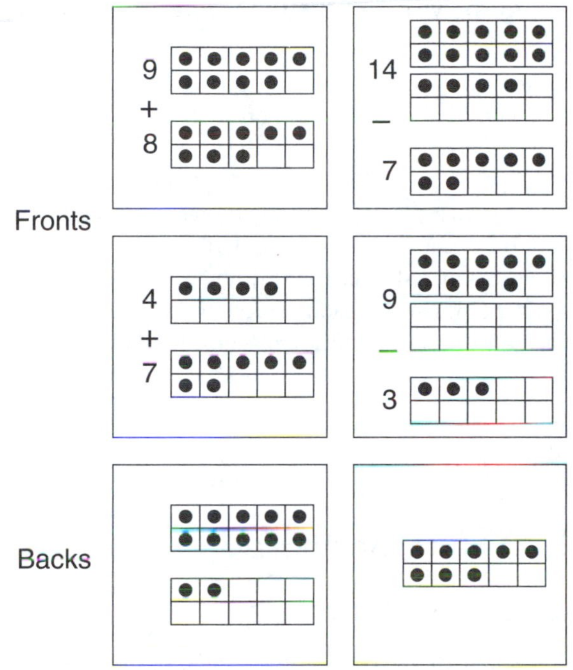

Fronts

Backs

Figure 6.1 Ten-Frame Addition and Subtraction Flash Cards

MATERIALS AND SET-UP

- Problem sets showing an addition or subtraction problem in numerical form along the left-hand side and ten frame representations of the numbers along the right-hand side. On the back of each card is a ten frame representation of the sum or difference (see Figure 6.1).

ASSESSMENT PROBE

1. The child picks a card, looks at the two numbers to add or subtract, and announces the sum or difference. Occasionally, ask her how she knows.
2. The child flips over the card to check her answer.

VARIATION

1. **What's My Number?** For addition cards, one child looks at the front of the card and announces one of the addends, and a second child looks at the back and says the sum. The child in back has to try to guess the second addend. For subtraction cards, the child in back announces the difference, and the child in front announces either, "The total amount is _____ ," or, "The amount subtracted is _____." The child in back has to guess the missing amount.

PD **pd** TOOLKIT™

Go to the PDToolkit to find the online templates referenced in this activity.

● What you are looking for

Does the child have the facts memorized?

Despite what some people think, I do care about children reaching automaticity on their addition and subtraction facts. That's everybody's goal; the debate is about how to get there. If the child is responding rapidly and confidently to the cards, it means either she has the facts memorized or she is using a number sense strategy that takes so little time and effort that it is functionally equivalent to memorization.

Is the child effectively using the visual of the ten frames to rapidly compute the answer?

The ten frames are designed to mirror the solution strategies we want children to use. Are the children who are not yet confident they know the addition/subtraction facts comfortable enough with the ten frames to glance at them and decide what the solution is without counting? If, for example, the child can't recall what $11 - 7$ is, does a glance at the frames tell her that the answer is 3 more than 7, plus 1 (i.e., replacing counting on with a bridging-to-10 strategy) or that 1 from the 11 takes you to 10, and 7 is 3 less than that 10 (i.e., replacing counting back with a bridging-to-10 strategy)? Does she see that adding $5 + 7$ looks like $5 + (5 + 2)$, or $(5 + 5) + 2$? Careful observation, plus an occasional question, will tell you whether the child is comfortable enough with the noncounting strategies to get off her fingers.

Assessment Probe

FACT FAMILY TRIOMINOES

MATERIALS AND SET-UP

- Stiff cards cut in the shape of an equilateral triangle. In the three corners, write the three numerals that make up an addition fact (e.g., 3, 8, and 11). Draw a dark circle around the numeral representing the sum.

Rather than doing the families in triangular form, you can write the three numerals horizontally on a strip of paper (with the largest numeral to the right), or you can even put them in a house arrangement, with the addends in two rooms on the main floor and the sum in the attic!

ASSESSMENT PROBE

1. Have a child choose a triomino without looking at it. He should pick it up by the corner so his fingers are covering up the number written there.
2. Ask the child to name the covered-up number. Ask him how he knows.
3. The child uncovers the number to check his answer and then picks up another triomino.

● What you are looking for

Does the child understand fact-family relationships?

The triominoes are a perfect representation of the intimate relationship three numbers have with each other. The two parts (e.g., 4 and 8) "belong" with the whole they make when they are joined together (12), and the four ways of expressing their relationship are so indistinguishable from one another that we call them a "family" of facts:

$$4 + 8 = 12$$
$$8 + 4 = 12$$
$$12 - 4 = 8$$
$$12 - 8 = 4$$

If the child can't tell you any one of these numbers given the other two, then he hasn't figured this out yet.

Does the child have the addition-subtraction facts memorized?

With the triominoes, there is no model to suggest the answer. Either the child knows the fact-family relationships, or he has to calculate the answer. If the child hesitates, try to figure out whether he is using a counting strategy or whether he has other tools he is confident using.

As always, it pays to separate the triominoes a child answers effortlessly from those where the child is hesitating. Those that are easy can be reviewed periodically to make sure they are still easy. Those that are hard can be set aside for the child to review and practice. Yes, this is just a variation on flash-card drills, but there is no pressure to get them all right or to do them fast, and you are not doing it as a public competition. You are simply observing carefully and helping sort the cards so the child can use them more efficiently in his private practice sessions.

Is the child "thinking addition" to answer all the problems?

If we wanted to, we could pretend subtraction doesn't even exist and never teach it to children. All problems could be considered addition problems or missing addend problems, and, in fact, children show a tendency to think addition even when we present them with a subtraction problem (see "Addition Trumps Subtraction" later in this chapter).

Assessment Probe

PARTS-OF CALCULATOR DRILL

MATERIALS AND SET-UP

- Any calculator that has a constant function programmed into it. Most calculators, no matter how inexpensive, do.

ASSESSMENT PROBE

1. The first child announces the number she wants to serve as the sum (e.g., 8) and enters it into the memory bank by hitting the keys [0][−][8][=].
2. The first child says: "I'm going to tell you a number and you have to tell me what the missing part of <u>8</u> is."
3. The first child announces a number equal to or less than the sum (e.g., 3) and simultaneously enters it into the calculator and hits equals: [3][=].
4. The second child says what the missing part is, and the child with the calculator checks to see if it matches what appears on the screen (in this case, 5).[1]
5. The first child continues to enter new numbers followed by [=], and the second child guesses the missing parts.

---

[1] What actually appears in [−5], but the negative sign is usually off to the left and should be ignored in this case.

Since the trinominoes are not set up to explicitly call for either addition or subtraction, it is a perfect opportunity to check how the child is thinking. For example, if you have the [6,8,14] triomino and cover up the 8, does the child say: "8, because 14 minus 6 is 8," or does he say: "8, because 8 plus 6 is 14." It doesn't matter which he says. It's just nice to know.

We now move on to the next Assessment Probe, "Counting-On Calculator Drill."

● What you are looking for

Can the child confidently tell you all the number combinations adding up to a given sum?

This is a perfect example of using the calculator to support acquisition of fluency rather than substituting for it. The subtraction function splits the two parts of a number on both sides of the zero on a number line (i.e., part stays a positive number, and part becomes a negative number).

This assessment should be done once the child is fairly comfortable with the number facts. It is reemphasizing the parts-of concept, which is central to mastery of addition/subtraction. Note that neither addition nor subtraction is being cued here, but rather that facts can be clustered in larger bundles than fact families around the part-whole concept, such as

$0 + 8 = 8$	$8 + 0 = 8$	$8 - 1 = 7$	
$1 + 7 = 8$	$7 + 1 = 8$	$8 - 2 = 6$	$8 - 7 = 1$
$2 + 6 = 8$	$6 + 2 = 8$	$8 - 3 = 5$	$8 - 6 = 2$
$3 + 5 = 8$	$5 + 3 = 8$	$8 - 4 = 4$	$8 - 5 = 3$
$4 + 4 = 8$	$8 - 0 = 8$		

Maybe we should call this an *extended* fact family!

Assessment Probe

COUNTING-ON CALCULATOR DRILL

MATERIALS AND SET-UP

- Any calculator that has a constant function programmed into it. Most calculators, no matter how inexpensive, do.

ASSESSMENT PROBE

1. The first child chooses a starter number (e.g., 46) and a number between 2 and 9 to skip count by (e.g., 7) and decides whether the task is to keep adding that number or to keep subtracting it (in this case, let's say adding). Simultaneously, the child punches the expression into the calculator: [46][+][7].
2. The second child starts doing successive subtraction or, in this case, addition: "53 ... 60 ... 67 ... 74 ... 81 ... 88 ... 95 ...." The child with the calculator keeps hitting the [=] button and checking whether the second child is correct.
3. Periodically, ask the second child to explain how he is coming up with the answers.

● What you are looking for

Can the child use the addition-subtraction facts and addition-subtraction strategies he knows to do mental math with larger numbers?

Again, this is an excellent example of a calculator being used to build mathematical power rather than serving as a crutch. Children would be much better off regularly doing these drills than doing Mad Minutes. Think about how a child might strategically be coming up with the answers to the example above: "46 plus 7 . . . 6 + 7 is 13, so the answer is 53 . . . then 7 more—that's easy, it's an even 60, which makes the next one 67, and then I see a doubles fact, so the next one is 74 . . . hmmm, 6 more would be 80 so the next one is 81, and the one after that is easy 88 . . . 2 more would hit 90, so the next one is 95 . . . ." There are other ways the child might be coming up with the answers, but all these strategies are useful and are amongst the ones fluent mathematicians bring to bear when doing nontraditional problems.

As you might suspect, successive subtraction is considerably harder than successive addition. Try it. This probably reflects the fact that most of us spent so much time using addition strategies to learn our subtraction facts that we have a hard time moving in the opposite direction.

Assessment Probe

ADDITION/SUBTRACTION WAR WITH PLAYING CARDS

MATERIALS AND SET-UP

- Ace–10 from two playing card decks.

ASSESSMENT PROBE

1. Children equally divide the deck and proceed to lay down two cards each. The player with the largest or smallest sum (or the largest or smallest difference) wins the trick.

Variations

1. Play with cards made from 1–10 ten frames.
2. **Red-Black War.** Black cards are positive (i.e., are added), and red cards are negative (i.e., are subtracted). For example, one child has [3 of spades, 2 of clubs], for a total of 5, and the other has [8 of diamonds, 5 of spades], for a total of —3. Note this will only work if children are comfortable with the notion of negative numbers.
3. Children score points based on how much larger or smaller their sum or difference is than that of their next closest opponent.

Go to the PDToolkit to find the online templates referenced in this activity.

● What you are looking for

What strategies do the children use to decide who has more and who has less?

In some cases, it is obvious which child should take the trick because the differences are so obvious. And if all the children have their addition and subtraction facts memorized, the outcomes are obvious. But usually children are somewhere in between, and it is fascinating to eavesdrop on the arguments they make to each other to make their case when the comparisons are close:

1. Sometimes they find the sums/differences and compare them: "My 8 and 7 is 15 because it's 1 more than double-7. Your 9 and 5 is 14 because 1 more than 9 is 10 and 4 more is 14. So I win."
2. Other times they do part-whole decompositions and recombinations to make card-by-card comparisons and bypass finding the sums or differences: "Look, your 9 is 1 more than my 8, but my 7 is 2 more than your 5, so I have 1 more than you. I win."

Using the ten frames helps support children as they continue to use number sense strategies to find answers. Red-Black War requires children to consider addition and subtraction simultaneously, which is always a challenge. There are some interesting debates that erupt as well when one child scores a high negative amount and the other scores a low positive amount. Is negative 14 larger or smaller than positive 4? Here's an opportunity for the children to figure it out.

Assessment Probe

ADDITION/SUBTRACTION USING A TORQUE BALANCE SCALE

Figure 6.2 Equation 8 + 4 = 2 + 10 on a Torque Balance Scale

MATERIALS AND SET-UP

- Torque balance scale (commercial product), with 10 numbered incremental hangers on each arm and a supply of 10-gram hanging weights (see Figure 6.2).
- Optional: Paper on which to record the solution as a number sentence.

ASSESSMENT PROBE

Addition

1. Place one or more weights on one arm of the torque balance (e.g., "Okay, I'm going to hang one weight on the 3 and two weights on the 6").
2. Hand the child one or more weights (e.g., "Here are two weights"), and ask her to tell you where she would hang them on the opposite arm to make the scale balance and to explain her choice.

3. After the child has made her predictions, have her hang the weights and see if the scale is in balance. If it is not, ask her which weight or weights she thinks she should move and why. Continue until scale balances.

4. Optional: After the child successfully balances the scale, ask her if there is anyplace else she could have hung the weights and still balanced the scale and why she thinks so.

Subtraction

1. Use the same process as for addition, except hang one or more weights on both arms of the scale so that the scale is out of balance by an amount equal to one of the hung weights. Ask the child which weight she would *remove* to bring the scale into balance and why.

VARIATIONS

1. The task is for the child to add weights to *both* sides of the unbalanced scale to bring it into balance.

2. The task is to remove one weight from one side of the unbalanced scale and choose where to place it on the other side to bring the scale into balance.

3. Place one or more weights on one arm of the torque balance. Hand the child two or more weights to place *on a single hook* on the other arm to bring the scale into balance.

4. Ask the child to record the initial set-up as sums on either side of an inequality sign (e.g., $9 + 7 > 10 + 5$) and then record her modification as a balanced equation (e.g., $9 + 7 = 10 + 5 + 1$).

● **What you are looking for**

Does the child use 10 as part of her solution?

If you have constructed a sum greater than 10 on one side of the scale, one thing to look for is whether the child uses the base-10 structure of the sum to construct her solution: "It's 17 on this side, so I'm going to put my three weights on the 10, the 3, and the 4 on the other side."

Can the child accurately construct running sums in her head?

This task requires that the child go beyond memorized addition facts, combining multiple addends to construct a total. Pay close attention to the strategies the child demonstrates in finding the total. Look especially for how she bridges the decades: "Let's see . . . 17 plus 4 more . . . well that would be 20 plus 1 more, so that's 21 . . . ."

What strategies does the child use to find the difference between the sums on the two sides of the balance?

Note that once the child knows the sums on both sides of the scale, she still has more math to do! Pay attention to the strategies the child uses to compare the sums and construct a solution. Does she use a counting-on method, or does she do something more sophisticated?

"So one side has 14, and the other side has 21. Well, 14 and 6 is 20, so the difference is 7."

And, if you have given the child more than one weight to put on the light side to balance the scale, she has one more step to complete:

" . . . so I'm going to put one on the 5 and one on the 2."

Or, if the child's task is to remove a weight from one side and put it on the other:

> " . . . so I'm going to take the weight off the 10 on this side and put it on the 3 on the other side."

Does the child use sophisticated strategies to simplify the problem?

Note that adding up all the weights on both sides of the scale is not the only—or necessarily the easiest—way to solve the problem of bringing the scale into balance. For example, if the scale has weights on the 10, 8, and 7 on one side and the 9, 7, and 2 on the other, the child might say: "Well, there's a 7 on both sides, so those balance each other. The 10 is 1 more than the 9, and the 8 is 6 more than the 2, so the left side is 7 more than the right side. I need to add a 7."

Can the child translate the solution into a number sentence?

It's important that children be able to see the relationship between physical models of addition and subtraction and the number sentences (i.e., equations) that capture the results. If, for example, the scale has $(9, 4, 1)$ on one side and $(5, 6)$ on the other, this would be initially recorded as

$$9 + 4 + 1 > 5 + 6$$

If the task is to add two weights to one side of the scale to bring it into balance, the child might then record

$$9 + 4 + 1 = 5 + 6 + 1 + 2$$

If, however, the task were to remove one weight to bring the scale into balance and the child chose to remove the 1, capturing this move would require recording

$$9 + 4 + 1 - 1 = 5 + 6$$

It is not inconsequential for the child to see that removing the weight requires that it be subtracted from that side and that the $+1$ and the -1 cancel each other out, equaling zero (i.e., the weight is no longer there).

More Teaching Tips

Addition Trumps Subtraction

In Chapters 5 and 6, I have been emphasizing that addition and subtraction are parallel processes. But in terms of how children attack problems, they are not equal. Children are much more comfortable doing addition than doing subtraction. This may be something genetic, having to do with relating much more to accumulation than to loss. But think about the process of modeling a Separate problem. If you have 13 and want to take away 5, you don't actually make the quantity 5; you take 5 out of the 13 that are already there.[2] Now you have 5 things over here, 8 things over there, and the 13 is gone. What's the answer?!

---

[2] Actually, in classroom practice, I have seen it done where the 5 *is* made. This is the appropriate way to model a Compare problem, not a Separate one. It yields the answer, but, conceptually, it violates the schema of taking the second quantity from the existing quantity. I think it is confusing for children to start solving $13 - 5$ by pulling out 18 counters.

Most likely, children go out of their way to solve a subtraction problem as an addition problem because we had them memorize their addition facts first and then their subtraction facts. If their number sense is sufficiently mature by the time we turn our attention to subtraction, they will think missing addend rather than memorize a new fact. For example, when asked what $13 - 5$ is, they will likely think: "What addition fact did I learn where 5 plus something was 13? $5 + 8$ is 13. *Eight!*" In other words, they have discovered the fact families.

So my advice is this: Teach addition and subtraction at the same time, and allow children to discuss their solutions in either addition or subtraction terms. But don't be surprised (or worried) if children gravitate toward solution strategies that sound a lot more like addition than subtraction.

The Perils of "Mad Minute" Drills

Many educators (and children) have a mistaken definition of *mental math*. Some call it mental math as long as they don't use manipulatives or their fingers, even when it's pretty obvious from their bouncing eyeballs that they're counting in their heads. Or a child says, "I just knew it," meaning the answer was memorized. Neither of these is mental math by my definition. Mental math, to me, is *strategic* math. It is something children do when they don't know the answer that is more sophisticated than simply counting.

In too many math classrooms today, children who are good at memorizing are told they are good at math, and those who are not good memorizers are left to believe they stink at it. Neither one of these is necessarily true. Good mathematicians have achieved *fluency*, not just automaticity. Fluency is a rapid-response system firmly embedded within a constellation of mathematical awarenesses and strategies. It is fluency that will carry children forward mathematically. Skillful counting will not.

Even after the math facts are memorized, what do children do if they temporarily forget one or are faced with a problem that doesn't use their memorized facts in a traditional way (e.g., counting on by 7's from a nontraditional number: "23 . . . 30 . . . 37 . . . 44 . . . 51 . . . ")? Children need recovery and sense-making fallbacks. Children who can solve a problem two or three different ways have a much greater grasp of mathematics than children who can solve it only one way—especially if that one way is a memorized answer or algorithm. You know something is off if the children in your class can't respond to a question like "How did you come up with that answer?" or "How would you explain to someone why that was the right answer?" The answer "Well, that's how the teacher taught us to do it" just doesn't cut it.

So what does all this have to do with speed drills? Children prematurely forced into speed drills are trapped in a desperate cycle of having to respond quickly when they don't have the answers memorized. Children will not give up counting until they are comfortable with something quicker and more reliable. Under conditions of stress, higher-order thinking shuts down, and more primitive instincts kick in. In desperation, the fingers fly. If, by chance, these children ever get to the stage where they can finger count fast enough to finish that page in time and error-free, what have they accomplished? Very little. Time is not the enemy— *counting* is.

It is truly sad to watch children doing this hour after hour, day after day, and year after year. It's our job to help them find a way out of the hole they've dug for themselves, not to endlessly remind them that they are stuck. It takes a truly strong child to not experience shame, anger, and resignation under this onslaught. Is it any wonder these children dread math time and only half-attend to what is going on during it?

My advice to you? Any time you see children in first or second grade routinely using counting to come up with answers to addition and subtraction problems (whether it be on their fingers, on a desk number line, or simply by bouncing their eyeballs as they mentally count), you should stop and direct those children to activities that will build their flexible part-whole awareness.

Bridging from the Concrete to Paper and Pencil

We tend to regard paper-and-pencil problems with numerals and plus or minus and equals signs as "real" math. For children, these are the most abstract form for representing mathematical relationships and therefore the hardest form for them to attack intelligently.

A good strategy for us to use to help children understand paper-and-pencil mathematics is to encourage them to record representations of problems they have first solved using concrete manipulatives. At first, these representations are dominated by drawings, which they then explain either verbally or in writing, but, increasingly, we should encourage them to also write a number sentence that summarizes the result. By connecting the actual experience first to the drawn version and then to the number sentence, we are helping them become comfortable with the reality that the number sentence is capturing. As a side benefit, their use of words, images, and symbols gives us a better window on their mathematical reasoning.

I must caution, however, against viewing math journaling as just another excuse to have them write. The children should spend the bulk of their math time on physical manipulations and mathematical conversations with you and their peers, not on silently writing in a journal. The primary focus of the journaling is for children to see the relationship between the problem solving they have done and addition-subtraction equations that represent their reasoning.

The Real Scoop on Those Dreaded Word Problems

It is a curious fact that, in the math world, we assume that children should be very comfortable solving paper-and-pencil equations before we ask them to tackle word problems. At one level, this makes sense. Often when teachers pose word problems in class, children look puzzled and say: "I don't understand. Should we add or subtract?" Then we start teaching them tricks like "If it says 'more,' then it's addition" or "It's a subtraction problem, so write the bigger number first." Many adults still wake up in a cold sweat after a nightmare in which they were back in grade school, being asked those incomprehensible word problems.

I'm convinced the problem is not that children don't understand problems describing real-world events; it's that children don't understand equations. As Frank Smith (1990) said, "When we say we cannot make sense of something, we mean that we cannot find the story in it, or make up a story about it. . . . This is the way we make sense of life, by making stories. It is the way we remember events: in terms of stories. Without stories, there would be no events" (as quoted in Whiten & Wilde, 1995). I have said at several points in this book that we should be careful to keep numbers in context as children go about their problem solving rather than treating them as abstract objects. Children show surprising intelligence in solving classroom mathematical problems that they could not solve on paper. Children often invent scenarios to make sense of problems they can't relate to in the abstract. And much of this book is about posing problems for children that involve manipulation of real-world objects in meaningful ways to make sense of mathematics.

That's why Chapters 5 and 6 discuss addition and subtraction simultaneously and why I most often refer to problems not as addition or subtraction problems but by the taxonomy developed by Carpenter and Moser (1983):

- **Join.** Two quantities are physically combined to make a new quantity. This is your prototypical addition problem. But it can be varied by making either the starting quantity or the quantity added to it be the unknown rather than the sum (e.g., "Sam had some apples. Sue gave him 5 more apples. Now Sam has 13 apples. How many apples did Sam start out with?").

- **Separate.** A quantity is removed from a starting quantity, with a quantity left over. This is your prototypical subtraction problem. But, again, varying which quantity is unknown can alter the complexity (e.g., "Sam had 13 apples and then he gave some to Sue. Now Sam has 8 apples. How many apples did he give Sue?").

- **Part-Whole.** An existing quantity is described in terms of two or more parts that make it up.[3] Again, there are nontraditional ways to present part-whole problems. ("There are 13 fruit in the basket. Eight of them are apples and some of them are oranges. How many oranges are in the basket?" As this chapter has emphasized, part-whole awareness is at the heart of developing fluency in addition/subtraction. Children often use part-whole strategies on the numbers in problems, no matter the problem type. For example, in a Join problem the child might think:"Let's see, Sam had 5 apples and then got 9 more. One more than 9 is 10, which leaves 4 left over. The answer is 14!")

- **Compare.** The magnitudes of two quantities are compared. This is probably the least common problem type presented to children, but it affords them an interesting opportunity to choose between addition and subtraction strategies. For example, consider this problem: "Sam has 8 apples. Sue has 5 apples. How many more apples does Sam have than Sue?" One child might think, "$8 - 5 =$ ____"; another might think, "$5 +$ ____ $= 8$"; and a third might think, "$8 -$ ____ $= 5$."

As math educators, it is imperative that we

1. Continuously mix up the problem types that children experience and which pieces of information in those problems are missing.[4]

---

[3] To many people, children see this as being no different than a Join problem. The only difference is that there is no action of joining involved. You are describing a set that already exists and is not being altered.

[4] It's a good idea to occasionally sprinkle in numbers extraneous to the problem posed. Children should not get in the habit of mindlessly scanning the problem for numbers and haphazardly plugging them into equations.

2. Ask children to create number sentences that mirror the ways they solved the problems rather than automatically treating them as addition or subtraction.

3. Avoid presenting addition and subtraction problems in a format that leads children to believe the equals sign means "Now solve the problem." Many children are caught totally off-guard when suddenly confronted with problems like these:

- ____ = 8 + 5
- ____ + 8 = 13
- 5 + 8 = ____ + 10

They shouldn't be.

Memorization Based on Number Sense

When we think about children intelligently tackling addition problems, it makes little sense for us to have them drill on a randomized deck of the 121 problems making up the addition facts 0 + 0 to 10 + 10. Awarenesses and strategies that allow them to respond rapidly and confidently, even if automaticity is not fully in place, come online in roughly the following sequence:

1. **The Zero Property of Addition.** Once confident that adding zero to a number doesn't change the quantity, 21 cards can be removed from the deck.

2. **Plus One.** Once children are comfortable with counting on from any given starting number, that means they know the answer is the number that comes right after any given number. This also covers 21 cards in the deck, including 20 not already removed. We're down to 80 cards.

3. **The Commutative Property of Addition.** Children discover the turn-around facts early on. Once they believe that 6 + 3 = 3 + 6, they can remove almost half the problems from the deck! The commutative property makes 55 of the 121 facts redundant, including 36 problems not yet removed from the deck. Down to 44 cards.

4. **Plus Two.** If children can count on, it requires very little time or effort for them to think: "It's not the number right after; it's the one after that." There are 21 plus two facts, including 9 not covered by the strategies already mentioned. Down to 35 cards.

5. **Plus Ten.** If we've been doing our job and helping the children realize that the teen numbers are ten plus a unit quantity, then the plus ten facts are understood as a property of numbers, not as facts to memorize. There are 21 plus ten facts, including 7 that are still sitting in our card deck. Down to 28 cards.

6. **Doubles Facts.** We're going to cheat a little bit here and talk about facts that are memorized rather than emerging from the development of basic number sense. Children delight in proving to us at an early age just how smart they are, and, for some reason, one of the ways they invariably do so is by proudly announcing: "I know how much six plus six is!" They seldom choose non-doubles facts to do this. Their fascination with the doubles facts is a fortunate accident for us because it opens up some of the more difficult number

combinations to strategic solution. There are 11 doubles facts in the total deck, including 7 we haven't yet removed. Down to 21 cards.

7. **Doubles Plus One (or Minus One).** On some problems where simpler strategies don't present themselves, children notice that they almost have a doubles fact; in other words, the two numbers are one apart. If they notice this, it is simple for them to recall the lower doubles and add one or the upper doubles and subtract one. There are a total of 20 doubles-plus-one facts in the deck, including 6 facts that don't lend themselves to simpler strategies.[5] Down to a mere 15 cards.

8. **Doubles Plus Two (or Minus Two).** At some point, some child will take a problem like $6 + 8$ and announce: "That's really the same as $7 + 7$. See, if you take 1 from the 8 and give it to the 6, they're both 7's!" This relationship is harder to notice intuitively, but there are 18 doubles-plus-two facts in the total deck, 5 of which we haven't pulled yet. Down to 10 cards.

9. **Bridging to 10.** For many of the facts that involve 8 or 9, children intuitively transform the larger number to 10 and then deal with the remainder. Sophisticated mental mathematicians frequently decompose and recombine numbers in order to work with "nice numbers" such as 10. There are 36 facts in the total deck that readily lend themselves to this strategy, including 7 of the cards we have not removed.

We're down to a measly 3 cards that maybe the children should simply memorize: $6 + 3$, $7 + 3$, and $7 + 4$. My point is this: Why do we spend so much time urging children to memorize their addition math facts? Automaticity flows through number sense, not memorization.

Teachers often complain that it seems awfully complicated to teach children all these strategies, and, when they do, the children don't necessarily start using them once the instructional session is over. I believe them. I think the problem is that they are trying to teach these as isolated skills rather than as reflections of the processes that are constantly being used by a classroom full of mathematicians set free to solve problems in ways that make sense to them. When you open yourself to the discussions among the children of how they approached a problem and encourage them to listen to each other, you become aware of the fact that these strategies are living, breathing things. The children realize that as well. They are much more likely to pay attention and be impressed by the intelligence and creativity of their peers than they are by a strategy suggested by a textbook. Occasionally, you need to do a mini-lesson to emphasize a particular strategy, and, occasionally, you may want to insist on children using a particular strategy so you can assess whether they are capable of using it. But, in the end, children develop their own individualized sense of which methods work best for them and make the most sense to them. And they have not just one solution strategy available to them, but many. They are mathematicians, ready to move on to bigger and harder problems.

---

[5] Actually, some of these facts lend themselves readily to the bridge-to-10 strategy, which in some children comes online earlier than the near-doubles strategy. For purposes of illustration, we'll stick with this sequence.

Study Group Discussion Starters: Secure Part-Whole Awareness and the Emergence of Addition/Subtraction Fluency

How dependent are your children on counting the answers to addition and subtraction problems?

What progress have you made in getting children off their fingers (or a number line) in solving addition and subtraction problem? In other words, do they show signs of *mentally* manipulating the quantities, or do they simply manipulate the quantities and count the answer? What has worked to get them comfortable with other approaches? Has it been your experience that children who stick with a counting strategy (either counting all or counting on) progress smoothly to fact mastery? In other words, is using a counting strategy followed by memorizing the basic facts a workable path to fluency?

Do your children tend to solve subtraction problems by adding?

When you ask children how they came up with the answer to a subtraction problem, what do they say? Do they refer to a known addition fact or treat it as a missing addend problem (for example, counting on from the subtracted amount to the beginning quantity)? Are there any disadvantages to them taking this approach?

What types of word problems do you pose?

Discuss your experiences with posing word problems outside of Join problems with the sum unknown (e.g., "Sally had 5 apples. Joey gave her 7 more. How many apples does Sally have now?") or Separate problems with the difference unknown (e.g., "Sally had 12 apples. She gave 5 of her apples to Joey. How many apples does Sally have now?"). Which ones do children find most difficult or most confusing? How have they gone about making sense of the problems? What role have manipulatives or drawing played? Have different children approached the problems using different strategies?

In this chapter, it has been suggested that word problems should precede solving addition and subtraction number sentences. Do you agree? Why or why not?

It has also been asserted that the key-word method is a poor strategy to teach. Again, do you agree? Why or why not?

What types of number sentence problems do you pose?

Do your children tend to interpret the equals sign as meaning "Now solve the problem"? In other words, have you experimented with varying where the missing information is located in a problem or how many operations are on either side of the equals sign? If you have varied the format in which problems are presented, what are some of the reasoning processes children have used to solve the problems? For example, if you posed the problem $7 + \underline{\quad} - 4 = 6 + 7$, could the children handle it? What range of solution strategies would you encounter?

Do your children spontaneously use part-whole strategies to quickly answer addition fact probes?

Do your children answer any addition fact probe quickly and accurately? Do you think they have the fact memorized, or do you suspect they are coming up with it some other way? How do you know? If you ask them to prove that a particular fact is correct, what strategy do they share? If you pose the question to a group, what range of strategies do you hear?

At what point is it important to emphasize speed in answering fact probes? Does there come a point where emphasizing strategies is counterproductive and children just need to spend time memorizing their facts? Have you experimented with diagnosing which problems the children are struggling to achieve automaticity with and limiting their memorization efforts to those problems?

What about subtraction? How much practice do children seem to need working on memorizing their subtraction facts after they are comfortable with their addition facts?

Can your children solve addition and subtraction problems beyond the basic facts?

Do you find that the children's comfort with the basic facts helps them make sense of problems with larger starter numbers? Do they tend to depend more on the memorized facts, or do they use mental math strategies? For example, when solving $37 + 6$, are they most likely to (a) count on from 37, (b) add 13 to 30, or (c) bridge to 40 and add 3?

PLACE-VALUE FLUENCY AND MULTIDIGIT ADDITION/SUBTRACTION LAUNCH POINTS

Concepts and Skills Being Reinforced in This Chapter

In Chapters 3 and 4, children began their explorations of the place-value system by revisiting the counting numbers 1–100. But it is not until they move past 100 that they truly start to understand how place value operates. The activities presented in this chapter have children working with models that help them understand the hundreds and thousands and begin to glimpse what lies beyond. More importantly, children begin to move fluidly between the place-value categories, solidifying the understandings that will form the foundation for mathematics to come.

The new Common Core standards (Council of Chief State School Officers & National Governors Association Center, 2010) call for children to have mastered adding and subtracting through the thousands by the end of second grade; in fact, after second grade, addition and subtraction cease to be a significant presence in the standards except where they apply to newly emerging concepts like fractions and decimals. It is therefore imperative that children see the "big picture" of how our number system is structured and see how the strategies they have developed for moving quantities across the units-tens interface apply to the general case. It is place-value understanding that will allow children to smoothly transition to the algorithms for multidigit addition and subtraction, to check whether the answers they generate using those algorithms make sense, and to strategically decide when *not* to use those algorithms.

You will find here a diverse set of manipulative models that can be added to the classroom to help children understand how quantities increase exponentially in a place-value system. Here is a summary of the place-value concepts children will gain mastery of through experiences such as those described in this chapter.

A Digit's Place Value Is Determined by How Many Positions It Is to the Left of the Units Column

2.NBT.1   *Understand that the three digits of a three-digit number represent amounts of hundreds, tens, and ones; e.g., 706 equals 7 hundreds, 0 tens, and 6 ones.*

2.NBT.4   *Compare two three-digit numbers based on meanings of the hundreds, tens, and ones digits, using >, =, and < symbols to record the results of comparisons.*

Until now, children have been able to get by with this schema: "The left digit is tens, the right digit is units." The numeral 100 is an exception—and not a big enough one to disrupt this misconception. When children first learn that the number after one hundred is one hundred one,[1] they assume it is written 1001; in other words, one hundred is for them a thing, not the beginning of a new place-value designator. Now that children are experiencing numerals of three or more digits, they are forced to adopt a true right-to-left place-value schema.[2]

Zero as a Placeholder

2.NBT.1b   *The numbers 100, 200, 300, 400, 500, 600, 700, 800, 900 refer to one, two, three, four, five, six, seven, eight, or nine hundreds (and 0 tens and 0 ones).*

2.NBT.3   *Read and write numbers to 1000 using base-ten numerals, number names, and expanded form.*

For a place-value number system to work, there needs to be a way to designate a column that is "skipped" when there are no quantities in that category—hence, the need for zero as a placeholder. Up to this point, children have only needed zeroes to indicate the decades. Now they are confronted with zeroes anywhere in a numeral (except to the left of the last non-zero digit).

The Maximum Face Value Is 9 in Any Place-Value Column

Our number system uses 10 as a base, but there is no symbol for 10. If more than 9 accumulate in any column, the place-value system has no means of representing that quantity with a single digit (and if a two-digit designator were used, it would throw off the place values of the other digits). To know the total quantity, exchanging must be done until there are 9 or less in each column.[3]

10:1 Exchange Rates

2.NBT.1a   *100 can be thought of as a bundle of ten tens—called a "hundred."*

2.NBT.7   *Understand that in adding or subtracting three-digit numbers, . . . sometimes it is necessary to compose or decompose tens or hundreds.*

As the previous concept suggests, it is possible to exchange items in one column for ones in another, but it is not a 1:1 swap; rather, the ratio is 10:1. Any

---

[1] See "The Counting Sequence in a Place-Value System" in this chapter.

[2] You have to count from right to left to determine the left-most digit's value, even though the numeral is read from left to right.

[3] Of course, it is totally understandable and sometimes useful to refer to a quantity as "three hundred seventeen tens and four units" rather than "four hundred seventy-four," but it is not standard notation. See "Expanded Notation Strip" in this chapter and "Wacky Numbers" in Chapter 8.

place-value quantity can be exchanged for 10 of the next column to the right (or 100 of the column two spaces over, etc.), and 10 of any place-value quantity can be exchanged for 1 of the next column to the left.[4]

Exponential Growth in a Place-Value System

Quantities continue to grow by a power of 10 as new digits are added to the left of the previous digit. Children got a glimpse of this truth when they learned to skip count by 10, but the effect becomes more dramatic the more place values you add—increments are in steps of a hundred in the next place value, and jumps happen a thousand at a time in the next column. In written form, the numbers don't look that much bigger. Look at the quantity those numerals represent, and the leaps are soon jaw-dropping.

The Counting Sequence in a Place-Value System

Each new iteration in a place-value digit requires counting through the entire sequence of place values that precede it. Children who have learned to count to 100 assume the next counting number is 200. It astounds them that they have to count another hundred numbers before they get to 200.

When Combining or Removing Quantities, Only Digits in the Same Place-Value Location Can Be Combined or Decreased

2.NBT.5 *Fluently add and subtract within 100 using strategies based on place value, properties of operations, and/or the relationship between addition and subtraction.*

2.NBT.6 *Add up to four two-digit numbers using strategies based on place value and properties of operations.*

2.NBT.7 *Add and subtract within 1000, using concrete models or drawings and strategies based on place value, properties of operations, and/or the relationship between addition and subtraction; relate the strategy to a written method. Understand that in adding or subtracting three-digit numbers, one adds or subtracts hundreds and hundreds, tens and tens, ones and ones; and sometimes it is necessary to compose or decompose tens or hundreds.*

2.NBT.8 *Mentally add 10 or 100 to a given number 100–900, and mentally subtract 10 or 100 from a given number 100–900.*

2.NBT.9 *Explain why addition and subtraction strategies work, using place value and the properties of operations.*

When children start doing addition and subtraction in a place-value system, they find they can't just randomly choose which digits to add or subtract. You can't subtract apples from oranges or add bananas and peaches—there's no name for the resulting collection. If you subtract hundreds from hundreds, you end up with hundreds, and if you add tens to tens, you end up with tens. This is why we need children to keep thinking place value rather than face value (i.e., the 4 in 43 is tens, but the 4 in 436 is hundreds) as they move into multidigit operations.

---

[4] In current texts, the terms *carrying* and *borrowing* have been replaced by the term *exchanging* or *trading*, which works for swaps in either direction. These terms are starting to be replaced in some standards documents with the more general terms *composition* and *decomposition* of numbers. I am sticking with the term *exchanging* in this book. I personally don't think the old terms did any significant damage to children's ability to understand place-value exchanges, but be aware the terminology has shifted.

Composing and Decomposing Bundles of Ten to Move Them from One Place-Value Category to Another Can Be Done at Any Level of the Place-Value System as a Tool of Problem Solving

2.NBT.7 *Understand that in adding or subtracting three-digit numbers, one adds or subtracts like units (hundreds and hundreds, tens and tens, ones and ones) and sometimes it is necessary to compose or decompose a higher value unit.*

2.NBT.11 *Compute sums and differences of one-, two-, and three-digit numbers using strategies based on place value, properties of operations, and/or the inverse relationship between addition and subtraction; explain the reasoning used.*

Children get a lot of practice making tens as they add and unbundling tens as they subtract, but they need time and experience, including manipulation of concrete models, to realize that this strategy extends to all levels of the place-value system. There are some manipulatives, such as Digi-Blocks, that are specifically designed to emphasize these transformations. It takes longer still for children to confidently and reflexively use this relationship as a problem-solving tool when faced with the need to "borrow" or "carry" a quantity to another position in the place-value hierarchy. Teaching the standard addition and subtraction algorithms without giving children sufficient time to visualize this transformation of the quantity's appearance (but not its total amount) is a mistake too often made in elementary mathematics.

Standard Algorithms Can Be Used to Efficiently Solve Multidigit Addition and Subtraction Problems, But Alternative Algorithms and Strategies Are Sometimes Preferable

2.NBT.7 *Add and subtract within 1000, using concrete models or drawings and strategies based on place value, properties of operations, and/or the relationship between addition and subtraction; relate the strategy to a written method.*

2.NBT.9 *Explain why addition and subtraction strategies and algorithms work, using place value and the properties of operations.*

Bridging from a conceptual understanding of addition and subtraction to the shorthand of the standard algorithms is a critical step in the achievement of fluency. Too often we believe the paper-and-pencil stage is the "real" math, and we shift our focus to automatic and error-free use of the algorithms. I agree that reaching the stage of effortless automaticity on standard algorithms is necessary and requires practice, but the trouble with automated skills is that we tend to cease monitoring their application or output. We must take steps to make sure two other aspects of fluency are not lost as children master the algorithms:

1. Pausing to see whether applying the algorithm is the most efficient way to come up with a solution and
2. Having a sense of the range within which the solution should fall and reexamining one's solution steps when it does not.

We don't want children blindly accepting ridiculous answers to posed problems just because that's the answer the algorithm spits out.

PD **pd** TOOLKIT™

Go to the PDToolkit to find the online template referenced in the following activity.

200 BOARD

MATERIALS AND SET-UP

- 10 × 10 grid of squares. The numeral 101 is printed in the upper left-hand square and the numeral 200 in the bottom right-hand square.
- 100 numeral tiles, numbered 101 to 200, with units digits in green, tens digits in blue, and hundreds digits in red (see Figure 7.1).

LAUNCH POINT

1. Ask a child who has gotten comfortable working with the hundreds board: "How would you like to count to a hundred a second time, but this time start with the number that comes *after* one hundred? What number do you think that is?"

2. If the child does not answer correctly, inform him: "The number that comes after one hundred is one hundred one, and it looks like this." Point to the numeral 101 on the board and at the three digits that make it up: "See? There is one hundred, no tens, and one unit." Have the child find the corresponding numeral tile and place it on the board.

3. "And what number do you think you will be on when you finish counting your second hundred?" Point to the 200 as a hint. "See, when you get to the

Figure 7.1 200-Board Numeral Tiles

last tile, you will have two hundreds, zero tens, and zero units."

4. Ask the child what number he thinks comes after 101 and what it looks like. Continue scaffolding the child's work until he is comfortable proceeding on his own.

Most children have no idea that getting from 101 to 200 requires counting as many numbers as it did to get from 1 to 100. It amazes them that all the tiles on the board except the last one start with a red 1 in the hundreds place.

Children at this level need a lot of experience reading three-digit numbers in terms of their tens and units values. This is a great activity for them to experience the pattern of the decades in a whole new way, seeing the units digit change each time but the tens digit staying constant for a set of 10 tiles. The manual task of finding the tiles disrupts the automaticity of oral counting and forces them to practice picking up the count in unfamiliar territory. The visual task of scanning for the proper tile forces them to find not just the right digits, but also the right digits in the right order (e.g., 147 rather than 174), strengthening the awareness of what place-value information is provided by each column.

To vary and extend the activity, you can

1. Provide a 300 board, and so on. I wouldn't bother going all the way to 1000, though seeing the whole layout of 10 boards would definitely be cool. I think

the primary benefit is achieved with the 200 board, and unless you made it a whole-class project, I don't think you would ever get a child to do the whole set.

2. Have the tiles in an opaque bag, and have the children pull them out one at a time and place them on the board. This requires them to focus on the units information to determine the column and the tens information to determine the row, just as they did with the original hundreds board.

3. Have children assemble the board by starting at the 200 and counting backward.

4. Give children a blank hundreds page on which to write the numerals 101–200 (or to continue on to 201–300, etc.). There is a different type of learning that happens when children write the numerals rather than visually searching for tiles and placing them. If, in doing the sheet, children start taking shortcuts like writing individual digits vertically or horizontally, don't interrupt them. They are demonstrating that they see a place-value-based pattern in the arrangement of the numbers.

Launch Point

MAKE YOUR OWN PLACE-VALUE MATERIALS

MATERIALS AND SET-UP

- Bowl of large pinto beans or small lima beans, dyed green.
- Bowl of craft sticks, dyed blue.
- 10 cm × 10 cm squares of stiff cardboard, colored red with a permanent marker.
- Bottles of glue.

It's not critical that the materials be colored, but I like to stay consistent with the color-coding scheme I use with the place-value numerals. I intentionally use beans that are too narrow for 10 of them to fill a craft stick when turned vertically, but too long for 10 of them to fit on the stick when they are turned horizontally (see Figure 7.2).

LAUNCH POINT

1. Invite the children to make their own ten stick. Show them the beans they will use for units. Show them how to place a single small drop of glue on the stick and push a lima bean into the drop, then another drop of glue, and so on.

2. After they complete each stick, say: "It's not really a ten-stick unless it's really ten. Show me." If they have made an error, have them correct it before proceeding.

3. Ask if they would like to make a hundred square by gluing ten-sticks on a red cardboard square. Have a discussion about how many ten-sticks are required to make one hundred.

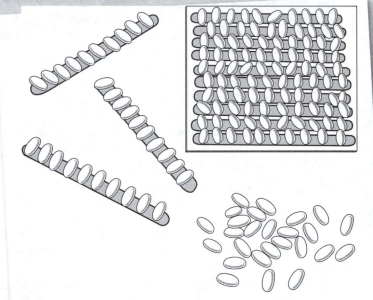

Figure 7.2 Make Your Own Place-Value Materials

4. When they have finished working with the materials for the day, they should set them in a safe place to dry. Their products are theirs to keep and take home, theirs to save and add to another day, or theirs to donate to the class "bank."

5. If children have assembled a hundred square, say: "It's not really a hundred square unless there are a hundred beans here." Have them count to verify the quantity.

5. Provide strips of large-square graph paper that are 10 squares tall and 1, 2, and 3 squares wide. Children can start at the number 1 and write numbers sequentially as far as they want to go, 10 numerals at a time (they tape the strips together, keeping the units columns aligned, to create a continuous strip). They are amazed that they need only one 1-column strip, nine 2-column strips, and then ninety 3-column strips before there is a need for a fourth column (to write 1000). And this linear array is a different way of seeing the patterns that exist in the place-value system.

The next Launch Point focuses on the problem with prefab place-value materials—which is that they are already assembled and named. Children accept at face value that they are what we say they are. Yes, they can see the hundred individual squares etched into the square piece of wood, but, in the young child's mind, it's too easy to think of it as an object called a hundred rather than as 100 individual units. And it is assumed that nobody messed up and put too many or too few squares on the wood.

In making their own materials, children are forced to decide what defines a ten-stick or a hundred square. You would be amazed how many children announce that they have a ten-stick because their stick is full, even though it has 8 or 12 beans on it. This is one of the few times when I have children check their work and correct it if they have made an error. One of the key objectives of the activity is for children to realize that what makes a ten-stick a ten-stick is that it has 10 units on it.

Another purpose of the activity is for children to realize how much 100 is. After finishing their first stick, they eagerly begin their second and then move on to their third. But usually by the sixth or seventh stick, they are counting and re-counting their completed sticks, surprised and annoyed that they haven't reached 100 yet. Counting the final product at the end drives home the point that the 10 ten-sticks, when put together, do in fact mean they have glued down 100 pinto beans—and it was a lot of work to do so!

To vary and extend the activity, consider the following:

1. Create a green cube with a hinged top, cut out of stiff cardboard or tag board. Ask the children who have completed a hundred square if they would like to make a thousand cube. Offer to build them their own thousand-cube box to keep if they complete all the hundred squares they need to fill it. I have had many children set out to have their very own thousand cube, but I have never had to build a box to give away. But what a great way to get children to appreciate how big a number 1000 is!

2. Have children bundle straws to make tens and bundle those bundles to make a hundred.[5] If you wish, you can provide enough straws so the hundreds bundles can be bundled to make a thousand. You could probably afford to let the children take their tens, hundreds, and thousands creations home if you have them bundle toothpicks rather than straws.

The next Launch Point focuses on why children need lots of practice shifting quantities across place-value categories. Treating the place-value supply shelf as a bank helps the children realize they can always take materials to the bank and

Go to the PDToolkit to find the online templates referenced in the following activity.

---

[5] Many classrooms do this with their calendar or days-in-school work—but children aren't normally allowed to *play* with those materials!

Launch Point

BANK GAME WITH PLACE-VALUE BLOCKS AND PLACE-VALUE CARDS

MATERIALS AND SET-UP

- **"Bank"**: Shelf supply of unit cubes, ten-bars, hundred squares, and thousand cubes (commercial products).
- Place-value cards 1–9, 10–90, 100–900, and 1,000–9,000, printed on glossy photo paper. Units digits and thousands digits are green, tens digits are blue, and hundreds digits are red. Have available both card sets in a layered deck format and sets that have been hole-punched and arranged sequentially on a key ring, with units digits aligned (see Figures 7.3 and 7.4).
- **Optional**: Place-value response wheels (see Figure 3.5).
- **Optional**: The ten-thousand bar made from folded display board, with thousands increments marked (see Figure 7.5); 10,000 place-value card (the ten-thousands digit is blue).
- Carrying trays (to transport bank materials).

Figure 7.3 Place-Value Card Set

Figure 7.4 Place-Value Flip-Card Set

LAUNCH POINT

<u>Introduction to the Materials</u>

1. Review the names of the units and decades, first with blocks and then with cards. Have a child count 10 units, place them in a column next to a ten-bar, and show that they match. Point out that the green zeroes on the 10–90 cards are the same color as the digits on the units cards because that is the units column. (*Note*: They have encountered this relationship previously with the teen, tens, and hundreds boards.) Review how 1–9 cards can be placed on top of 10–90 cards (as was done with the teen and tens boards) to make two-digit numerals. Review how corresponding quantities can be made with the place-value blocks.

2. Introduce hundred squares and hundreds cards. Have children take ten-bars and, while skip counting by ten, place them side by side until they reach one hundred. Then lay a hundred square on top of the 10 ten-bars to show the equivalency. Emphasize that the green and blue zeroes on the hundreds cards are in the units and tens columns, respectively. Show how the units and tens cards can be layered on the hundreds cards to

Figure 7.5 Ten-Thousand Bar with Thousand Cube

make three-digit numerals and how corresponding quantities can be made with place-value blocks.

3. Go through the same steps to introduce the thousand cubes and thousands cards.

4. If you wish, also introduce the ten-thousand bar and ten-thousand card. Point out that just as the thousand cube looks like a giant unit cube (and the thousands digit on the cards is color-coded green, like the units column), the ten-thousand bar looks like a giant ten-bar, and the digit in the ten-thousands

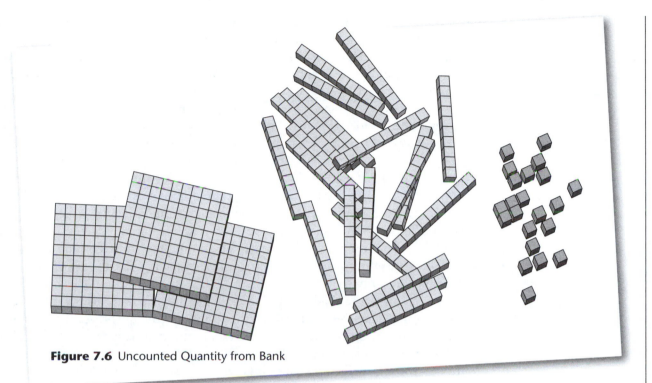

Figure 7.6 Uncounted Quantity from Bank

column is colored blue, just like the tens column.

Bank Game, Starting with Quantities

1. Have children put a random quantity of units, tens, hundreds, and thousands blocks on their carrying trays (see Figure 7.6). Ask them to figure out how many blocks they have all together.

2. Children make exchanges at the bank for categories of material they have 10 or more of, then find the place-value card that goes with each category (see Figure 7.7), and finally layer the place-value cards and read the numeral to you (see Figure 7.8).

Bank Game, Starting with Place-Value Cards

1. Have the children form a three- to four-digit numeral on their carrying trays, using the place-value cards (occasionally leaving one of the categories blank). You can either orally name the number you want them to make, or you can show it using the place-value response wheels.

2. Ask the children to read the numeral to you, then go to the bank and retrieve the necessary place-value materials to make that quantity, and finally put the appropriate place-value cards on top of each stack.

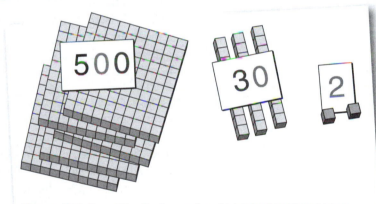

Figure 7.7 Quantities Exchanged and Matched to Place-Value Cards

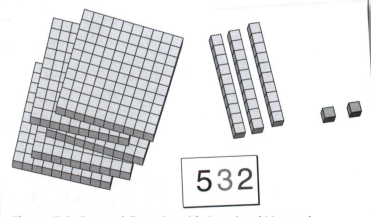

Figure 7.8 Counted Quantity with Associated Numeral

make a fair-trade exchange (i.e., the change in materials will not alter the quantity in their possession). It also drives home the point that we have the no-more-than-nine-in-any-category rule in our numbering system not because there aren't times we violate that rule, but because we cannot name the quantity in standard terminology without limiting each category to nine or less.

Note that my version of the place-value cards puts a comma between the thousands and hundreds digits. This is not standard in commercial place-value card sets, but I do so for an important reason. As the place-value categories expand, we recycle the words *units*, *tens*, and *hundreds*. For example, the seventh through ninth place-value positions represent units of millions, tens of millions, and hundreds of millions. These three-digit sets are called *periods*, and our standard notation for segmenting multidigit numerals into periods is to use commas.[6] The periodic nature of the place-value numerals is reflected in the patterned color-coding of the digits; for example, the units column and thousands column are both colored green, and the tens and ten-thousands columns are both colored blue.

Less obvious to the children (and to many teachers) is that this periodic cycle is also seen in the place-value materials we use to model the quantities. The thousand cube is the unit of the second period, just as the unit cube is the unit of the first period. By placing a ten-thousand rod in the classroom, we make clear that tens of thousands look just like tens, only bigger. If you wanted, you could construct a 1 meter × 1 meter × 0.1 meter box that would represent one hundred thousand (i.e., a giant hundred square) and a 1 meter × 1 meter × 1 meter box that would represent the unit of the next period, one million (i.e., a *really* big unit cube).

Use the following to extend children's flexible use of the place-value materials:

1. **Exchange Games.** Construct card decks (or game boards) that have children *Get* a certain amount from a central pot of place-value materials (e.g., *Get 90*) or *Give* a certain amount back to the pile (e.g., *Give 200*). Make sure there are significantly more *Get* than *Give* cards, so the children are acquiring an increasing stash of place-value materials. A few cards should be inserted that say *Exchange*. When that card comes up, all players exchange place-value quantities with the central supply until they have nine or less in each category.

    If you make exchange game boards, children roll a die or spin a spinner to move. Once children understand the structure of the boards you introduce, they enjoy using their imaginations to make their own theme-based boards to use with their peers, complete with shortcuts, trap doors, and so on.

2. **Race to a Thousand.** This is an extension of Race to 100 (see Chapter 3). In this case, there is a central pot of units, tens, and hundreds and just one thousand cube, with the goal being to be the first to exchange all your blocks for the cube. Children use a cup that has seven lima beans in it to determine the quantity they gather each turn. The beans are marked on one side with a line (signifying a ten) and on the other side with a dot (signifying a unit). If a child tossed the beans and got four lines and three dots, she would take four tens and three units from the pot. The pot shouldn't contain an endless supply of

---

[6] In some other parts of the world, periods are used.

units and tens, forcing the children to periodically replenish the pot by trading some of their units for tens and some of their tens for hundreds. This allows them to see how close they are to their goal.

As with Race to 100, it is possible to play Race to Zero instead, where each player starts with a thousand cube and tries to get rid of it as quickly as possible. It is also possible to do a money version of this same game (Race to $10) or a metric weights version (Race to a Kilo).

The next Launch Point, "Place-Value Materials Sorter Tray," perhaps more than any other, demonstrates to the children the power of the base-10 system to organize a large collection of materials in a way that makes the total instantly

Go to the PDToolkit to find the online templates referenced in the following activity.

Launch Point

PLACE-VALUE MATERIALS SORTER TRAY

MATERIALS AND SET-UP

- Construct a shallow cardboard box that is slightly more than 10 cm wide (i.e., slightly wider than a ten-bar is long) and at least 20 cm long (i.e., at least as long as two ten-bars).
- A cardboard insert that is as wide and tall as the box.
- Place-value blocks (commercial set).
- Place-value cards (see Figure 7.3).

LAUNCH POINT

1. Have the children dump a quantity of tens and units have altogether (see Figure 7.9).
2. Have the children gently shake the box and move materials around with their fingers until the blocks form a solid layer that extends to both walls, with no holes (see Figure 7.10).
3. If there are more than 10 rows of materials, have the children place the cardboard insert between the 10th and 11th rows.
4. Ask the children whether they want to change their estimate of how many they have and, if so, why. If they wish, they can count the entire set. When they are finished, ask them to form the corresponding numeral with the place-value cards.

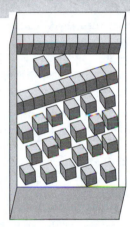

Figure 7.9 Unsorted Place-Value Materials in a Sorter Tray

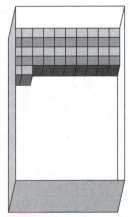

Figure 7.10 Sorted Place-Value Materials in a Sorter Tray

Go to the PDToolkit to find the online templates referenced in the following activity.

recognizable. We are not having them do any exchanges or asking them to deal with all the units before moving on to the tens. The box doesn't neatly put all the units in one place and the tens in another. Rows made up of ten units are intermingled with rows made up of one ten. Yet the materials clearly indicate there are a certain number of hundreds, tens, and units present. Children are amazed that they can name this rather large quantity of materials with a minimum of counting.

Launch Point

HUNDRED AND THOUSAND EXTENSIONS OF TEN FRAMES AND HAND GAME CARDS

MATERIALS AND SET-UP

Ten Frames

- **100 Frame.** On red card stock, arrange 10 ten frames that are turned vertically into two rows of five. (That is, make a ten frame out of the ten frames—see Figure 7.11. If you use the online template, you can print the black-and-white page directly onto red card stock).

- **1000 Frame.** Modify the hundreds sheet so all the interior lines are of equal thickness and only the borders are thicker. Print 10 of the modified hundreds sheets on green card stock. On a green sheet of art paper, arrange the 10 sheets in two rows of five (i.e., make a ten frame out of the hundreds sheets—see Figure 7.12). Use tape to reinforce the spaces between the hundreds sheets, and fold first in half and then accordion-style.

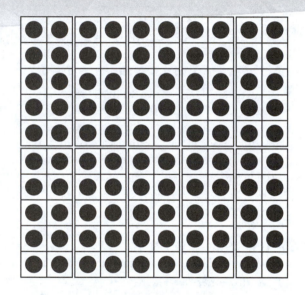

Figure 7.11 A 100 Frame Using Ten Frames

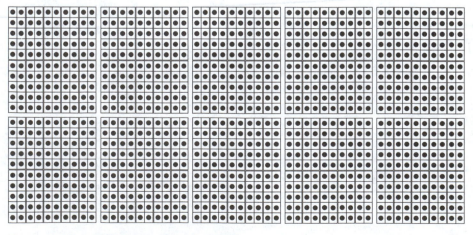

Figure 7.12 A 1000 Frame Using Ten Frames

Hand Game Cards

- **100 Frame.** On red card stock, arrange copies of the ten-fingers card in two columns five cards high (i.e., make a ten frame out of the 10 images—see Figure 7.13. Either leave a small space between each of the ten-fingers cards, or make a thicker line showing the divisions between the cards. If you use the online template, you can simply print the page directly on glossy photo paper.

- **1000 Frame.** Print 10 of the 100 frames made from the ten-fingers cards on green card stock. On a green sheet of art paper, arrange the 10 100

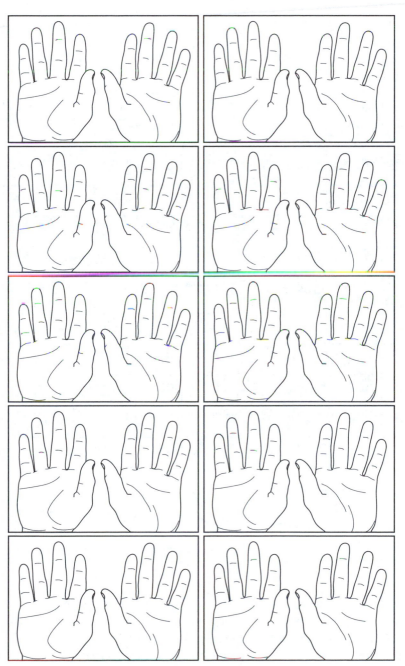

Figure 7.13 A 100 Frame Using Ten-Fingers Cards

frames in two rows of five (i.e., make a ten frame out of the 100 frames—see Figure 7.14. Use tape to reinforce the spaces between the 100 frames, and fold first in half and then accordion-style.

- Place-value cards.

LAUNCH POINT

1. Use the Hand Game cards and ten frame sets as alternative ways of displaying and combining quantities. For example, you could do the following problem:

 a. Show 437 as 4 hundred-fingers sheets, 3 ten-fingers cards, and 1 seven-fingers card.

 b. Show 685 as 6 hundred-fingers sheets, 8 ten-fingers cards, and 1 five-fingers card.

 c. Show that
 - The unit fingers combine to make 1 ten-fingers card and 1 two-fingers card;
 - The 12 ten-fingers cards combine to make 1 hundred-fingers sheet with 2 ten-fingers cards left over;
 - The 11 hundred-fingers sheets make 1 thousand-fingers poster with 1 hundred-fingers sheet left over;
 - This results in 1 thousand-fingers poster, 1 hundred-fingers sheet, 2 ten-fingers cards, and 1 two-fingers card;
 - These can be shown with the place-value cards as 1,000 + 100 + 20 + 2, or 1,122.

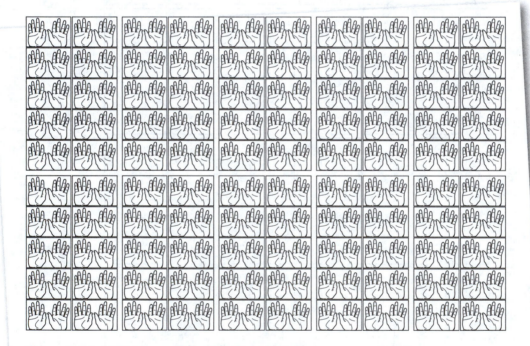

Figure 7.14 A 1000 Frame Using Ten-Fingers Cards

The ten frame is such a powerful tool in the early development of number sense that it is a shame to not continue the model in working with quantities past 99. Arranging tens in the same ten frame configuration to make 100 and arranging hundreds in the same ten frame configuration to make 1,000 are a powerful demonstration that large numbers can be displayed in other ways than with place-value blocks. It may even be a superior model, since each new power of ten mirrors the dimensions of the preceding level (much like the popular Digi-Blocks materials do—see _www.digi-blocks.com_). And unlike the place-value blocks or Digi-Blocks, the thousands frame keeps all 1000 units visible, making a much stronger impression of just how much a thousand is.

A similar case can be made for the images of hands displaying 10 fingers. The frame showing 100 pairs of hands displaying a total of 1,000 fingers is an almost dizzying visual. I like that. And I think that demonstrating how children's earliest counting tool can be used to display really big numbers is a plus, as well. If you wanted to make the display even more real for children, you could have 10 children stand in two rows of five with their 10 fingers up and count their fingers by tens; then show how the hundreds sheet does the same thing. It would be a wonderful event to pool the resources of multiple classrooms to display on the playground 10 clusters of 10 children, all with their fingers up, and take a picture of what 1000 fingers really look like!

Both these sets make it possible for children to display the quantities that accompany numerals without the time and/or expense and/or inconvenience of using the real things. We move too quickly into having children work just with the numerals because of the hassle of buying, storing, and manipulating hands-on displays. These materials are a valuable bridge between the concrete and the abstract.

Go to the PDToolkit to find the online template referenced in this activity.

Launch Point

EXPANDED NOTATION STRIP

MATERIALS AND SET-UP

- A long card that folds accordion-fashion. When folded, the card has four laminated squares showing, followed by the word *units* (see Figure 7.15). When completely extended, the words *thousands*, *hundreds*, and *tens* are also showing (see Figure 7.16).
- Wipe-off marker and eraser.
- Place-value blocks.

2	7	4	6	units

Figure 7.15 Folded Expanded Notation Strip

LAUNCH POINT

1. Have the children write a digit on each of the four squares of the folded strip and then name the four-digit numeral (e.g., the strip shows *4 . . . 3 . . . 7 . . . 2 units*, and they say, "Four thousand three hundred seventy-two").

2. Have the children unfold the strip completely (e.g., it now shows *4 thousands . . . 3 hundreds . . . 7 tens . . . 2 units*), and have one child make the quantity with the corresponding place-value blocks.

3. Have another child refold a portion of the strip to show a new configuration (e.g., it now shows *43 hundreds . . . 7 tens . . . 2 units*). Have a child make the quantity with the indicated place-value blocks.

4. Repeat with other folded patterns and other place-value block collections.

5. Ask the group: "Are each of these the same, or does one have more than the others? How do you know?"

2	thou	sand	7	hund	reds	4	tens		6	units

Figure 7.16 Unfolded Expanded Notation Strip

This clever device for showing expanded notation in both standard and non-standard forms suggests in concrete form that all these are equivalent representations of the same quantity. We tend to not give children enough practice working with nonstandard place-value quantities, but only by doing so can they become comfortable with the 10:1 ratios that exist across the place-value spectrum.

This is a great activity to help children continue to think in place-value terms about the total value of a set rather than simply compare the total number of objects in each of the place-value categories. For example, *2 hundreds 23 tens 4 units* is more than *3 hundreds 9 tens 6 units* even though it has fewer hundreds.

This is also a great way for the children to physically experience how efficient the place-value system is for displaying large quantities. It is physically much quicker to construct 2,673 by displaying 2 thousand cubes, 6 hundred squares, 7 ten-bars, and 3 units than it would be by displaying, for example, 26 hundreds and 73 units. They are both the same amount, but one is obviously the easier way to go.

Ways to broaden and extend the children's work with this device include:

1. Have the children use a calculator to add up their different arrangements. Using the example given in the Launch Point, the children would punch in

   4000 [+] 300 [+] 70 [+] 2 [=] and the display would show, progressively,

   > "4000"
   > "4300"
   > "4370"
   > "4372"

2. If they did a nonstandard configuration for 2,673 (see Wacky Numbers in Chapter 8), they could punch in

   > 1000 [+] ("1000" appears in display)
   > 1500 [+] ("2500" appears in display)
   > 150 [+] ("2650" appears in display)
   > 23 [=] ("2673" appears in display)

Note that they have to do some nonlinear thinking to figure out how to enter something like "15 hundreds" into the calculator. That, too, is a good learning experience.

We will now turn our attention to the next Launch Point, "Modeling Multidigit Addition/Subtraction with Exchanging." As important as it is to use physical manipulatives to solve mathematical problems, it is equally important to bridge to the paper-and-pencil ways of solving problems. It may seem cumbersome and involve too many steps to model the transformations that go into addition and subtraction with exchanging, but it is the best way to make the operations that are coded into the standard algorithms understandable. Even most adults are amazed to find that the steps in the algorithm are actually the same steps that would be taken if the problem were being solved physically. Using the place-value mats helps to maintain the reality of the place-value categories, as does the use of the place-value cards. It is important that children approach the algorithm not as a process of manipulating digits but as one of manipulating place-value quantities—mat and blocks give meaning to place-value cards, which in turn give meaning to the numbers generated on the recording sheet.

Although the examples I give are for three-digit problems requiring exchanging, obviously one would start with simpler problems, such as two-digit problems and problems that don't require the exchanging steps. But I caution against

PD TOOLKIT™

Go to the PDToolkit to find the online template referenced in the following activity.

MODELING MULTIDIGIT ADDITION/SUBTRACTION WITH EXCHANGING

$$
\begin{array}{r}
287 \\
+146 \\
\hline
13 \\
120 \\
+300 \\
\hline
\end{array}
$$

Figure 7.17 Adding 287 and 146 Using Join Model

MATERIALS AND SET-UP

- Place-value blocks: unit cubes, ten-bars, hundred squares, and thousand cubes.
- Place-value mat.
- Place-value cards.
- Recording paper or wipe-off board.

LAUNCH POINTS

Addition (Join model)

1. Write the addition problem on a recording sheet to the right of the place-value mat (e.g., 287 + 146).
2. Model both quantities on the place-value mat, one underneath the other, along with the place-value cards representing those quantities.
3. Push the quantities and cards in each place-value column together. If there are 10 or more blocks within a particular category, position them in the form of the next place-value category (i.e., make 10 of the 13 units look like a ten-bar and 10 of the 12 ten-bars look like a hundred square).
4. Replace the place-value cards from the addends with place-value cards representing the quantity in each column (i.e., use a 10-card and 3-card to form 13, a 100-card and 20-card to form 120, and a 300-card—see Figure 7.17).
5. Write the three partial sums on the recording sheet.
6. Move the like quantities and like cards into their respective columns (i.e., move the 10 units and the

10-card into the tens column, and move the 10 ten-bars and 100-card into the hundreds column) and find the cards to represent the sum (i.e., 433).
7. Write the sum on the recording paper, under the partial sums.
8. Later stage: Skip the place-value cards and partial sums, and record each step taken with the blocks using the standard algorithm (i.e., after pushing the units together, move 10 units to the tens column, record a 3, and "carry" the 1; after combining the tens, move 10 tens to the hundreds column, record a 3, and "carry" the 1; then combine the hundreds and record a 4).

Subtraction (Separate model)

1. Write the subtraction problem on a recording sheet to the right of the place-value mat (e.g., 346 − 187).
2. Model the first quantity on the place-value mat, along with the place-value cards representing that

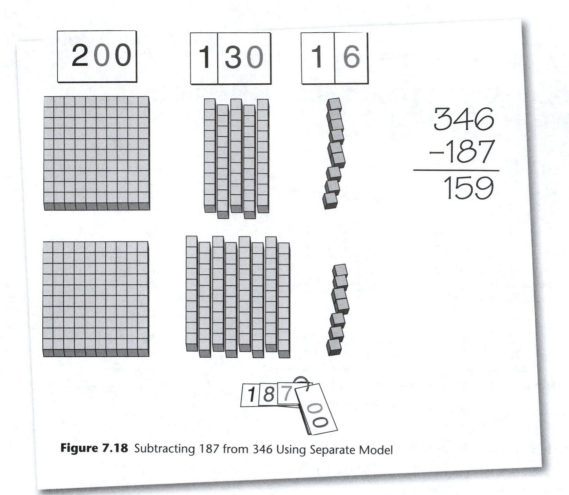

Figure 7.18 Subtracting 187 from 346 Using Separate Model

quantity (i.e., 300, 40, and 6) and, beneath those, the cards for the quantities to be removed (i.e., 100, 80, and 7).

3. Starting with the units, remove the indicated quantities. If there are not sufficient blocks to do so, move one of the blocks from the column to the left and change the place-value cards to reflect the new arrangement; then remove the indicated quantity (i.e., move a ten-bar to the units column, show the new amounts by covering the 40-card with a 30-card and adding a 10-card to the 6-card to form 16, and then remove 7 units[7]—see Figure 7.18; similarly, move a hundred square to the tens column, show the new amounts by covering the 300-card with a 200-card and adding a 100-card to the 30-card to form 130, and then remove 8 tens).

4. Form the difference with place-value cards (i.e., 159).

5. Write the difference on the recording sheet.

6. Later stage: Skip the place-value cards, and record each step taken with the blocks using the standard algorithm (i.e., to subtract the units, cross out the 4 in the tens column and write a 3 above it and then mark a 1 next to the 6 in the units column; to subtract the tens, cross out the 3 in the hundreds column and write a 2 above it and then mark a 1 next to the 3 in the tens column).

Subtraction (Compare model)

1. Write the subtraction problem on a recording sheet to the right of the place-value mat (e.g., 346 – 187).

2. Model both quantities on the place-value mat, one underneath the other, along with the place-value cards representing those quantities.

3. Starting with the units, lay the quantities for the smaller number on top of the blocks representing the first number. If there are not enough blocks in a category to cover, move one of the blocks from the next higher category into the column, and start covering it (i.e., after covering the six units, move one of the ten-bars into the units column and cover the lowest

---

[7] Note that to actually remove the 7 units, the ten-bar will have to be decomposed into ten units.

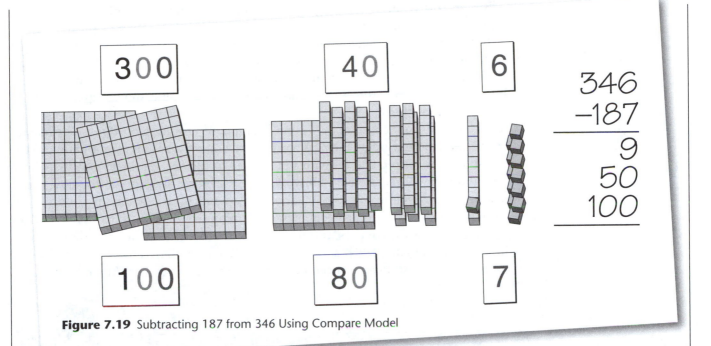

Figure 7.19 Subtracting 187 from 346 Using Compare Model

unit; after covering the remaining three ten-bars, move a hundred square into the tens column and cover five of the tens; then cover one of the remaining hundred squares—see Figure 7.19).

4. Find the place-value cards to represent the portions that have *not* been covered (i.e., 100, 50, and 9).

5. Write the difference on the recording sheet.
6. Later stage: Skip the place-value cards, and record each step taken with the blocks using the standard algorithm (same as in the Separate problem).

artificially staying with the simpler varieties and then switching to those that always require exchanging. Doing so causes children to lock into rote repetition rather than continuing to evaluate what the problem calls for.

Note the important role played by the intermediary step of forming the partial sums. When solving the tens portion of 287 + 146, counting a total of 12 tens and writing the partial sum 120 maintains the actual quantity much better than writing a 2 in the second column and writing a 1 at the top of the next column, and keeping the extra ten from the 13 units in the units place makes the relationship between 40 + 80 and 120 visually clear. Another reason the partial sums are a good intermediate step is something I haven't mentioned yet. It is a well-established research finding that children, left to their own devices, prefer to solve addition problems starting with the larger quantities rather than with the units. The reason we teach them to start with the units is so the standard algorithm will work. But one can easily generate the partial sums starting from the left—it's just as easy to write 300 plus 120 plus 13 as it is to write 13 plus 120 plus 300.

In fact, the temptation to work from the left to the right is so strong that many children intuitively figure out how to make it work for subtraction as well, even when exchanges are necessary. Take, for example, the problem we solved above, 346 − 187. A child could approach the problem this way: "First, I subtract 100 from 300 and get 200. Then I subtract 80 from 40, and that's minus 40, so I don't have 200, I have . . . let's see . . . 160. Then I subtract 7 from 6, but that's minus one, so the answer is 1 less than 160. The answer is 159." I would feel really good about the future prospects of a child who is able to think his way through the problem like that. In the next activity, I will discuss the save boxes children sometimes use to avoid the cumbersome steps required by the standard algorithms.

This next Launch Point is a good example of encouraging the use of mental strategies without forcing them. What you are hoping for is that some children will see an easy way to come up with the answer to the first problem and that those who did not will see the possibility of using that same strategy on the next problem. In the examples given, Set A starts with a doubles fact that many children will recognize. By the fourth problem, you are hoping they will work from the doubles fact and add 3 rather than trying to work the problem from the right, which involves exchanging. Set B starts with two problems that zero out the units column, letting the students concentrate on how the tens are changing. By the fourth

Launch Point

MENTAL MATH PROBLEM SETS

MATERIALS AND SET-UP

- A card showing a series of addition or subtraction problems to solve, the first couple arranged to make a particular solution strategy useful and subsequent ones less obviously so.

For example, Set A might be designed to encourage use of a doubles fact:

$$25 + 25$$
$$25 + 26$$
$$25 + 23$$
$$25 + 28$$

Set B might encourage a mental strategy to avoid the need to "borrow"

$$143 - 13$$
$$264 - 24$$
$$174 - 45$$
$$582 - 43$$

Set C could suggest how to use a close-to-a-hundred strategy to simplify problems

$$142 + 499$$
$$199 + 442$$
$$449 + 197$$
$$397 + 205$$

And Set D could encourage making sets of 10 to simplify multiple-addend problems

$$6 + 4 + 2$$
$$2 + 8 + 5$$
$$9 + 27 + 1$$
$$2 + 7 + 8 + 3$$
$$14 + 5 + 5 + 6 + 4$$

LAUNCH POINT

1. Present the first problem, asking the children to solve it in their head (i.e., they should use *mental* math, not paper-and-pencil algorithms).
2. After suitable wait time, ask the children to share with each other the strategies they used to come up with a solution. Let *them* resolve any disagreements as to the correct answer (i.e., don't tell them, and don't take sides, but do help them listen to and understand each other).
3. Move on to the next problem.

problem, you are looking for them to see the possibility of doing the same thing by temporarily changing the problem into a simpler problem (e.g., "582 minus 42 is 540 . . . ") and then adjusting their answer to match the actual problem (" . . . but I have to subtract 1 more, so the answer is 539"). Set C encourages a similar compensation strategy, first solving the problems as if one of the numbers was actually the near-hundreds number ("142 plus 500 is 642 . . . ") and then compensating (" . . . but the answer is 1 less than that, 641"). Set D encourages combining addends to make tens, so by the final problem many of the children are saying, "5 and 5 are 10 and 6 and 4 are 10, so the answer is 14 plus 20, or 34."

These won't be the only strategies shared, of course, but by having them modeled by their fellow classmates, you are demonstrating to the children that these strategies are useful in a very authentic way, and you are encouraging the habit of pausing for a moment and looking for shortcuts before diving in and using the standard algorithm. Note that these sets are encouraging estimation using "nice numbers," which in most life circumstances is more important than knowing how to compute the exact answer.

When reviewing children's solutions, you might find it useful to try to capture on a wipe-off board or the overhead the solutions being offered so the children can see what the solutions look like written down. This might also help children see that the "new" solution being offered is essentially the same as one that has already been shared. Modeling the strategies using other classroom materials, such as number lines, Unifix cubes, or place-value blocks, can help the children relate to the mental strategy being shared in a more visual way.

When writing down the steps in a child's mental math strategy, consider using a *save box* to symbolize the need to do the compensation step. For example, in the third problem in Set B (174 − 45), point out that the child reenvisioned the problem as 174 − 44 − 1 and put the − 1 in memory, to do at the end. By actually drawing the −1 in a save box, you are making it clear that the intermediate answer is off by 1 and the final step should be to subtract 1, not add 1. In similar fashion, show that, for the first problem in Set C (142 + 499), the child reenvisioned the problem as 142 + 500 − 1 and put the −1 in a save box, to do at the end.

It is much more useful to have children do these exercises where they solve problems flexibly in their head than to have them do page after page of paper-and-pencil tasks using the standard algorithm. Yes, they have to learn how to do that, too, but if they get locked into thinking that is the only way to solve the problem, they will not see the opportunities for more elegant solutions when they arise.

The next Launch Point is titled "Decimeter Rods, Meter Rods, Centimeter Rods, Metric Measuring Tape, and Meteric Trundle Wheel." The decimeter rods were used in my earlier book (Nelson, 2007), along with number rods, as part of the early exploration of the quantities 1–10. Now they are being used as part of a larger system of base-10 materials that can be used to measure.

The metric system of measurement is a perfect vehicle for practicing place-value awareness. Children of this age are not just developing number sense, but also learning to measure (and to deal with fractions). Here is a golden opportunity to address all those concepts, as well as setting the stage for what will eventually be known as decimals (e.g., the above measurement could be recorded as 2.85 meters). Here children are being given measurement tools that are following the same 10:1 ratio they have been wrestling with in their number sense work. It is quite striking to put out the 10 centimeter rods and 10 decimeter rods, and the first 10 meters on

Launch Point

DECIMETER RODS, METER RODS, CENTIMETER RODS, METRIC MEASURING TAPE, AND METRIC TRUNDLE WHEEL

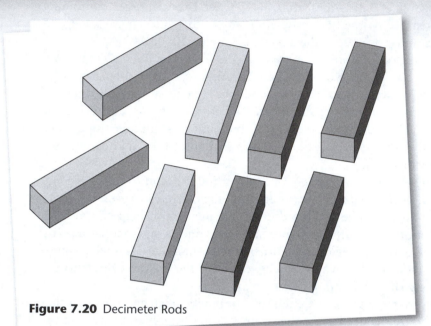

Figure 7.20 Decimeter Rods

MATERIALS AND SET-UP

- **Decimeter Rods.** These are wooden rods 2.5 cm × 2.5 cm × 10 cm.[8] Half the rods are painted red and half blue (see Figure 7.20). You need at least 10 of these.
- **Meter Rods.** These are wooden rods 2.5 cm × 2.5 cm × 1 m, painted either red or blue. You only need a few of these (see Figure 7.21).
- **Centimeter Rods.** These are red and blue counting tiles 2.5 cm × 2.5 cm × 1 cm (commercial product—see Figure 7.22). You need at least 10 of these.
- **Metric Measuring Tape** (commercial product— see Figure 7.23). Several manufacturers make a 50-meter measuring tape on a spool that has a handle for winding the tape up. On the numbered side of the tape, use permanent markers to color the first meter red, the second meter blue, the third meter red, and so on. On the back side of the tape, use the markers to color

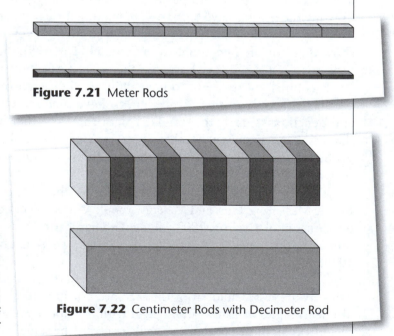

Figure 7.21 Meter Rods

Figure 7.22 Centimeter Rods with Decimeter Rod

---

[8] Another way to make decimeter and meter rods is to buy half-inch doweling from the hardware store and cut it to length, or you can simply make the materials from stiff cardboard wrapped with colored duct tape. I was first introduced to what she called *discrete rods* by Peggy Leoffler, who shocked her Montessori colleagues by daring to cut up a set of precious red-and-blue number rods in order to explore their impact on the standard math sequence.

the first 10 meters red, the second 10 meters blue, and so on.

- **Metric Trundle Wheel** (commercial product—see Figure 7.24). A trundle wheel is a wheel with a handle attached to it. The wheel is rolled along a surface to measure distance—often long distances or distances that do not follow a straight path. The metric trundle wheel is 1 meter in circumference, with the rim marked in centimeter increments. To measure, start with the zero on the wheel touching the starting point. As the wheel is pushed along, each completed revolution is signaled by an audible click, meaning another meter has been added. To know the total length, count the clicks and add the number of centimeters indicated by the numeral sitting on the end point.

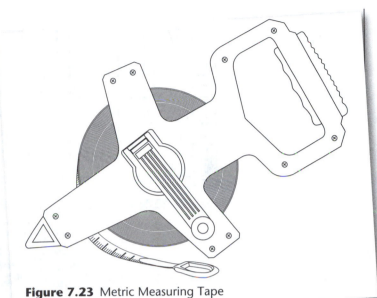

Figure 7.23 Metric Measuring Tape

LAUNCH POINT

Introducing the Measuring Tools

1. Stand the centimeter rods on their edge, and put them flush with each other in alternating red and blue sequence. Show that 10 centimeter rods equal 1 decimeter rod.
2. Line up the decimeter rods in alternating red and blue sequence. Show that 10 decimeter rods equal 1 meter rod.
3. Show how the meter rods can also be lined up end to end in alternating red and blue sequence (if you don't have 10 of them, move on to the next step).
4. Pull out the metric measuring tape. Show how it is marked off in alternating red and blue sequence. Show that 10 meters (indicated on the front of the tape) equal 1 decameter (i.e., the first red strip on the back of the tape).

Using the Metric Rods to Measure

1. Choose something to measure.
2. Choose the rod set so that it will take at least 1 rod but less than 10 rods to measure the distance. In other words, for small things start with the centimeter rods, for medium-sized things start with the decimeter rods, and for large things start with the meter rods.

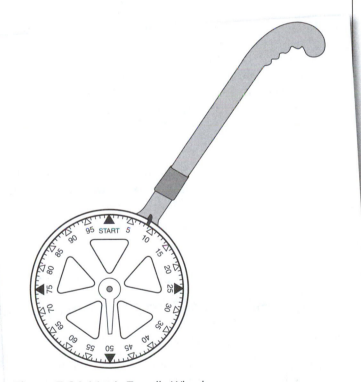

Figure 7.24 Metric Trundle Wheel

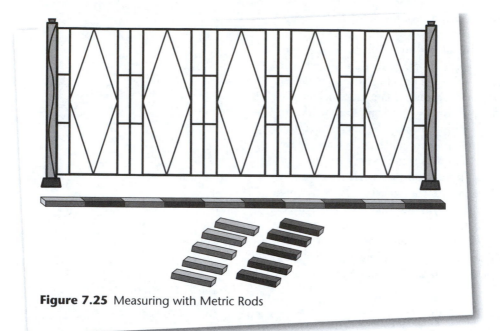

Figure 7.25 Measuring with Metric Rods

3. Count as many whole units as possible with the chosen measuring rods.
4. Measure the leftover portion with the next smaller set of measuring rods. For example, if you were measuring the stairway banister, you might lay down 2 meter rods, see that a third meter rod would be too much, and then start laying out decimeter rods. Let's say 8 of those fit, but there's still a little space left. You then could use 5 of the centimeter rods to fill that gap (see Figure 7.25).

the measuring tape simultaneously and see the exponential growth in scale. The more ways we can bring this concept into children's lives and into their day-to-day work, the better they will internalize it.

Launch Point

READING AND WRITING REALLY BIG NUMERALS

MATERIALS AND SET-UP

- Cards with very long numerals written on them, with periods indicated (e.g., "97,104,293,000,621, 508").
- Cards with very large quantities written in word form (e.g., "Ninety-seven quadrillion, one hundred four trillion, two hundred ninety-three billion, six hundred twenty-one thousand, five hundred eight").

LAUNCH POINT

- Children pick a card and either read the numeral aloud or write the numeral named.

I mentioned in an earlier chapter that children are fascinated at an early age with the doubles facts. They are equally fascinated with really big numbers, but we do little to feed and nurture this innate interest. For children to truly understand the decades pattern of our counting system and appreciate the efficiency with which we recycle the numerals 0–9 and the nomenclature of tens and hundreds, we must allow them to move beyond four-digit numerals. They can't appreciate the forest if we only let them look at a few trees.

It takes little time and a very simple classroom display to introduce the terms *millions*, *billions*, *trillions*, *quadrillions*, and so on into the children's vocabulary and to show which periods those names represent. Having children read or write a few of these numbers is an excellent sponge activity to use in the classroom when there is a lull in the classroom and you want the children to briefly revisit the world of really big numbers. They are quite proud of themselves when they demonstrate they can do this.

To expand and extend the children's work with large numbers, you can

1. Be on the lookout for large numbers in the news. You'd be surprised how many examples are out there, once you start looking for them. Often the numbers are given in word form (e.g., "3 trillion dollar deficit"). Have the children read them, write them, and discuss them in the context of the news article—this can be a great crossover to science, social studies, or some other subject. *Note:* You will often see numbers that include a decimal component (e.g., "4.5 billion acres") or that include a fraction (e.g., "4 and a half trillion cicadas"). Interesting conversations will ensue as the children grapple with what those mean and how to represent them. In the process, they are spontaneously readying themselves for concepts schools have decided they are not yet "ready" for.

2. Consider making a *Book of One Million*, containing one million zeroes. I have put a page with 4,000 zeroes on it in an online template. If you make 250 copies of that page (i.e., 125 duplexed pages), you have a million zeroes! Color in a random zero on each page of the book, and write the corresponding numeral in the margin. This way children can practice reading numerals 1–999,999, while at the same time appreciating where that numeral fits in a 1–1,000,000 sequence—and, perhaps most important of all, getting a feel for how big one million really is. There are also several really great children's books that explore large numbers, which you can periodically share with children to feed their hunger for the numbers in our world that go beyond a measly hundred or thousand.

Go to the PDToolkit to find the online template referenced here.

PLACE-VALUE FLUENCY AND MULTIDIGIT ADDITION/SUBTRACTION CHECKPOINTS

HUNDRED SQUARE IN A CAVE GAME

MATERIALS AND SET-UP

- Opaque box or small storage bin. The box is set upside down and has a cutout to serve as the entrance to the cave.
- One hundred-square, 9 ten-bars, and 10 units.

ASSESSMENT PROBE

1. Hide the ten-bars and units behind your back, and place the hundred square on top of the cave. Tell the child: "Close your eyes. When you open your eyes, some of the hundred square will still be sitting on top of the cave, but some of it will have moved inside the cave. You job will be to try to guess how much of the hundred square is inside the cave."
2. The child closes his eyes. You hide the hundred square and place some of the tens and units on top of the cave and some inside.
3. The child opens his eyes and guesses. Ask him how he knows. Raise the cave to reveal the actual quantity. Put the ten-bars and units together to show they do indeed equal a hundred square.
4. Repeat with a new problem.

VARIATION

1. Thousand Cube in a Cave.

● What you are looking for

Can the child find the missing part of one hundred by mentally decomposing one hundred into tens and units?

This involves conservation of quantity at a fairly sophisticated level. Children always have a harder time talking about the quantity they don't see than about the quantity they do see. And note that there are only 9 ten-bars, not 10, since 1 ten-bar has been decomposed into 10 units. A child who sees 3 ten-bars and 7 units on top of the cave may be tempted to answer "73" rather than the correct "63" for what's inside the cave. It is from the child's explanation of his response that you will know how he is decomposing the single hundred square into a composite of ten-bars and units. For example, he might say:

> "Well, there are 3 tens here, so that means 7 tens are missing. But one of those ten-bars is partly here (pointing to the 7 units)—only 3 of that ten are missing. So that means 6 tens are missing, plus 3 more. Sixty-three."

Or he might work from the other direction:

> "These 7 mean one ten was removed from the hundred to make units, and 3 of those are missing. That leaves 9 tens, and 3 of them are here, so 6 of them must be in the cave. Sixty-three."

Assessment Probe

WACKY NUMBERS

Go to the PDToolkit to find the online templates referenced in this activity.

MATERIALS AND SET-UP

- Optional: Place-value blocks.
- Optional: Place-value cards or response wheels.

ASSESSMENT PROBE

1. Show or say a number more than three tens and less than ten thousand. Ask the children to show alternative combinations of units, tens, hundreds, and thousands that are equivalent (for example, given the prompt 2,673, they could show or say 1 thousand, 15 hundreds, 17 tens, and 3 units).

VARIATIONS

1. Present the quantity or numeral in nonstandard groupings, and have the children identify the standard notation.
2. Ask a series of nontraditional questions about place-value equivalencies; for example:

   "How many tens in a thousand?"
   "How much is one hundred tens?"
   "How many hundreds in ten thousand?"
   "How many ten-thousands in a million?"

3. **Wacky Numbers Concentration.** Create matching sets of cards, one showing a numeral in standard form and another showing a nonstandard arrangement. Children find the cards that match.

4. **Wacky Numbers War.** Use cards similar to those described above, and have the children each turn over a card and decide whether one is greater than the other or whether they are of equivalent value.

5. **Wacky Numbers Bingo.** Same premise, only the caller calls a quantity in nonstandard form and the players need to see whether they have the equivalent standard version on their playing cards (either the numeral or a quantity shown visually using a place-value stamping set).

● What you are looking for

Can children readily see the equivalency of quantities across place-value categories?

In Chapter 7, I described how nonstandard representations are modeled using the expanded notation strips, but children need many more opportunities to practice this skill. Having children purposefully violate the "rules" of standard notation is perhaps the best way to see if they truly understand what standard notation means. More importantly, competence and confidence in doing this task signal that the children are comfortable composing and decomposing place-value quantities, which is an essential mental construct for them to start adding and subtracting multidigit numbers.

Assessment Probe

"I HAVE, WHO HAS?" GAME

MATERIALS AND SET-UP

- Cards to distribute to the children. At the top of each card is a numeral, in standard notation (e.g., "4,366"). At the bottom of the card is the phrase "Who has . . . ," followed by the description of a quantity in nonstandard notation (e.g., "Who has 2 thousands, 23 hundreds, 5 tens, and 16 units?"—which would clue the child holding the card with the standard notation for that quantity to say, "I have four thousand three hundred sixty-six. Who has . . . "). Cards are designed such that they form a chain that will loop back to the numeral on the card that was read to start the activity.

ASSESSMENT PROBE

1. Notice how quickly children respond, and scaffold conversations as children debate whether their numerals fit the description or not.

● What you are looking for

Do children recognize place-value quantities when they are presented orally in nontraditional form?

This is yet another chance for children to experience place-value quantities in nontraditional arrangements, a pivotal aspect of place-value understanding. In one sense, this activity puts children on the spot in front of their peers, which is something I tend to avoid. The good thing about "I Have, Who Has?" games, however, is that no other child has the same number (so no one else is competing to read the numeral on their card) and everyone is mentally working the problem. If the silence drags on too long, you can scaffold a class conversation of what they think the answer is and why, which will give the child holding the card a chance to chime in with confidence and keep the game going.

Assessment Probe

PARTS-OF CALCULATOR DRILL

MATERIALS AND SET-UP

- Calculator.

ASSESSMENT PROBE

1. Decide on the place-value target number that you will be making parts of (e.g., 100, 1000, 200, 500).
2. Enter into the calculator 0 [−] target number [=].
3. Announce a parts-of number, which can be any number less than the target number. Enter it into the calculator, and then hit equals. The child then tries to guess what numeral you see displayed on the screen (e.g., if 100 were entered as the target, when you enter 46 and then hit equals, "−54" will be displayed).
4. Announce a new number less than the target number, type it into the calculator, and then hit equals. The child guesses the displayed numeral.

VARIATION

1. Practice other important anchor numbers, such as 20 and 50.

● What you are looking for

Can the child find the missing part of a multidigit number by mentally decomposing it into tens and units?

This is essentially the same task as was practiced in Hundred Square in a Cave, but the constant function on the calculator allows many more problems to be practiced in a shorter span of time. Reserve this task for children who have become comfortable with solving the more concrete task.

Assessment Probe

SKIP-COUNTING CALCULATOR DRILL

MATERIALS AND SET-UP

- Calculator.

ASSESSMENT PROBE

1. Choose any non-decade number between 1 and 999 as the start number. Enter that number into the calculator (e.g., 718).

2. Choose which place-value position you will skip count by (+10, +100, +1000). Enter that constant function into the calculator (e.g., +100), and then hit equals (the display will show 818). The child says what number he thinks is displayed (e.g., "Eight hundred eighteen").

3. Keep hitting the equals sign to check as the child's continue skip counting (e.g., "Nine hundred eighteen, one thousand one hundred eighteen, one thousand two hundred eighteen . . . ").

VARIATIONS

1. Have the child skip count backward from a high starting number.

2. Switch the skip-count category in a patterned basis from thousands to hundreds to tens to ones to thousands, and so on. For example, if the starting number were 318, the child would count:

   318, 1318, 1418, 1428, 1429, 2429, 2529, 2539, 2540, 3540, 3640 . . .

   Note: You won't be able to use the constant function on the calculator as a check. You would be better off using the place-value cards or response wheels for this one if the child needs a visual aid to keep track of what number he's on.

● What you are looking for

Can the child mentally keep track of which place-value quantities are staying constant and which are changing when skip counting from a nontraditional base number?

We have children practice counting "10, 20, 30, 40 . . . " and "100, 200, 300, 400 . . . ," but there are two problems with limiting ourselves to these verbal chants:

1. These become a simple, memorized verbal string.

2. They lead some children to form false ideas, such as that the number that follows 100 is 200.

A much better test of a child's ability to skip count by a certain place value is to have him practice doing so from a messier starting point. A child who develops a comfort with this more sophisticated version of skip counting puts it to good use in solving a problem such as 148 + 34 by saying, for example: "First I counted up from 148—158, 168, 178. Then I counted up four—179, 180, 181, 182. So I knew the answer was 182."

Can the child successfully bridge the place-value transition points when he reaches them?

The hardest part of this skip-counting task comes when the child must alter two place-value positions simultaneously: (1) resetting the count from 9 back to 0 in the category he is skip counting by and (2) increasing the next place-value position by one. If the child can manage that transformation while still remembering the portions of the count that are not changing, you can be quite sure he is comfortable with place-value transformations.

Can the child switch skip counts fluidly?

Variation #2 above is a particularly complex task, but an important one. Many children who can comfortably get into the rhythm of a particular skip count have difficulty switching to a different counting system in midcount. We encounter this when we have children learning to tell time on an analog clock (counting 5, 10, 15, 20, 21, 22, 23) or counting the value of a handful of change (25, 50, 75, 85, 90, 95, 96, 97). Practicing that skill in a place-value context is an excellent way to judge just how comfortable the child is with a hierarchical counting system.

Assessment Probe

TARGET GAME

MATERIALS AND SET-UP

- Cards showing six to eight numerals, an operations designator ("add" or "subtract") at the top, and a target number at the bottom.
- Optional: Calculator.

ASSESSMENT PROBE

1. Have the child select which pair of six to eight given numbers she thinks will get her closest to the target number. For example, for an addition card, the options might be

42   104   93   130   116   71

with the target number being

200

2. Ask the child for her rationale. Have her add/subtract her chosen numbers using the calculator and discuss how close she came.
3. Have her check other likely pairings and discuss the results.

VARIATION

1. Have a card deck where the child uses trios of numbers to try to come as close to the target as possible.

What you are looking for

Can the child estimate how place-value quantities combine (or differ) reasonably accurately?

In setting up the cards, choose numbers such that the child can't rely only on the greatest digit to make the best selection. In other words, her thinking should be forced to consider the relative impact of competing information given in different place-value categories. For example, in processing the example given in the Assessment Probe, the child might say: "I looked at 104 and 116, but that would be 200 plus 16 plus 4, which would be 220, and that doesn't seem very close. 93 is pretty close to a hundred but a little less, and 104 is pretty close to a hundred but a little more, so I thought those two might be the closest. But then I saw 130 and 71, and I know that's just one more than 200, and that's about as close as you can get. I'm sure it wasn't 116 plus 71 because 116 is close to a hundred but 71 isn't." Dismissing the last possibility indicates the child has difficulty moving off the anchor numbers; still, her level of reasoning indicates she is well on her way to becoming mathematically proficient.

As usual, reasoning when the operation is subtraction is considerably more difficult. What if, in the example given, the operation had been subtraction and the target had been 50? Here is the kind of thinking that might be shared with you: "104 is close to 100, and 42 is close to 50, so maybe that's the best pair. I'm not sure though. What if you started with 130 and you took away 71? It seems that would be pretty close, too. I'm not sure."

Does the child have a sense of the magnitude of difference between her choice and the target number?

Once the child has made her choices and checked them on the calculator, she still needs to decide whether they were close enough to be the best option. Some children will just assume their choice was good ("The target was 200 and my answer was 200 something, so I did pretty good"). Others will take a more critical approach ("Hmmm, my answer was more than 50 too high . . . I bet there's a closer match than that").

A particularly interesting problem occurs when one answer is higher than the target and the other is lower. Let's say the operation is subtraction, the target is 1,000, and the choices are

$$522 \quad 3,097 \quad 1,188 \quad 2,104 \quad 1,583 \quad 4,502$$

Maybe the child would first choose $1,583 - 522$ (=1,061) but then wonder whether $2,104 - 1,188$ might be a better choice (=916). Which is closer to 1,000, 1,061 or 916? The answer requires some fairly sophisticated thinking, like this: "I choose 1,061. I think that is the best one because I missed by about 60 and the other is more than 80 less than 1,000. See? 920 plus 80 would be 1,000."

Assessment Probe

"WHAT'S WRONG WITH THIS PICTURE?" SETS[1]

MATERIALS AND SET-UP

- Cards showing a sequence of problems solved by a fictitious child. For example:

Case 1: Charley

47	126	38
+92	+27	+104
139	396	484

Case 2: Jessica

^{1}37	^{1}46	^{2}^{1}159
+38	+89	+63
165	225	2112

Case 3: Albert

365	856	53
−47	−325	−28
322	531	35

Case 4: Benita

^{5}$^{13}_{}$64^{1}2	^{2}$^{14}_{}$35^{1}5	$^{8}_{}$9^{1}6
−268	−182	−54
374	1613	312

[1] For more examples of common error patterns, see Ashlock (2002).

ASSESSMENT PROBE

1. The child looks at the problems on the card and explains what the fictitious child did, why that way of solving the problems doesn't work, how that child should have solved the problem, and why that way works.

VARIATIONS

1. Ask the child whether he could tell one of the solutions was wrong even before looking at *how* it was solved.
2. Ask the child to generate another problem solved incorrectly, using the fictitious child's strategy.
3. Have the child use base-10 manipulatives to prove that his method of solving the problem is the correct one.

● What you are looking for

Does the child know how and why the standard algorithms work?

Algorithms are designed to be quick and efficient. They are not designed to be conceptually transparent. A child need not think about why each of the steps in the algorithm works every time he uses it, but if he is incapable of doing so, he has no way of recovering when his recall of what to do next fails. It is by remembering the place value of the digits, not just the face value, that a child can talk through the algorithm for Jessica's problem $37 + 38$, saying:

> "Well, first you add 7 and 8 and get 15. So I write the 5 in the units place and I make 1 more ten in the tens column. Then that 1 ten plus 3 more tens plus 3 more tens makes 7 tens, so I write a 7 down here. So the answer is 75."

Or in the case of Benita's problem $355 - 182$, he might say:

> "Look, I start over here with the units. If I take 2 away from 5, I get 3, so I write a 3 down here. Then I subtract the tens, but I can't subtract 8 tens from 5 tens, so I get 10 more tens from the 300, leaving me with 2 hundreds and 15 tens. If I subtract 8 tens from 15 tens, I get 7 tens, so I write a 7 down here. Then 1 hundred from 2 hundred is 1 hundred, so I write a 1 down here. The answer is 173."

Can the child explain, in place-value terms, how the fictitious child went wrong?

It might be said that you can't completely master an algorithm without having explored all the ways to mess it up. As children are exposed to an increasing number of algorithms, similar features start to migrate from one algorithm to another. Just as children go through a phase of sprinkling their writing with commas everywhere after learning how to use them, children also move through the phase of using exchanging to solve addition and subtraction problems with a vengeance, even when it's not required (as was the case with Benita earlier). This tendency is exacerbated if we teach skills in isolation (e.g., first we teach how to solve problems that don't require exchanging, and then we teach how to solve problems that do) or if we teach algorithms as a series of mindless steps. Benita was probably taught to solve her first problem, $642 - 268$, with words that sounded like this: "You can't subtract 8 from 2, so cross out the 4, write a 3 above it, and put a 1 next to the 2. Then 12 minus 8 is 4. You can't subtract 6 from 3, so cross out the 6, write a 5 above it, and write a 1 next to the 3. Then 13 minus 6 is 7. And 5 minus 2 is 3. You're done." Sounds like magic to me. It probably did to her too.

As children are working problems, moments of doubt often arise, and they ask themselves: "Now how did that next part go?" If they have only the memorized steps to guide them, all they can do is plunge ahead and hope for the best. When subtracting, children should be asking themselves: "Do I have enough in this place-value category to subtract, and, if not, where will I get more?" This requires staying grounded in place-value understanding. Similarly, when combining quantities in a place-value category (i.e., adding), they should be asking themselves: "Do I have too many in this place-value category, and, if so, where should I put the extras?" Simply crossing out digits and replacing them or putting little hash-marks next to digits, without understanding what those actions mean in place-value terms, leaves too many options open for generating silly answers.

Can the child estimate the sum or difference before working the problem?

Three of the four fictitious children above should have had a "Wait a minute!" moment after writing down some of their answers. Charley should have said to himself: "No way is 126 plus 27 equal to 396!" Jessica should have said: "I must be doing something wrong, since 159 and 63 should be around 200, not 2,000!" And Benita should have noticed: "If I'm subtracting from 96, how can the answer be bigger than 96?" By maintaining a basic sense of what the operations of addition and subtraction are doing to numbers and by having a sense of the relative magnitude of the numbers they are working with, they are in a position to know that something has gone wrong in the memorized algorithm, so they take a second look at their steps and see which one doesn't make sense. Albert, unfortunately, doesn't have a glaring anomaly to warn him that something has gone wrong. The fact that he has made a mistake will have to be pointed out to him.

None of us who have mastered algorithms for solving different types of math problems think about the sense of each step in the algorithm each time we use it. The whole point of the algorithm is to allow us to solve problems quickly, efficiently, and mindlessly. I don't think about every keystroke as I'm typing this or every muscle movement when I'm driving a car, but if I don't have monitoring systems in place to tell me when to stop operating on autopilot and turn my brain back on, I'm eventually going to get into trouble.

 **inal Teaching Tips**

Words Matter

Mathematics is a language, and, like any language, it works best when it is used with precision. This is not a matter of quibbling over picky definitions. It is about the ability of members of a math community to communicate with each other effectively. In that spirit, I would like to briefly revisit some of the terminology used in this text.

I have been careful to distinguish between *number* and *numeral*.[2] Number is a quantity of objects (e.g., "thirty-five blocks"). We teach children about numbers by letting them explore quantities physically. Numeral, on the other hand, is a written symbol representing a certain quantity (e.g., "35"). Numerals are more abstract than numbers. Children know what to do if I show them thirty-five blocks, take seven of those blocks away, and then ask them how many blocks they have left. They are likely to be at a loss, however, if I show them "35 − 7 = ____" and ask them to provide the answer. We can avoid a lot of unnecessary confusion in our conversations with our fellow educators if we make clear whether we are referring to a quantity of thirty-five blocks or the numeral 35.

---

[2] I don't insist that *children* make the same distinction, nor am I always careful to say numeral rather than number when talking with them. It sounds less formal to say *number* 46 when pointing at the hundreds board than to say *numeral* 46, even though I am clearly referencing the symbol, not the quantity.

In the discussions of place value, I consistently use the term *units* rather than *ones*. They mean the same thing—the right-most digit in a multidigit numeral or loose counters (i.e., ones that have not been bundled into tens, hundreds, etc.). I use the term *units* for two reasons:

1. There is potential confusion between "one" and "ones." "One" is a counting number, and "ones" is potentially ungrammatical in this context (e.g., you would say, "I have several" rather than saying, "I have ones"). "Ones" is acceptable when referring to place value, but using a new term, "units," for this concept helps avoid confusion.

2. When we later refer to even higher numbers, we refer to "units of millions, tens of millions . . . ," not "ones of millions, tens of millions. . . ."

There is also a distinction between *numerals* and *digits*. The children are entering the stage of math where it is important to make the mathematical distinction between *face value* and *place value*. Digits (e.g., 3 and 7) occupy place-value positions in numerals (e.g., 37). I refer to the *units column*, which is occupied by the *digit in the units column* or the *units digit*, and to the *tens column*, which is occupied by the *digit in the tens column* or the *tens digit*. Let's revisit the numeral "37" as an example. The digit 3 occupies the tens column. It has a face value of 3, but it has a place value of 30. In contrast, the digit 7 occupies the units column, so it has both a face value and a place value of 7. If we want children to start attending to the place-value nature of our counting system, we need to make clear from the start that digits 3 and 7 are very different animals. Therefore, 37 is not the same as 73, and in adding 37 and 19, we are not adding 3 and 1—we are adding 30 and 10.

I have followed another place-value convention that you may not have noticed and may seem trivial in early childhood, but becomes important when the children hit late elementary school. When reading a number that goes into the thousands, you should not say "and" between the hundreds and tens places. For example, when reading 1,437, you should say, "One thousand four hundred thirty-seven," not "One thousand four hundred *and* thirty-seven." It feels awkward until you get used to it, but mathematicians reserve the word *and* for separating the whole number portion from the decimal portion of a number (e.g., "Two *and* thirty-seven hundredths"). Why encourage the children to develop a bad habit teachers in the upper-elementary grades will struggle to break them of?

There are also times when it is important *not* to be a stickler for proper nomenclature. A case in point is in the naming of two-digit numbers. We are striving mightily to have children at this age think of 23 not just as a set of discrete units, but as 2 tens and 3 units. If, in reading the numeral 436, they say, "Four hundreds, two tens, and three units" rather than "Four hundred twenty-three," I would not correct them, because they are doing what I want them to keep doing. At most, I would use indirect correction: "Yes, it's four hundreds, two tens, and three units, which we could also say as four hundred twenty-three."

And, finally, one last pet peeve: Please do not talk about *plusing* or *minusing* numbers. There are no such words! This phrasing comes from our fixation with the paper and pencil rather than the concrete. The numbers become nouns (seven) rather than adjectives (seven apples), and the operations signs become verbs (to plus) rather than operations symbols (to combine, compare, or be grouped with other parts). The closer you keep children to the real world, the smarter mathematicians they are!

Keeping Children Fluid

The root word for *fluency* is *fluid*, or liquid. Fluids move about easily, but with purpose—they adjust to the container they find themselves in, filling the deepest regions first, all the while hugging the edges and working toward a smooth, calm skin at the surface. I like that imagery. That's probably why the informal label for Csikszentmihalyi's (1990) explorations of how we behave at times of optimal functioning is *flow theory*. When we flow, we use our talents to the maximum. We are most primed to act and to learn. We are the best we can be.

I like to use a states-of-matter analogy to describe my role as teacher, as well. First, a brief physics lesson: All matter can, at any given moment, exist as a solid or a liquid or a gas. Heat a solid enough, and it will turn into a liquid. Heat a liquid enough, and it will turn into a gas. So temperature is the key. And what is temperature? Temperature is in fact the measure of how fast the molecules in the substance are moving and colliding with each other. In a solid, the molecules are rather sluggish, and they pretty much stay where they are. In a liquid, they are moving fast enough and colliding often enough that the molecules are changing their positions quite freely. In a gas, the movement is so swift, the collisions so violent, and the changes so rapid and so extreme that it's hard to track the position of a single molecule.

Back to my role as a teacher. I believe it is my job to keep children in a liquid state. I do that by controlling the energy level in the room. If I do not give them enough freedom to decide, to think, to interact, and to ponder really intriguing questions, the children will become solid. I will definitely know they are in the room, but learning is not optimized. If I allow the energy level in the room to get too high, the children are unable to focus, they are at a loss as to how to proceed, and they act and interact with high energy, but without direction. They may be having a good time, but learning is not optimized. So if the level of activity is too sluggish, pump some energy into the room. If the buzz is getting too frantic, settle things down. Teacher as pressure valve—who knew?

Actually, we all know this. Much current educational theory is based on the same premise. In Piagetian psychology, we talk about skillfully using *discrepant events* to create moments of *disequilibrium* so the children will revisit and rethink their prior ways of understanding. Vygotsky's *zone of proximal development* basically tells us that we need to adjust learning tasks so children are neither too frustrated nor too bored. For children to become fluent, you need to help them stay fluid.

Teaching as Improv

I'm sure I frustrate students in my early childhood education courses all the time because it seems that half the time I tell them they have to walk into the classroom every day with a well-defined plan and the other half of the time I tell them they need to be following the children's lead. It's not that I'm changing my mind; it's that both need to be true at the same time.

The type of teaching I am advocating requires an enormous amount of mindfulness and preparation. Making sure the room contains what each child needs, gently encouraging children to engage in activities that will truly benefit them, and responding to children's comments and questions appropriately require a lot of forethought. But when the curtain rises, it must be you and the children who inhabit the room, not your preconceived script.

I read a wonderful article once that described well-functioning classrooms as similar to what happens in good improv (Lobman, 2003). In improv, there is no script. The rules are that you must react honestly and authentically to what the previous actor has just done. You can't ignore it and proceed in the direction you thought you were heading. You can't decide it makes no sense. You can't ask for an explanation. Your next move must fit comfortably with the new reality you have been handed, but now it's your turn to take the scene someplace the other players did not anticipate. And so the play unfolds.

The danger in being overprepared is that you become too intent on having the children adjust to your reality rather than being equally amenable to adjusting to theirs. You have this great sequence in mind where this lead-in will set the stage to make this point or develop this concept. I laugh when I see lesson plans written like this: "The teacher will say . . . " and "The children will say. . . ." The only way that script will ever see the light of day is if the teacher runs roughshod over the children's ideas and intentions and marches blindly from point A to point B. That is not teaching. Teaching is a play in which you are just one of the actors. There is no director. There is no script.

Collaboration and Transformation

Transforming your practice is a hard thing to do alone. As stated in the National Research Council (NRC) report *Adding It Up* (2001):

> Learning to teach well cannot be accomplished once and for all in a pre-service program; it is a career-long challenge. . . . Regular time needs to be provided for teachers to continue their professional development, conferring with one another about common problems and working together to develop their teaching proficiency. They need access to resources and expertise that will assist them in improving their instruction. (p. 12)

It is hard for teachers in isolation to puzzle out what just happened in their classrooms and what to do next without other sets of eyes and ears to compare notes with. Find a similar-minded colleague, or, better yet, make a commitment as a staff to give this approach a serious attempt. Either by informal arrangement or as a schoolwide initiative, read sections of this book and discuss their implications for your own classrooms. Debate, problem solve, compare notes, and share cases. Consciously try out some of the ideas, and bring the results back to the group for further discussion and problem solving.

- Think about ways you can transform your physical space and your scheduling of "math time" to maximize the mathematical potential of your room.
- Use your district-adopted curriculum, but use it with a critical eye—in many cases, it is a transformation in how you and the children are doing the activities and talking about your experiences that makes the difference. You will not only find your way more quickly to a smoothly functioning system, but also have a support group and cheerleading section to soften your lows and celebrate your highs.
- Consider basing more of your assessment on your detailed observations of children at work rather than relying on paper-and-pencil tests. As the NRC (2001) stated:

Materials for instruction need to develop the core content of school mathematics in depth and with continuity. In addition to helping students learn, these materials should also support teachers' understanding of mathematical concepts, of students' thinking, and of effective pedagogical techniques. Mathematics assessments need to enable and not just gauge the development of proficiency. . . . Every school should be organized so that the teachers are just as much learners as the students are. (p. 13)

Support each other in the difficult waters of understanding mathematics. Increasingly, see the mathematics being done through the eyes of the children rather than from your own vantage point. It gets easier over time, but getting started is tough. As a group, you can transform your practice, better understanding the true nature of mathematics and the role of children's work in bringing it to life.

Keeping Your Eye on the Prize

> Teaching is the highest form of learning.
> —*Aristotle*

We have to be careful not to interpret benchmarks as a laundry list of things to be taught (or things to avoid teaching). The skills children are currently working on came from someplace, and those they are currently mastering are leading somewhere. We know a lot these days about the developmental progression of mathematical skills. That's why those at the cutting edge talk about learning trajectories or learning horizons. Children's learning has structure and direction. It is not just a collection of things that were taught yesterday and things that will be taught tomorrow.

We may be stuck in an educational system that plops children of the same age in the same classroom and pretends they are all the same, but we shouldn't fool ourselves. As good as some detailed mathematical scope-and-sequence documents such as the *Common Core State Standards for Mathematics* (Council of Chief State School Officers & National Governors Association Center, 2010) are, we would be better served by spending the bulk of our time focusing on documents that summarize the developmental research on which they are based, such as *Mathematics Learning in Early Childhood* (NRC, 2009). That's why this book is designed to help you diversify the mathematical offerings of your classroom rather than providing a set, linear sequence of lessons to teach. When children are set free in a rich, supportive mathematical environment, they will endlessly surprise you, both with misconceptions that are still lingering and with mathematics that is supposedly beyond their reach that they are starting to access.

In this new paradigm, your main task is to recognize the mathematics children are doing when you see it so you can validate it, support it, and gently nudge it to the next level. This method of mathematical instruction does not relieve you of the responsibility to teach. Far from it. But it does mean you will spend much less time teaching and practicing isolated skills, evaluating children's responses strictly based on whether they successfully mimic the approach just taught. It means that you are open to the diversity of responses and strategies children share with you and that you are ready to ponder their validity, recognize their shared features, and learn from them what to do next. It requires you to plan for the future but not to forget the past, to know where you want to get to but to understand the journey will not be in a straight line and not all the children will arrive at the same time. It requires patience, intelligence, empathy, and quick reflexes. But that's what it takes to turn math inside out. Good luck.

Study Group Discussion Starters: Extending Place-Value Awareness and Addition/Subtraction Beyond the Hundreds

Do your children know the place-value pattern?

What evidence do you have that children do or do not understand the 10:1 relationship between place-value categories? What examples have you seen of them misapplying exchanging rules or treating one place-value category as another?

Have you tried some of the suggested alternative models for place-value quantities (e.g., hand cards, ten frame extensions, metric measuring devices, Digi-Blocks)? If so, have these representations broadened or deepened their understanding of the base-10 structure of the place-value system?

Do your children have a sense of what comes after the thousands—and why? Have they heard of larger numbers such as millions, billions, or trillions? What relationship do they think those numbers have to the ones they are currently working with?

Can your children generate nontraditional arrangements of place-value quantities?

How comfortable are your children moving back and forth between the standard nomenclature of multidigit numerals and equivalent alternative arrangements? For example, can they easily take some of the tens in 458 and move them into the units column (e.g., 4 hundreds, 3 tens, and 28 units)? Can they easily move equivalent quantities more than one place value (e.g., 3 hundreds, 5 tens, and 108 units)? How much time do you think should be devoted to developing this skill?

How smooth is the transition from two-digit addition and subtraction to operations involving three or more digits?

In your experience, once children have learned to solve two-digit addition and subtraction problems, do they easily transfer those skills to harder problems? If so, what was it about how that earlier instruction was presented that made for a smooth transition? If, on the other hand, children seem bewildered when the solution steps increase in number and complexity, what was it about the way they were taught to solve the simpler problems that is not working? What have you had to do to get them fluent with multidigit operations?

Can your children estimate the solutions to multi-digit operations?

Do your children understand the operations of addition and subtraction and the relative magnitude of place-value quantities well enough to know approximately what the outcome of an operation should be? How often do you find children noticing that their computed answers don't make sense and using place-value reasoning to do so? How important is it to encourage children to estimate answers before doing computations or to check the reasonableness of their answers as a final step?

Can your children interpret the steps in the multi-digit addition and subtraction algorithms?

Do your children understand what all those cross-outs and small numbers mean as they use the standard algorithm? How long and how often do you think you should speak of the operation steps in place-value terms (e.g., " . . . then you subtract the 30 from the 80 . . . " rather than " . . . then you subtract the 3 from the 8 . . . "), and when is it safe to simply focus upon the steps of completing the algorithm accurately? When children make errors in applying the algorithms, is it okay to simply show them how to fix their errors, or should you spend time focusing upon why the errors don't make sense?

What have been your biggest challenges and successes?

Share with each other what you have seen children struggling with the most as you have pushed their numeracy explorations into the realm of bigger numbers and how to add and subtract them. What have you tried? What confusions or misunderstandings have persisted? Also share with each other your greatest success stories. What sudden breakthroughs have you seen children make? What was it they did, their peers did, or you did that made the difference?

Do you think the numeracy goals of the Common Core standards for second graders are reasonable? How many of the children you work with seem to be capable of this level of mathematical thinking and problem solving by the age of eight?

Should children who are struggling continue to work on the types of activities discussed in this part until they demonstrate place-value understanding of multi-digit problems, or is some other strategy called for to help them catch up? If children continue to be confused by the explanations of algorithms you provide them and other children share with them, is it okay to just move on and concentrate on error-free practice with the algorithms? Which is the more important goal?

Research-Based Teaching-Learning Paths[1]

There are three *Core Areas* in the number sense strand—Number, Relations, and Addition/Subtraction Operations—each with four developmental *Steps*, roughly translating to ages 2–3, preK, K, and grade 1.[2] Core mathematical ideas are so named because, in the words of the committee:

1. *"They are foundational mathematically and developmentally.*
2. *They are achievable for children of those ages. . . .*
3. *They are consistent with children's ways of thinking, developing, and learning when they have experience with mathematics ideas. . . .*
4. *They are interesting to children."* (p. ii-1)

As the charts that follow makes clear, a large number of foundational skills are needed in the number core in order for understandings of relations and operations to emerge.

---

[1] Content reprinted in a reorganized format with permission from *Mathematics Learning in Early Childhood: Paths Toward Excellence and Equity* (2009) by the National Academy of Sciences, courtesy of the National Academies Press, Washington, D.C.

[2] However, the committee emphasizes that there is great variability in the timeline of mastery both between and within individuals, and "much of this variability stems from differences in opportunities to learn and to practice these competencies, and we stress how important it is to provide such opportunities to learn for all children" (p. 5–23).

Chart 1   Number Core Path

Sub-Path 1: *Cardinality* (i.e., being able to recognize and name quantities)

- proceeds from being able to visually recognize and name quantities of five or less (Step 1),
- extends up to ten if groupings of five (e.g., fingers) are used. Other simple part/ whole combinations are also possible, such as 2 and 2 making 4 (Step 2),
- progresses into the teens, when groupings of ten are made available (Step 3),
- and finally extends up to 100, when quantities are grouped in tens and units (Step 4).

Sub-Path 2: *Number Word List* (i.e., being able to orally count without naming errors)

- starts with being able to recite the numbers up to five or six and shortly after up to ten (Step 1),
- then correct oral counting extends to the teens and possibly up through the twenties and thirties (Step 2),
- until children proudly recite their numbers all the way to 100 (Step 3),
- also showing that they can orally count by tens to 100 (Step 4).

Sub-Path 3: *1:1 Counting Correspondences* (i.e., being careful, when counting objects, to say the next number name only when a new object is being pointed to, and being careful to count all the objects without re-counting any of them)

- starts with very small sets of physical objects and gradually extends to other categories of counting (e.g., pictures, physical movements) up to six items (Step 1),
- proceeds to accurate counting of sets larger than ten, into the mid-teens, especially if the objects are arranged to facilitate accurate counting (Step 2),
- gradually increasing countable set sizes into the twenties (Step 3),
- and on to sets in the higher decades. A parallel skill that develops is being able to count larger numbers arranged by place value by first skip-counting through the decades (e.g., counting a set of 4 tens and 5 units as "10, 20, 30, 40, 41, 42, 43, 44, 45").

Sub-Path 4: *Written Number Symbols* (i.e., being able to write and recognize numerals)

- starts with random numerals that the child recognizes or attempts to write (Step 1),
- progressing to where 1–10 are recognized and written, though writing attempts are perhaps awkward or contain reversals (Step 2),
- then recognition or writing of numerals extends through the teens, with numerals 20–100 beginning to be recognized when they are presented in a chart organized by tens (Step 3),
- gradually including an appreciation of the place-value structure of the numerals 1–100 (Step 4).

Sub-Path 5: *Coordination of Sub-Paths* (i.e., starting to develop advanced number concepts as a result of practicing all the skills mentioned above)

- for example, starting to realize that the last name said when counting a set tells how many things are in the set (Step 1),
- later being able to not just count sets presented but also to count up to a specified number and stop (Step 2),
- later still re-conceptualizing the teen numbers as not just bigger numbers but as numbers containing a ten (e.g., $18 = 10 + 8$), as well as getting comfortable with the fact that ten ones really is equivalent to one ten (Step 3),
- until finally this emergent place-value awareness extends up to 100 (e.g., $68 = 60 + 8$).

Chart 2   Relations (More Than/Less Than/Equal To) Core Path
Step 1. Starts with learning the vocabulary of more and less and applying it to concrete experiences, although these judgments are often made based on perceptual features rather than relative quantity.
Step 2. Gradually, children start to develop more quantity-based judgments of more and less, most commonly using a matching strategy (match the objects in both sets, and see if either set has objects that don't have a match). Children start to use the counting strategy of counting both sets and then making the judgment of which has more, although this requires other skills such as (a) remembering the first number while counting the second and (b) knowing which of the two counted numbers is a larger cardinal number (e.g., "The first set had six in it. This set has eight. But I don't know if six is bigger than eight or if eight is bigger than six!").
Step 3. Children's ability to judge which set is greater extends to larger quantities, especially if the quantities are displayed in bar graph or side-by-side fashion. Children's exposure to part/whole aspects of the numbers they know paves the way for a broad range of relational concepts, such as an intuitive understanding of the commutative property, or "turn-around facts" (e.g., that $3 + 5 = 5 + 3$) and re-conceptualizing some addition facts as general principles, such as that $+1$ just results in the next higher cardinal number and $+0$ changes nothing.
Step 4. Other more sophisticated number sense principles eventually emerge, such as re-conceptualizing subtraction as missing-addend addition (e.g., given the problem $9 - 4$, the child thinks "4 plus what equals 9?"), getting comfortable with the counting on strategy (meaning that when two sets are combined the first set doesn't need to be recounted), and recognizing that 10 can be a useful bridge number in solving some problems (e.g., given the problem $9 + 7$, the child could realize that if 9 were one more, it would be 10, and if that one were taken from the 7 it would be 6, and the child knows that $10 + 6$ is 16).

Chart 3 Addition/Subtraction Operations Core Path

Step 1. Children show that they can understand and solve simple addition and subtraction situations using numbers five or less, if they are presented in meaningful contexts using objects, often using visual solution strategies.

Step 2. Children add drawings and finger counting to their solution strategies, starting to understand a wider variety of phrases implying addition/subtraction such as *all together* or *are left*. To a lesser extent, children can solve *decontextualized problems* (e.g., "Two and three make how many?" With small sums and differences, children start to apply part-whole understandings (e.g., "There are six there now; if those three are taken away that will leave three") and counting on (e.g., "I'm putting those four and those over there together, and then I'll have four, five, six, seven, . . . ").

Step 3. Children start to solve modeled or drawn addition and subtraction problems with totals up to ten. Using five as an anchor number (e.g., $6 = 5 + 1$, $7 = 5 + 2$, etc.) is common, as are applications of other part-whole relations to flexibly decompose numbers (e.g., "I know that 7 is 6 and 1 . . . ") and recompose numbers (" . . . so if I combine 7 and 6, it's just like combining 6 and 6 with one more. I know 6 and 6 is 12, so 7 and 6 must to 13.") They are starting to be able to write their solution strategies in standard format (e.g., $4 + 7 = 11$), though problems posed in that format are still difficult for them to solve without modeling the situation. They are starting to know some number combinations by heart.

Step 4. Children are becoming more comfortable using the counting on or counting back strategy with any number. Missing addend strategies for solving subtraction problems are common (e.g., thinking of $13 - 6$ as 6 plus something equals 13). Strategies such as double plus one (e.g., $5 + 6 = [5 + 5] + 1 = 11$) or bridging to ten (e.g., $9 + 6 = 10 + 5 = 15$) are increasingly available to quickly solve larger sums, especially to children who have had extensive experience with part-whole activities and thinking of the teen numbers in place value terms. Relative difference problems involving larger numbers (e.g., how much larger is 23 than 18) are still relatively difficult for them to solve.

Assessment Templates

Use for Individual Child, Tracking Progress over Time

Secure Place-Value Awareness

Rating Scale:

1 – concept has been introduced (indicate date)
2 – child struggles with concept, hesitating or making occasional errors (indicate date)
3 – child is comfortable with the concept and answers confidently (indicate date)

Child's Name:			
Can:	1	2	3
Instantly interpret teen numerals in terms of tens and units.			
Instantly name teen quantities represented as one ten plus loose units.			
Orally count by tens to 100 and backward from 100.			
Instantly interpret numerals up to 99 in terms of tens and units.			
Instantly name quantities up to 99 represented as tens plus loose units.			
Distinguish between 47 and 74 and explain why they are different amounts.			
Confidently make greater than/less than judgments for pairs of numerals up to 99 (e.g., 29 and 41) and explain their reasoning in place-value terms.			
Explain what each of the digits in the numeral 100 means.			
Count forward and backward comfortably through the decades (e.g., . . . 38, 39, 40, 41 . . . and . . . 82, 81, 80, 79, 78 . . .).			
Restate quantities presented in nonstandard groupings (e.g., 3 tens 27 units) in standard notation (i.e., 57) and do the reverse (e.g., name 73 as 4 tens and 33 units).			
Count forward and backward by tens from a non-decade starting point (e.g., 58, 68, 78, 88 . . . or 82, 72, 62, 52 . . .).			
Make reasonable estimates of quantities up to 100 displayed as loose units (e.g., estimate 50 for a display of 66 buttons; estimate 30 for a display of 28 cotton swabs).			

Notes:

Secure Part-Whole Awareness and the Emergence of Addition-Subtraction Fluency

Rating Scale:

1 – concept has been introduced (indicate date)
2 – child struggles with concept, hesitating or making occasional errors (indicate date)
3 – child is comfortable with the concept and answers confidently (indicate date)

Child's Name:			
Can:	1	2	3
Take a given single-digit number apart in multiple ways.			
Treat turn-around facts as equivalent (i.e., understands the commutative property).			
Understand addition and subtraction as inverse operations (i.e., understands fact families).			
Given one part of any number 10 or less, name the missing part.			
Given an addition or subtraction number sentence, represent the problem with manipulatives.			
Solve *Join word problems* of all types, including those with the starting quantity or amount added unknown; represent the problem with materials; and write the solution as a number sentence.			
Solve *Separate word problems* of all types, including those with the starting quantity or amount taken away unknown; represent the problem with materials; and write the solution as a number sentence.			
Solve *Compare word problems* of all types, including those where one of the quantities being compared is unknown; represent the problem with materials; and write the solution as a number sentence.			
Solve *Part-whole word problems* of all types, including those where one of the parts is unknown; represent the problem with materials; and write the solution as a number sentence.			
Name the doubles facts from memory.			
Explain and use the *bridging to ten* strategy.			
Explain and use the *doubles plus one* strategy.			
Explain and use the *doubles plus two* strategy.			
Quickly name any sum for expressions $0 + 0$ to $10 + 10$ by some means other than counting on.			
Solve basic addition and subtraction problems in both horizontal and vertical format, with the missing piece in any position in the problem.			
Use knowledge of basic addition facts to add a single-digit number to a two-digit number (e.g., $37 + 6$).			
Solve single-digit addition problems with multiple addends.			

Notes:

Extending Place-Value Awareness and Addition/Subtraction Beyond the Hundreds

Rating Scale:

1 – concept has been introduced (indicate date)
2 – child struggles with concept, hesitating or making occasional errors (indicate date)
3 – child is comfortable with the concept and answers confidently (indicate date)

Child's Name:			
Can:	1	2	3
Name the quantity represented by any of the digits in a four-digit number.			
Represent any four-digit number with place-value materials.			
State any number in expanded notation (e.g., 4,692 is 4 thousands, 6 hundreds, 9 tens, and 2 units).			
Explain what zeroes in a numeral represent (e.g., the zero in 3,607 means there are no tens).			
Explain how much a quantity in one place-value column would be if it were moved to an adjacent place-value column (e.g., how many tens would 2 hundreds be? 30 units would be how many tens?).			
Count forward and backward through place-value transition points (e.g., 803, 802, 801, 800, 799, 798 . . . or 998, 999, 1,000, 1,001, 1,002 . . .).			
Skip count in any place-value column (e.g., 377, 387, 397, 407, 417 . . .).			
Explain that 1,000 is the units place of thousands and that the next category would be tens of thousands and then hundreds of thousands.			
Name the missing part of 100 (e.g., given 34, the missing part of 100 is 66) and of 1,000 when the units place of the given part is zero (e.g., given 460, the missing part of 1,000 is 540).			
Rename place-value quantities in nontraditional arrangements (e.g., 941 is 8 hundreds, 13 tens, and 11 units).			
Explain why, when addition or subtraction problems are written in vertical format, the place-value digits must line up.			
Explain his or her solution of multidigit addition or subtraction problems in place-value terms.			
Provide a reasonably accurate estimate of multidigit sums and differences before computing the exact answer.			
Accurately use the standard algorithm for multidigit addition and subtraction, both with and without exchanging.			
Explain the steps in the standard algorithm for addition and subtraction in place-value terms.			

Notes:

Assessment Templates

Use for Whole Class, Tracking Outcomes of a Particular Lesson or Activity

Secure Place-Value Awareness

Rating Scale:

1 – child cannot do without continuous hints, reminders, and scaffolding
2 – child struggles with concept, hesitating, making occasional errors, or requiring occasional hints
3 – child is comfortable with the concept and answers confidently and independently

Code for skill(s) being monitored:

Child can:

A. Instantly interpret teen numerals in terms of tens and units.

B. Instantly name teen quantities represented as one ten plus loose units.

C. Orally count by tens to 100 and backward from 100.

D. Instantly interpret numerals up to 99 in terms of tens and units.

E. Instantly name quantities up to 99 represented as tens plus loose units.

F. Distinguish between 47 and 74 and explain why they are different amounts.

G. Confidently make greater than/less than judgments for pairs of numerals up to 99 (e.g., 29 and 41) and explain their reasoning in place-value terms.

H. Explain what each of the digits in the numeral 100 means.

I. Count forward and backward comfortably through the decades (e.g., . . . 38, 39, 40, 41 . . . and . . . 82, 81, 80, 79, 78 . . .).

J. Restate quantities presented in nonstandard groupings (e.g., 3 tens 27 units) in standard notation (i.e., 57) and do the reverse (e.g., name 73 as 4 tens and 33 units).

K. Count forward and backward by tens from a non-decade starting point (e.g., 58, 68, 78, 88 . . . or 82, 72, 62, 52 . . .).

L. Make reasonable estimates of quantities up to 100 displayed as loose units (e.g., estimate 50 for a display of 66 buttons; estimate 30 for a display of 28 cotton swabs).

Secure Place-Value Awareness

Task:				Date:

Indicate codes for skills at tops of columns; sort names of children into levels

Level	Skill ____	Skill ____	Skill ____	Skill ____
1				
2				
3				

Notes:

Secure Part-Whole Awareness and the Emergence of Addition-Subtraction Fluency

Rating Scale:

1 – child cannot do without continuous hints, reminders, and scaffolding
2 – child struggles with concept, hesitating, making occasional errors, or requiring occasional hints
3 – child is comfortable with the concept and answers confidently and independently

Code for skill(s) being monitored:

Child can:

A. Take a given single-digit number apart in multiple ways.

B. Treat turn-around facts as equivalent (i.e., understands the commutative property).

C. Understand addition and subtraction as inverse operations (i.e., understands fact families).

D. Given one part of any number 10 or less, name the missing part.

E. Given an addition or subtraction number sentence, represent the problem with manipulatives.

F. Solve *Join word problems* of all types, including those with the starting quantity or amount added unknown; represent the problem with materials; and write the solution as a number sentence.

G. Solve *Separate word problems* of all types, including those with the starting quantity or amount taken away unknown; represent the problem with materials; and write the solution as a number sentence.

H. Solve *Compare word problems* of all types, including those where one of the quantities being compared is unknown; represent the problem with materials; and write the solution as a number sentence.

I. Solve *Part-whole word problems* of all types, including those where one of the parts is unknown; represent the problem with materials; and write the solution as a number sentence.

J. Name the doubles facts from memory.

K. Explain and use the *bridging to ten* strategy.

L. Explain and use the *doubles plus one* strategy.

M. Explain and use the *doubles plus two* strategy.

N. Quickly name any sum for expressions $0 + 0$ to $10 + 10$ by some means other than counting on.

O. Solve addition and subtraction problems in both horizontal and vertical format, with the missing piece in any position in the problem.

P. Use knowledge of basic addition facts to add a single-digit number to a two-digit number (e.g., $37 + 6$).

Q. Solve single-digit addition problems with multiple addends.

Secure Part-Whole Awareness and the Emergence of Addition-Subtraction Fluency

Task: _____

Date: _____

Indicate codes for skills at tops of columns; sort names of children into levels

Level	Skill _____	Skill _____	Skill _____	Skill _____
1				
2				
3				

Notes:

Extending Place-Value Awareness and Addition/Subtraction Beyond the Hundreds

Rating Scale:

1 – child cannot do without continuous hints, reminders, and scaffolding
2 – child struggles with concept, hesitating, making occasional errors, or requiring occasional hints
3 – child is comfortable with the concept and answers confidently and independently

Code for skill(s) being monitored:

Child can:

A. Name the quantity represented by any of the digits in a four-digit number.

B. Represent any four-digit number with place-value materials.

C. State any number in expanded notation (e.g., 4,692 is 4 thousands, 6 hundreds, 9 tens, and 2 units).

D. Explain what zeroes in a numeral represent (e.g., the zero in 3,607 means there are no tens).

E. Explain how much a quantity in one place-value column would be if it were moved to an adjacent place-value column (e.g., how many tens would 2 hundreds be? 30 units would be how many tens?).

F. Count forward and backward through place-value transition points (e.g., 803, 802, 801, 800, 799, 798 . . . or 998, 999, 1,000, 1,001, 1,002 . . .).

G. Skip count in any place-value column (e.g., 377, 387, 397, 407, 417 . . .).

H. Explain that 1,000 is the units place of thousands and that the next category would be tens of thousands and then hundreds of thousands.

 I. Name the missing part of 100 (e.g., given 34, the missing part of 100 is 66) and of 1,000 when the units place of the given part is zero (e.g., given 460, the missing part of 1,000 is 540).

J. Rename place-value quantities in nontraditional arrangements (e.g., 941 is 8 hundreds, 13 tens, and 11 units).

K. Explain why, when addition or subtraction problems are written in vertical format, the place-value digits must line up.

L. Explain his or her solution of multidigit addition or subtraction problems in place-value terms.

M. Provide a reasonably accurate estimate of multidigit sums and differences before computing the exact answer.

N. Accurately use the standard algorithm for multidigit addition and subtraction, both with and without exchanging.

O. Explain the steps in the standard algorithm for addition and subtraction in place-value terms.

Extending Place-Value Awareness and
Addition/Subtraction Beyond the Hundreds

Task: _____   **Date:** _____

Indicate codes for skills at tops of columns; sort names of children into levels

Level	Skill _____	Skill _____	Skill _____	Skill _____
1				
2				
3				

Notes:

References

Andrews, Angela, & Trafton, Paul. (2002). *Little kids—Powerful problem solvers: Math stories from a kindergarten classroom.* Portsmouth, NH: Heinemann.

Annenberg Foundation. (1997). *Teaching math: A video library K–4.* Boston: WGBH. *www.learner.org/resources/series32.html?pop=yes&pid=908#*

Ashlock, Robert. (2002). *Error patterns in computation: Using error patterns to improve instruction* (8th ed.). Upper Saddle River, NJ: Pearson.

Baretta-Lorton, Mary. (1976). *Mathematics their way: An activity-centered mathematics program for early childhood.* (Out of print)

Bredekamp, Sue, & Copple, Carol (Eds.). (1997). *Developmentally appropriate practice in early childhood programs* (rev. ed.). Washington, DC: NAEYC.

Brenneman, Kimberly, Stevenson-Boyd, Judi, & Frede, Ellen C. (2008). *Math and science in preschool: Policies and practice* (NIEER Policy Brief). Washington, DC: National Institute for Early Education Research.

Burns, Marilyn. (2003). *Mathematics: Assessing understanding, part 1* [DVD]. Sausalito, CA: Math Solutions.

Cadwell, Louise. (2002). *Bringing learning to life: The Reggio approach to early childhood education.* New York: Teachers College Press.

Carpenter, Thomas, & Moser, J. (1983). The acquisition of addition and subtraction concepts. In R. A. Lesh & M. Landau (Eds.), *Acquisition of mathematics concepts and processes* (pp. 7–44). Orlando, FL: Academic Press.

Clements, Douglas, & Sarama, Julie. (2009). *Learning and teaching early math: The learning trajectories approach.* New York: Routledge.

Confer, Chris. (2005). *Teaching number sense: Kindergarten.* Sausalito, CA: Math Solutions.

Copley, Juanita (Ed.). (1999). *Mathematics in the early years.* Reston, VA: NCTM.

Copley, Juanita. (2000). *The young child and mathematics.* Washington, DC: NAEYC.

Copley, Juanita (Ed.). (2004). *Showcasing mathematics for the young child: Activities for three-, four-, and five-year-olds.* Reston, VA: NCTM.

Copley, Juanita, Jones, Candy, & Dighe, Judith. (2007). *Mathematics: The creative curriculum approach.* Washington, DC: Teaching Strategies.

Council of Chief State School Officers & National Governors Association Center for Best Practices. (2010). *Common core state standards for mathematics.* Downloadable at *www.corestandards.org/the-standards/mathematics*

Csikszentmihalyi, M. (1990). *Flow: The psychology of optimal experience.* New York: Harper Collins.

Dacey, Linda, & Eston, Rebeka. (1999). *Growing mathematical ideas in kindergarten.* Sausalito, CA: Math Solutions.

DeVreis, Rheta, Zan, B., Hildebradt, C., Edmiaston, R., & Sales, C. (2002). *Developing constructivist early childhood curriculum.* New York: Teachers College Press.

Fernandez, C., & Chokshi, S. (2002, October). A practical guide to translating lesson study for a U.S. setting. *Phi Delta Kappan,* pp. 128–134.

Fosnot, Catherine Twomey, & Cameron, Antonia. (2007). *Games for early number sense: A yearlong resource.* Portsmouth, NH: Heinemann.

Fosnot, Catherine Twomey, & Uittenbogaard, Willem. (2007). *Minilessons for early addition and subtraction.* Portsmouth, NH: Heinemann.

Geary, David, Drew, B., & Hoard, M. (2009). Predicting mathematical achievement and mathematical learning disability with a simple screening tool. *Journal of Psychoeducational Assessment, 27*(3), 265–279.

Gelman, Rochel, & Gallistel, C. (1978). *The child's understanding of number.* Cambridge, MA: Harvard University Press.

Ginsburg, Herbert, Lee, Joon Sun, & Stevenson Boyd, Judi. (2008). Mathematics education for young children: What it is and how to promote it. *Social Policy Report, 23*(1).

Hardy, G. H. (1940). *A mathematician's apology.* Cambridge: Cambridge University Press.

International Association for the Evaluation of Educational Achievement. (1997). *Mathematics achievement in the primary school years: IEA's Third International Mathematics and Science Study (TIMMS).* Boston: TIMSS & PIRLS International Study Center, Lynch School of Education, Boston College. *http://timssandpirls.bc.edu/timss1995k/TIMSSPDF/amtimss.pdf*

International Association for the Evaluation of Educational Achievement. (2006). *TIMSS advanced 2008 assessment frameworks.* Boston: TIMSS & PIRLS International Study Center, Lynch School of Education, Boston College.

Kamii, Constance. (1985). *Young children reinvent arithmetic.* New York: Teachers College Press.

Lobman, Chris. (2003, May). The bugs are coming! Improvisation and early childhood teaching. *Young Children,* pp. 18–24.

Mokros, Jan, Russell, Susan Jo, & Economopoulos, Karen. (1995). *Beyond arithmetic: Changing mathematics in the elementary classroom.* White Plains, NY: Dale Seymour.

NAEP. (2010). *NAEP Mathematics Assessment, 2009. http://nces.ed.gov/nationsreportcard/mathematics*

NAEP. (2011). *The nation's report card: Mathematics 2011.* Washington, DC: National Center for Education Statistics, Institute of Education Sciences, U.S. Department of Education.

NAEYC & NCTM. (2002). *Early childhood mathematics: Promoting good beginnings* (Joint Position Statement of the National Association for the Education of Young Children and the National Council for Teachers of Mathematics). Downloadable at *http://208.118.177.216/about/positions.asp*

National Governors Association Center for Best Practices and the Council of Chief State School Officers. (2010). Common Core State Standards.

National Mathematics Advisory Panel. (2008). *Foundations for success: The final report of the National Mathematics Advisory Panel.* Washington, DC: U.S. Department of Education.

NCTM. (2000). *Principles and standards for school mathematics.* Reston, VA: NCTM.

NCTM. (2006). *Curriculum focal points for prekindergarten through grade 8 mathematics: A quest for coherence.* Reston, VA: NCTM.

Nelson, Greg. (2007). *Math at their own pace: Child-directed activities for developing early number sense.* St. Paul, MN: Redleaf Press.

NRC, Committee on Early Childhood Mathematics. (2009). *Mathematics learning in early childhood: Paths toward excellence and equity* (Christopher T. Cross, Taneisha A. Woods, & Heidi Schweingruber, Eds.). Washington, DC: National Academy Press.

NRC, Mathematics Learning Study Group. (2001). *Adding it up: Helping children learn mathematics* (Jeremy Kilpatrick, Jane Swafford, & Bradford Findell, Eds.). Washington, DC: National Academy Press.

Polya, George. (1957). *How to solve it: A new aspect of mathematical method* (2nd ed.). Princeton, NJ: Princeton University Press.

Richardson, Kathy. (1998). *Developing number concepts: Book 2. Beginning addition and subtraction.* New York: Dale Seymour.

Richardson, Kathy. (2002a). *Math time: A look at children's thinking.* Norman, OK: Educational Enrichment.

Richardson, Kathy. (2002b). *A look at children's thinking* [DVD]. Bellingham, WA: Math Perspectives.

Shoseki, Tokyo. (2007). *Mathematics for elementary school, grade 1.* Madison, NJ: Global Educational Resources.

Smith, Frank. (1990). *To think.* New York: Teachers College Press.

Van de Walle, John, & Lovin, LouAnn. (2006). *Teaching student-centered mathematics, grades K–3.* Upper Saddle River, NJ: Pearson.

Vygotsky, L. S. (1934/1936). *Thought and language.* (A. Kozulin, Ed. and Trans.). Cambridge, MA: MIT Press.

Whiten, David, & Wilde, Sandra. (1995). *It's the story that counts: More children's books for mathematical learning, K–6.* Portsmouth, NH: Heinemann.

Index